The Medium
Is the Monster

The Medium Is the Monster

Canadian Adaptations of Frankenstein and the Discourse of Technology

Mark A. McCutcheon

AU PRESS

Copyright © 2018 Mark A. McCutcheon
Published by AU Press, Athabasca University
1200, 10011 – 109 Street, Edmonton, AB T5J 3S8

Cover image: Deadmau5 live in San Francisco. Copyright © 2015 by Maurizio Pesce.
Cover design by Marvin Harder
Interior design by Sergiy Kozakov
Printed and bound in Canada by Friesens

ISBN 978-1-77199-236-7 (cl.)   978-1-77199-224-4 (pbk.)
ISBN 978-1-77199-225-1 (PDF)   978-1-77199-226-8 (epub)
doi: 10.15215/aupress/9781771992244.01

Library and Archives Canada Cataloguing in Publication

McCutcheon, Mark A., 1972-, author
          The medium is the monster : Canadian adaptations of Frankenstein and the discourse
of technology / Mark A. McCutcheon.

Includes bibliographical references and index.
Issued in print and electronic formats.

          1. Shelley, Mary Wollstonecraft, 1797–1851—Adaptations. 2. Shelley, Mary
Wollstonecraft, 1797–1851—Influence. 3. Shelley, Mary Wollstonecraft, 1797–1851.
Frankenstein. 4. McLuhan, Marshall, 1911–1980—Adaptations. 5. McLuhan, Marshall,
1911–1980—Influence. 6. Technology in popular culture. 7. Technology in popular
culture—Canada. 8. Technology in literature. 9. Technology and civilization. 10.
Technology and civilization in literature. I. Title.

PR5397.F738M33 2018   823'.7   C2018-900180-1
                                             C2018-900181-X

This book has been published with the help of a grant from the Federation for the
Humanities and Social Sciences, through the Awards to Scholarly Publications Program,
using funds provided by the Social Sciences and Humanities Research Council of Canada.

We acknowledge the financial support of the Government of Canada through the
Canada Book Fund (CBF) for our publishing activities and the assistance provided by the
Government of Alberta through the Alberta Media Fund.

Canadä   Albertan
          Government

For Dr. Leslie Robicsek, to whom I promised long ago to dedicate my first book. (I'm sure neither of us then envisioned that my first book would look like this, but writing is full of surprises and unexpected turns, which may be one reason why Mary Shelley described it as "hideous progeny.")

Even the most abstract categories, in spite of their validity for all epochs—because of their abstract nature—are yet in the precise terms of this abstraction themselves as much the product of historical conditions and possess their full validity only in respect of and within these conditions.

Karl Marx, *Grundrisse* ([1857] 1983, 390)

The Québec film-maker, Jean-Claude Labrecque, once said of the threat of cultural obliteration posed by new technologies of communication: "It's like snow; it keeps falling and all you can do is go on shoveling." Technology as snow, or maybe as a nuclear winter; that's the Canadian, and by extension, world situation now.

Arthur Kroker, *Technology and the Canadian Mind* (1984, 129)

The malicious horizon made us the essential thinkers of technology.

Dionne Brand, *No Language Is Neutral* (1990, 23)

Contents

Acknowledgements

I want to thank many individuals and institutions for supporting the work that's gone into this book. Thanks to Daniel Fischlin, at the University of Guelph, for introducing me to the capacious field of adaptation studies. Thanks to Barbara Schmidt-Haberkamp, of the University of Bonn, and the Association for the Study of the New English Literatures (ASNEL) for inviting the keynote talk I gave at ASNEL's 2007 conference, where I first formulated this book's argument. Thanks to Alan Filewod at Guelph, and to Joel Faflak, at Western University, for supervising the doctoral and postdoctoral work that went into fleshing out that argument—and thanks to SSHRC for their doctoral and postdoc support. Thanks to my Athabasca University colleagues, to the Research Office, and to the Athabasca University Faculty Association. Thanks to Libraries and Archives Canada for letting me probe their McLuhan holdings. Thanks to Catalyst Theatre for sharing script materials from their superb stage version of *Frankenstein*. Thanks to the many friends, colleagues, mentors, and students I've bounced these ideas off; and thanks to the organizers who have accepted and the audiences who have attended preliminary communications of the study's findings at conferences held by ACCUTE, Athabasca University, CACLALS, CSDH-SCHN, the Cultural Studies Association (US), MLA, NASSR, Philipps-Universität Marburg, the TransCanada Institute, the University of Otago, and Western University. Thanks to the editors of the ASNEL proceedings series, of the journals *SFFTV* and *Continuum*, and of the book *Popular Postcolonialisms*, in which earlier versions of chapters, passages, or spinoffs of this research were previously published. Thanks to Siobhan McMenemy for early feedback on the project, and massive thanks to the manuscript's peer reviewers, to editor *par excellence* Pamela Holway and everyone at Athabasca University Press, and to indexer *extraordinaire* Louise Fairley. And last, but very far from least, my deepest thanks to my parents, to my daughters, and to Heather: for everything.

The Medium
Is the Monster

Introduction

The question that animates this book might at first sound like the start of a joke: what do modern technology, Mary Shelley's *Frankenstein*, and Canada have to do with one another? The short answer is "Marshall McLuhan," and much of what follows will be devoted to explaining this punchline. I want to venture a twofold argument: first, that Shelley's *Frankenstein* effectively "reinvented" the meaning of the word "technology" for modern English; and, second, that Marshall McLuhan's media theory and its receptions, especially in Canadian popular culture, together constitute a tradition in adaptations of *Frankenstein* that has globalized this Frankensteinian sense of the word. So my two main tasks here are to provide a concrete account of the historical origins and transformation of the definitively modern word "technology" and, by closely reading *Frankenstein* and its Canadian adaptations, many of which also adapt McLuhan, to model new directions for adaptation studies.

I aim to show how *Frankenstein*, technology, McLuhan, and Canadian popular culture relate to one another, in historical and cultural contexts, and to explore the implications of this interrelation. I start with an historical account of the modern meaning of "technology," a word that organizes not only whole scholarly fields but also the political economies of whole nation-states—yet a word whose meaning is often ambiguous in scholarly literature and ambivalent in popular culture. Technology, a term that initially used to denote the study of any art or technique, has come, in modernity, to describe machines, industrial systems, and media. Contrary to extant definitions (such as that in the *OED*), which locate the word's redefinition in the late nineteenth century, this book shows that its modern "reinvention" emerged in the early nineteenth century—specifically, in the wake of *Frankenstein*'s publication. *The Medium Is the Monster* analyzes *Frankenstein* as a founding intertext for technology in its own time and in adaptations that popularized the story by simplifying it as a cautionary tale of technology run amok (Baldick 1987, 7). My argument then turns from *Frankenstein* in its period to its postcolonial adaptations in Canadian popular culture, anchored in McLuhan's work. If *Frankenstein* helps us to understand the modern transformation of the discourse of technology, then Canadian adaptations of *Frankenstein* help us to understand the globalized transfer of this discourse, a transfer effected largely by McLuhan's media theory, together with its myriad adaptations.

The impetus for this investigation derives from two areas of interest: first, a preoccupation with the rich variety of *Frankenstein*'s receptions and adaptations, which abound in Canada and repay postcolonial study in this national context; and second, an interest in—and a dissatisfaction with—the ways the word *technology* is used in popular culture and scholarly literature. In popular culture and everyday speech, references to technology regularly strike a sometimes subtle, sometimes strident chord of ambivalence. In scholarly literature on technology, and in popular literature too, the word enjoys great elasticity of meaning, as an abstraction, sometimes a convenient one—sometimes even an unexamined one. It is alternately presumed to be self-evident, defined commonsensically, conceptualized idiosyncratically or speciously, or theorized critically. The effects of the word's ambivalence and multiple meanings have profound and sometimes pernicious effects and implications. Prominent in humanities and social science scholarship, prevalent in everyday language, and privileged in political policy, the word *technology* adapts readily to the service of imaginative culture, incisive critique, or ideological mystification. Discussing one of technology's most intimately related counterpart keywords, *media*, John Guillory states that his aim is "to describe the philosophical preconditions of media discourse" (2010, 321). If we substitute "technology" for "media" (a rhetorical switch that recurs throughout McLuhan's work, incidentally), Guillory's statement could aptly summarize the aim of the first chapters here.

A representative instance of the word's use in popular culture illustrates the ambivalence and ambiguities of technology and suggests how to connect the conceptual dots among technology, *Frankenstein*, and Canada. The 2 February 2009 episode of Viacom's cable news-comedy program *The Daily Show* (Stewart et al. 2009) featured a segment called "Future Shock": a report on military robotics. *Daily Show* host Jon Stewart introduces the segment like this: "Technology: technology's allowed us to do everything from land on the moon, to fake landing on the moon. Now technology may be about to solve one of our most vexing problems of all." Over footage of assembly lines and vacuum cleaners, the segment's correspondent, Samantha Bee, says: "Robots. They've already revolutionized the way we clean our homes and spot-weld. Now they're about to help us cross the last frontier of human unpleasantness: killing." Bee's segment reports on a government military contract awarded to iRobot, the corporation that makes the "Roomba" robot vacuum. The segment stages a satirical drama of technological imperative versus technological risk, juxtaposing interview footage with the iRobot CEO against an interview with Noel Sharkey, a robotics professor at Sheffield, whom Bee names among those who "actually see a downside to having robots do our killing." The segment's production parodies the conventions of the cable-news "technology report," with quick cuts, footage of high-tech gadgetry, and strobe-like interstitials flashing the segment's "Future Shock" title. At one point in the interview, the iRobot CEO describes a cyberpunk future straight out of William Gibson's 1984 novel *Neuromancer*: "Wouldn't it be cool to be able to have, look, a memory chip that you could put in the back of your neck. You could augment yourself with some robot technology—all of a sudden you understood calculus." This speech shifts to voice-over as the video cuts to a special-effects sequence that farcically visualizes it: a wide shot of Bee cuts to a close-up of a prop-dummy head (a wig-draped chicken carcass) being drilled and stuffed with wires. A wide shot turns the figure around as Bee, now sporting horn-rimmed glasses and an armload of textbooks, exclaims, "I totally get it!" Correspondent Jason Jones, costumed as a "jock," walks past, slapping the books out of her hand and shouting "Nerd!" As Jones exits screen left, she frowns and points a finger at him. Bee's finger—visually referencing a joke about *The Terminator* from earlier in the segment—then morphs, via computer graphic effects, into a machine gun and opens fire.

The *Daily Show* sketch uses a mix of clichés, news genre conventions, and satirical commentary and imagery to dramatize a symptomatic convergence of subjects: the modern discourse of "technology"; the iconic figure of *Frankenstein*; and the contribution of Canadian labour to globalized popular culture. Stewart's introductory invocation of the term technology suggests its sensational "headline" value and presumes the transparency of its meaning, in his illustrative references to space exploration and digital simulation. As the episode unfolds, it then dramatizes, in all its ambivalence, the Utopian techno-fetishism of cyborg empowerment and the dystopian techno-phobia of murderous robots run amok. The iRobot CEO represents the former position, in statements premised in *technological instrumentalism*: the "most widely accepted view of technology," as Andrew Feenberg notes, "based on the commonsense idea that technologies are 'tools' standing ready to serve the purposes of their users" (2002, 5). Professor Sharkey represents the latter position, with statements suggesting the wary reservations of *technological determinism*: the view that technology acts independently of human agency to determine social conditions. This contrast in views on technology is dramatized according to *Frankenstein's* "skeleton story" of technology in revolt (Baldick 1987, 7). This dramatization entails alluding to prior adaptations of *Frankenstein*, which is a widely recognized source for the *Terminator* films parodied here (Picart 2003, 9), for the discourse of robotics (Hitchcock 2007, 136), and even for science fiction as such (Aldiss 1986, 26). Lastly, the episode demonstrates the crucial—but characteristically inconspicuous—contribution of Canadian labour to globalized popular culture: the episode features Canadian actors Bee and Jones, and its "Future Shock" title reproduces the title of Alvin Toffler's 1970 book, a book that owed its success largely to the prior success of McLuhan. One of the effects of the episode's coordination of these subjects is to simultaneously reproduce and satirize the view of *technological substantivism*, which goes further than determinism to suggest that technology has become autonomous, or even that—in the triumphal words of Henry Frankenstein in the iconic James Whale film (1931)—"It's alive!"

That 2009 *Daily Show* episode illustrates the connections among technology discourse, *Frankenstein*, and Canadian popular culture that this book maps out. How such an episode makes these connections, in its adaptation of multiple intertextual sources and references, is a question of theory and method that chapters 1 and 2 take up in depth. Many such popular cultural images of technology could be offered, and later chapters will look at some key examples in detail. Likewise, in the scholarly and popular bodies of literature on technology, we see similar presumptions of the word's meaning and similar ambiguity and ambivalence in its usage, as well as similar connotations of its uncanny autonomy. I want to suggest that it has been one of the distinctive contributions of Canadian adaptations of *Frankenstein* to disseminate and popularize these presumptions, connotations, and ambiguities—which, taken together, I call the *modern discourse of globalized technology.*

To put the matter plainly, I hold that we cannot talk about technology without conjuring *Frankenstein*, and that Canadian adaptations of *Frankenstein* have popularized, even globalized, this modern, fundamentally Frankensteinian discourse of technology. Adaptations of *Frankenstein* have long proliferated, and continue to proliferate, across media and around the world. What this study hopes to contribute to the literature on *Frankenstein* adaptation is a historicized analysis of *Frankenstein's* founding traces in the modern discourse of technology and attention to the interstitial and liminal fields of cultural production—between extensive and ephemeral modes, between scholarly and popular registers—at which much contemporary *Frankenstein* adaptation takes place. As we'll see, in the contexts of technology discourse and Canada's postcolonial popular culture, Shelley's hideous progeny has engendered a diffuse and decidedly strange brood of mutations, replicants, and other intertextual adaptations of its story, both extensive and ephemeral. As globally significant articulations of technology discourse, Canadian *Frankensteins* reveal a strange interface of postcolonial literary adaptation and techno-Romantic popular culture. Canadian adaptations of *Frankenstein* organize popular ideas of technology and structure images of the global technological crises in which Canada is embroiled—from copyright to climate change.

To argue and illustrate this claim, *The Medium Is the Monster* unfolds as follows. Before examining *Frankenstein* or its adaptations in detail, the first chapter elaborates on two key discursive and social contexts for my argument—technology discourse and Canadian culture—and, in the process, contextualizes how subsequent chapters triangulate these terms with *Frankenstein* and its numerous popular cultural progeny.

Chapter 2 further develops this study's premises and method by elaborating on my approach to the theory and practice of adaptation studies—the analysis of how different media, genres, and other cultural forms are used to tell and retell a story like *Frankenstein*. My approach to adaptation studies challenges some key premises of the field in order to build its capacity to analyze the many forms adaptation can take, from the extensive (like feature film versions of Shelley's novel) to the allusive or ephemeral (like pop songs that sample audio from *Frankenstein* films, or even just develop instrumentation traditions that evoke *Frankenstein*). A critical term I adopt to theorize such a range of adaptations is the "Frankenpheme": an image or idea derived from *Frankenstein,* represented in another text or form (Morton 2002, 47). This chapter surveys a spectrum of sound and image adaptations—focusing on Afro-Futurist music and Canadian rap—for a few reasons: to model an approach to adaptation studies that is sufficiently expansive and materialist to account for the vast cultural diffusion of a text like *Frankenstein,* to detail textual and contextual criteria for reading texts as "Frankensteinian," and thus to suggest how Canadian *Frankenstein* adaptations both circulate globally and inform the discourse of technology.

Chapter 3 focuses on Mary Shelley's novel, documenting the modernization of the meaning of *technology* as a discursive effect of the novel and its early stage adaptations. I retrace the word's "reinvention" (from describing the study of any art or technique to describing industrial machines and systems) and argue that Shelley's characterization of the monster through five tropes—shock, revolution, utility, inhumanity, and contagion—in turn characterizes the "reinvented" meaning of technology with affective anxiety and a negative moral valence and contributes to its fetishization (that is, the treatment of technology as if it were a living thing). Transatlantic *Frankenstein* adaptations and technology references in the period then represent technology in terms of industrial monstrosity, and the period's theatrical *Frankenstein* productions dramatize technology's uncanny liveness in their spectacular use of special effects. The chapter tracks the discursive origins of a word now valorized as a policy imperative and naturalized as virtually biological.

In chapter 4, I turn from Shelley's time to the postwar period, McLuhan, and his media theory. This chapter details the intertextual and historical contexts of McLuhan's work and closely reads how McLuhan represents technology as a Frankenpheme in his best-known texts. The reading illuminates the underappreciated Romanticism in McLuhan's media theory, and its focus on some of his most popular statements highlights the global influence of his work in shaping and popularizing the modern discourse of globalized technology, a discourse that I summarize as the *McLuhanesque Frankenpheme of technology.* A crucial globalizing dimension of McLuhan's popularization of a Frankensteinian sense of technology is his press presence and counterculture influence in the 1960s. This chapter documents the receptions of McLuhan by the journalistic establishment and the performative, mediatized scenes of the counterculture, which mobilized McLuhan's ideas for social change, but, in the process, also furnished the corporate news media with sensational images of "tuned in" radicalism that amplified McLuhan's idea of technology as a Frankensteinian menace and caricatured McLuhan as a kind of mad scientist of media.

In chapter 5, the work of US expatriate novelist William Gibson links the counterculture of the 1960s to the technoculture of the 1980s. Gibson has openly acknowledged McLuhan's counterculturally informed influence on his 1984 novel *Neuromancer* (see Foster 1999 and Rapatzikou 2004). A close reading of *Neuromancer*'s borrowings from both McLuhan and *Frankenstein* invites a comparison of Gibson's work to David Cronenberg's contemporaneous "cult" film *Videodrome* (1983). In these texts—both globally renowned touchstones for digital culture—I identify a shared pattern of intertextual adaptation, narrative strategy, and new media theorization. Gibson and Cronenberg combine and juxtapose references to Shelley's novel and McLuhan's theory—not only in *Neuromancer* and *Videodrome* but also throughout their oeuvres—and so consolidate and reproduce McLuhan's Frankenpheme of technology.

Chapter 6 tracks this distinctive pattern of pairing *Frankenstein* and McLuhan references through Canadian science fiction, with readings of illustrative works by writers like Larissa Lai (2009), Nalo Hopkinson (1998), Margaret Atwood (2003), and Peter Watts (2006). How these writers' texts adapt both *Frankenstein* and McLuhan echoes the adaptation pattern established by Gibson and Cronenberg and shows the propagation of McLuhan's Frankenpheme of technology across Canadian science fiction.

In chapter 7, I shift from print adaptations of the McLuhanesque Frankenpheme of technology to its amplifications in electronic dance music (EDM) culture, where the work of several key producers and DJs both evokes the technological sublime of ghosts in the machine and enacts what music critic Simon Reynolds calls "techno-Romanticism" (1999): the subcultural synchronization of hedonism and high technology. Two notable acts in this respect are the house music producer Deadmau5 (a.k.a. Joel Zimmerman) and the Paladin Project (a.k.a. Len Jaroli), a spectacular DJ persona who played "dark and hard" dance music at Canadian raves and clubs. These performers reveal the subcultural circulation of McLuhanesque *Frankenstein* adaptations, as does Matthew MacFadzean's 2001 fringe play *richardthesecond*, whose dance culture milieu points to the further amplification of McLuhan's Frankenpheme of technology in Canadian pop culture.

Chapter 8 analyzes how the Frankensteinian discourse of technology has informed and structured popular cultural representations of the Alberta tar sands industry. It is the world's biggest resource extraction project, and, as such, it presents a vast industrial spectacle of "the technological sublime": the experience of "awe and wonder, often tinged with an element of terror, which people have had when confronted with particular natural sites, architectural forms, and technological achievements" (Nye 1994, xvi). Accordingly, a variety of cultural representations of Big Oil and the tar sands do not just evoke the industry's technological spectacle, but do so in ways that amplify its Frankensteinian aspects too.

Finally, the conclusion moves beyond Canadian texts and contexts to survey an international selection of scholarly receptions of McLuhan as an important means of globally distributing McLuhan's Frankenpheme of technology. Langdon Winner's *Autonomous Technology* (1977) and Avital Ronell's *Telephone Book* (1991) both explicitly link McLuhan and *Frankenstein*. I then consider the reception of McLuhan in Europe—acknowledging the difficulties of translation—with reference to Jean Baudrillard (1983) and Friedrich Kittler ([1986] 1999). The study then closes by reflecting on the implications of Canadian adaptations of *Frankenstein* for reconceiving Canada's "technological nationalism" (Charland 1986) as *technocratic transnationalism* in order to better describe the increasingly corporate and globally focused priorities of Canada's governance and cultural production. This proposed notion of technocratic transnationalism helps to highlight some notable commonalities among Canadian *Frankenstein* adaptations: besides their consistent pairing of Shelley and McLuhan, they also share preoccupations with media, corporate business, and globalization. Finally, I point to some further directions for studying *Frankenstein* adaptations, and for reconceiving adaptation studies more expansively, which richly rewards paying close attention to more varied forms of adaptation in cultural production.

1. Technology, *Frankenstein*, and . . . Canada?

Because of technology's ambiguities, the scholarly literature that takes technology as its main subject sometimes pays special attention to definitions and terminology, and, in the process, it articulates different premises. One thing many writers agree on is that, as W. Brian Arthur says, "we have no agreement on what the word 'technology' means" (2009, 13). Langdon Winner observes that the word "is applied haphazardly to a staggering collection of phenomena" (1977, 10). For French cultural theorist Jacques Ellul ([1954] 1964) and *Wired* cofounder Kevin Kelly alike, the word is "too small" (Kelly 2011, 11), too specific for their purposes, so they coin more expansive terms that encompass and exceed technology, like Ellul's concept of *technique*. For Alvin Toffler, the inverse obtains: "Technology," he specifies, "includes techniques" (1970, 25).

Technology: A Shape-Shifting Signifier

Three major premises for definitions and theories of technology prevail: the *instrumentalist* premise sees technology as mere, value-neutral tools that can be put to different uses, ethical or otherwise, by users; the *determinist* premise holds that technology is not value-neutral but rather determines and organizes its uses according to its own logic or priorities; and the *substantivist* premise "claims that not only does technology operate according to its own inherent logic, but also that this logic is at the expense of humanity" (Lorimer, Gasher, and Skinner 2008, 253). McLuhan, in his writings, defines and theorizes the terms technology and media, which are major keywords and closely related in his work; McLuhan's thinking on technology has been characterized sometimes as determinist, sometimes as substantivist.

Other definitions are worth glossing here for their variety. Winner provides a pragmatic, three-part definition of technology as apparatus, techniques, and organizations (1977, 11), on which he then builds a substantivist theorization. Carl Mitcham excavates an exhaustive etymology of the word and its meanings, from its ancient roots in Aristotle to the nineteenth century, in his survey of the philosophy of technology (1994, 128). George Grant, in *Technology and Empire*, defines the word as follows: "by technology I mean 'the totality of methods rationally arrived at and having absolute efficiency (for a given stage of development) in every field of human activity'" (1969, 113). Grant is quoting from Ellul's 1954 *La Technique*, translated into English as *The Technological Society* (1964). But Ellul and his English translator take pains in the English edition to specify that the keyword is not technology but *technique*, which "does not mean machines, technology, or this or that procedure for attaining an end" ([1954] 1964, xxv), but the aforementioned "totality of methods." For Grant, technology is synonymous with a word that, for Ellul, surpasses and subsumes it; Grant's English misappropriation of French theory resonates with Canadian irony.

Samuel Weber (1989) notes a similar contingency of translation with "The Question Concerning Technology," the prevailing English translation of Martin Heidegger's 1954 essay "Die Frage nach der Technik," by William Lovitt, published in 1977. Heidegger's essay has become a founding text for contemporary fields of technology studies; however, Weber argues, technology is narrower and more theoretical than the German *Technik*, which also means "technique, craft, skill" (1989, 981). Cursory as this critique of translation is, in the context of Weber's larger argument, it has wide-reaching implications for the considerable amount of scholarship on technology that has been influenced by Heidegger's essay since its anglophone debut. Even the translator's decision to translate *Technik* as "technology" set a scholarly precedent; it recurs, for instance, in the English translation of Arnold Gehlen's "Philosophical-Anthropological Perspective on Technology" ([1983] 2003, 213).

Perhaps strangely, there are also major contributions to scholarly literature on technology that offer neither working nor detailed definitions of this pivotal keyword, but instead leave its fundamental meaning presumed and implied. Donna Haraway's 1991 essay "A Cyborg Manifesto: Science, Technology, and Socialist-Feminism in the Late Twentieth Century" uses technology as a keyword throughout, referring variously to telephones, housework, and biotechnology. Most often, Haraway pairs the word with science, to describe the nexus of practices privileged by white capitalist patriarchy. But the reader must infer from these references what's meant by technology: Haraway supplies neither definition nor theorization, only references amidst which the reader must triangulate the term's usage and meaning. Late in the essay, Haraway acknowledges something of the particular moral valence of the term—a valence I will argue here belongs to its *Frankenstein*-conditioned history—in her suggestive closing advisory that we should refuse "a demonology of technology" (1991, 181).

Theorizations are sometimes offered in lieu of concrete definitions. Scholars often take a position on technology, contextualize their approaches to it, or reflect on its place in critical, philosophical, or political tradition, without considering its linguistic contours: its denotations and connotations, its material referents. In *Transforming Technology*, Feenberg (2002) argues for a critical theory of technology that transcends what he sees as a dialectical stalemate between instrumental and substantive theories. Feenberg develops a critique of the assumptions and functions of both these schools of thought, as well as his own persuasive and significant critical theorization, but, throughout, he refers to technology in a way that presumes the reader comes to the discussion already knowing what is meant by its key term of reference.

What is vexing about such ambiguity and presumption is the malleability they afford a writer to make one's own idea of technology into a convenient abstraction that can best suit one's own research project, critical argument, or ideological agenda. Kevin Robins and Frank Webster, in *Times of the Technoculture*, introduce the subject of their study as "the discourse of technological revolution" (1999, 1), and their ensuing critique extensively problematizes the cultural functions and political contexts of change and "revolution" in representations of modern technology. But they take the term technology to be self-explanatory and derive from it a constellation of coinages, like "technoscape" (Appadurai 1990) and "technoculture." Where Robins and Webster do pause to clarify how they "think about the nature of technologies," they make this clarification in theoretical terms: they reject instrumentalism and situate their approach as more deterministic or substantive, emphasizing that "technologies always articulate particular social values and priorities" (1999, 4). But what they mean by "technologies" per se goes unspecified, although the context of their discussion implies that they use the term as abstract shorthand for the information and communication technologies (ICTs) that serve and structure capital.

Definitions often make an appearance in books about technology for general audiences too, where they also produce variable results and conclusions. In *The Real World of Technology*, Ursula Franklin defines technology as system and practice, more "multifaceted entity" than merely "material components": "It includes activities as well as a body of knowledge, structures as well as the act of structuring" (1990, 14). Technology is more than anything else here a scalable theoretical tool, as easily invoked to discuss the specific "technology of Chinese bronze casting" (15) as to conclude with the vast generalization that "the world of technology is the sum total of what people do" (123). And although Franklin takes care in her arguments to emphasize social context and to resist determinism (57), such determinism nevertheless flashes through, in the statement that "technology has muddled or even destroyed the traditional social compass" (14), or the claim that "many technological systems, when examined for context and overall design, are anti-people" (76). The ideological implications of popular writing on technology can be particularly pronounced.

Arthur's *The Nature of Technology* surveys and rejects dictionary definitions—and claims (rather preposterously) that "a theory of technology" is "missing" from the literature on the subject (2009, 14). Arthur proposes a three-part definition of technology—as purposive means, as combinations of practices and components, and as a culture's totality of said combinations (28)—which then establishes the basis for what he claims is a new theory of technology as an evolutionary system (its "nature"). And yet neither Arthur's definition nor theory are actually new: the former clearly echoes Winner's three-part definition, while the latter extends the substantivist theoretical tradition of Ellul—and of McLuhan (whose theory of technology is of central concern in what follows). Similarly, Kelly's *What Technology Wants* grounds an argument for technology's autonomy as a "living system" (2011, 15) in an unfortunately oversimplified synopsis of Mitcham's account; while Mitcham traces the meanings of technology through medieval and early modern Europe, Kelly claims that the term simply vanished after Aristotle and was spontaneously "resurrected" by the late-eighteenth-century scholar Johann Beckmann (8). The language of resurrection is noteworthy here, in the context of the present study's claims for *Frankenstein*'s role in framing how we talk about technology.

So we find similar notes of ambivalence, amorphousness, and anxiety both between and within the bodies of popular and scholarly writing that focus on technology as their main subject. With this observation, I don't mean to denigrate the valuable work done by scholars, critics, and other writers and artists on the subject of technology, let alone dismiss science and technology studies (STS) or other fields of study organized around this subject. Language, definitions, and discourse are not everyone's main concern, and understandably so—given the prevailing "technological imperative" of modern state governance and economic policy, the determining force of technology in everyday life, the myriad current problems and crises of technological risk, and the need to assess, make sense of, and critique these and technology's other social roles, relations, and functions. But in the quite variable forms of attention given to and worked out of the language of technology, discourses on technology pose their own risks to public knowledge and epistemology, in the ease or eagerness with which such discourses can produce and reproduce not clearer understandings of technology but, rather, further fetishizations, reifications, and other mystifications of it. Technology has been fetishized and reified even by analyses that are otherwise quite cogent critiques of technology, its political economic functions, and its socio-cultural effects. Examining technology first and foremost as a discourse, instead, this book offers a genealogy of this discourse, from the redefinition of technology at the advent of industrial modernity to its current privilege as a central keyword in the hegemony of globalized neoliberal capitalism.

Numerous examples of this privilege abound: for instance, in the contemporary, corporatizing university's relative political and economic prioritization of science, technology, engineering, and mathematical disciplines (as well as professional fields) over those of the humanities and social sciences (Sigelman 2016). One striking, concise illustration of the privilege technology enjoys in policy and business—and in their mutual constitution under global capital—is provided by a 2017 Canadian government press release, which states that "technology and the innovation it helps promote are key to the future of Canada's economy" (Canada 2017). Yet even here a Frankensteinian shadow looms, in this press release's specification of investment in "clean technology"—this is a common enough compound noun meaning energy production that doesn't exacerbate climate change, but as a compound it also implies that there may be something dirty about "technology" per se.

As dramatized by the example of *The Daily Show*, the privilege so widely enjoyed by technology today has its countervailing shadow; as Neil Postman put it, "every technology is both a burden and a blessing" (1993, 4). To borrow a fitting metaphor from the field of STS itself, the word *technology* is its own linguistic "black box": it works effectively and persuasively in everyday speech, popular culture, and scholarship, even when its inner workings remain unexamined or inaccessible. The elastic and ambiguous word *technology* combines with successive waves of technological development—and with technology discourse's nontextual vocabulary of sound and image—to give rise to generalized representations of technology per se that are based mainly in specific, current "high tech" trends and developments of the day.

The sound and image vocabulary of technology discourse complements the textual vocabulary of technology in that the word evokes a certain visibility of novelty in what it's applied to—as, by the same token, certain sound- and image-based social and cultural practices evoke the technological more clearly or conventionally than others. The word technology, in everyday language, usually refers to tools, systems, and products that are new, that exhibit a spectacular quality, that are made via industrial and postindustrial processes—tools, systems, and products that are, in other words, "high tech." In contemporary parlance, "technology" is not a term commonly applied to, say, wheels or chalkboards, although both could qualify as such according to the varied theoretical parameters and criteria mentioned above. Observing this "shorthand" use of the word, Jeremy Gilbert and Ewan Pearson identify a hierarchizing function in the language of technology, what they call technology's effect as an "index of visibility." "Some items," they write, "are considered more technological in status than others"; for example, "a drum machine is more technological than a drum." Conversely, more established tools and systems are rendered "invisible as technologies" (1999, 112).

Correspondingly, some image- and sound-based practices of representation appear and sound more technological than others. Films that make extensive use of computer graphic imaging (CGI); images of industry, machinery, computers, motorized vehicles, automation, robotics, and cybernetics; holograms: these images visualize what is now seen as "high tech"—as, for earlier historical audiences, did images of automata, silent films, and jukeboxes. In the milieu of sound, the electronic dance tracks of Deadmau5 sound more technological than the country songs of Taylor Swift, although very similar instruments and sound engineering practices may be used in the recording and performance of each (for instance, drum machines, multitrack recorders, mixing boards, and speaker towers). The audibility of technology has long belonged to popular music's politics of authenticity, from the first phonographs—which were understood by band musicians as a direct threat to their livelihood, the threat of automation—to the complex fallout of disco's "death" at the end of the 1970s: rejected ostensibly for its artifice, but ideologically for its queerness, disco returned to the dance underground, where its artificiality was not jettisoned but rather intensified, to re-emerge in the 1980s as house, techno, and the spectrum of sounds now known as "EDM"—electronic dance music. The complexities EDM has brought to pop music's politics of authenticity, in terms of "liveness," are explored in chapter 7.

Given the cultural functions and effects of technology's "index of visibility," the discourse of technology as I theorize it in this book includes some sound and image productions and practices as well as textual articulations. While Deadmau5's house tracks make only scant reference to "technology" in their lyrical content, the discourse of technology audibly pervades the production, performance, and reception of this music. "Technology" occurs only once in the script of Cronenberg's 1983 film *Videodrome*—but the discourse of technology visibly permeates the whole film, in its sensational imagery of consumer home electronics that grow grotesquely monstrous. So this study investigates Frankensteinian figures of technology, not exclusively in textual constructions but also in selected sound- and image-based cultural productions: film, music, and photography, some examples of which are compared in chapter 8.

This visibility or spectacular character of technology discourse has its epistemic roots in *Frankenstein*'s monster and the nascent industrialism it figures. As David Nye notes, in the nineteenth century, "the English were prone to view industrialization in terms of satanic mills, frankensteinian monsters, and class strife" (1994, 54). Marxist readers of Shelley's novel have shown how Frankenstein's monster, as a reanimated collage of corpses, became legible as a monstrous image of the working class. "In the anatomist's assembly of the monster," writes David McNally, Shelley "imaginatively reconstructs the process by which the working class was created: first dissected (separated from the land and their communities), then reassembled as a frightening collective entity . . . the proletarian mob" (2011, 95). But Shelley's monster was composed—not coincidentally—during the Luddite machine-breaking disturbances of the mid-1810s (O'Flinn 1986), so the monster has also become legible as a figure of the industrial, technological mode of capitalist production that yielded the working class: a mode of production that incorporated alienated labour, automation, Fordist assembly lines, Taylorist management, the increasing mobility of capital and labour, and the consolidation and ascent of corporate business structure. Sometimes figuring the "vampiric" leadership of corporate capitalism, sometimes figuring the zombie-like labour of industrial workers, and sometimes figuring both at once—as in Marx's famous, grotesque image of capital as "dead labour which, vampire-like, lives only by sucking living labour" ([1867] 1976, 342)—Shelley's vividly imaginative construct has spawned its own "hideous progeny" in many representations and mediations of technology and technological change under capitalism.

As illustrated by the many examples found in major compendia of *Frankenstein* in popular culture (for instance, Forry 1990; Hitchcock 2007; Morton 2002), *Frankenstein* has established and disseminated a vivid vocabulary of not just textual but multimodal, multimedia images of technology: from an 1821 cartoon placing a bound edition of *Frankenstein* among dental instruments (fig. 1), to the oeuvre of Cronenberg's "body horror" films, discussed in chapter 5, to the cultural hostilities over the aura of "liveness" versus the audibility of automation that are perennially enacted between new and established music-making practices (see chapter 7). As mediated by the classic cinematic adaptations of *Frankenstein*, even the image of throwing a switch exemplifies an image of technology that embeds an evocative Frankensteinian subtext. "When all is ready, I throw this switch": this line from a 1938 radio show about Superman, sampled by Coldcut in their 1987 remix of Eric B. and Rakim's rap track "Paid in Full," occurs early, right before the first instance of the lyrical refrain "Pump up the volume." The sample about switch throwing thus lends a Frankensteinian tone to the rest of the track as a dense collage of audio samples all grafted together and fused with major components of the rap artists' original single.

Figure 1 A. E. "Tugging at a ~~High~~ Eye Tooth." Coloured etching by G. Cruikshank, after A. E. 1821. Note the copy of *Frankenstein* on the bookshelf. Image courtesy of the Wellcome Collection. Photo CC4.0 licensed from Wellcome Collection.

Sometimes, textual articulations of technology combine with visual and other representational strategies to reinforce and reify the popular understanding of technology as the latest in high tech, which as of this writing encompasses largely consumer-oriented, digital, networking tools and systems, things like mobile devices and social media. And sometimes, too, these multimodal representative strategies converge to suggest something else about what technology means. Consider Larry Rosen's 2012 book *iDisorder: Understanding Our Obsession with Technology and Overcoming Its Hold on Us*. The title and subtitle themselves suggest a lot about what's meant here by "technology": the "i" in "iDisorder" connotes Apple's branding, which together with the word "obsession" suggest that by "technology," Rosen means consumer digital electronics and systems. Furthermore, "obsession" and the trope of "overcoming its hold" suggest a dialectic of desire and danger; technology is implied to be an agent or enabler of something like addiction. The trope of "overcoming" a "hold" suggests that technology is an adversarial power the reader is wrestling with or struggling against. The cover image shows the black silhouette of a tortured soul trapped in the white screen of a Blackberry-like device (which maybe also suggests the book isn't just blaming Apple?). The vague and inclusive "us" commonly found in general-audience and self-help books implies the book's target market to be middle-class users of networked mobile devices who think there's a problem with their use. In his book's introductory chapter, Rosen quickly establishes that by technology he means digital, networked devices. He sums up his book's aim as an effort to "demonstrate how the technologies that we use daily coerce us to act in ways that may be detrimental to our well-being" and "to recognize the craziness that technology can promote and discover new ways to stay sane" (2012, 5–6). Or, as the publisher's blurb about the book, quoted on the author's webpage, puts it, "Rosen teaches us how to stay human in an increasingly technological world" (Rosen 2011). I am neither supporting nor disputing Rosen's ideas or his expertise in technophobia and what he has termed "technostress" (2012, 6); my point here is that his study of technology-conditioned psychological disorders and how to alleviate their "symptoms" (6) itself exhibits a symptomatic sense of technology, in not only its writing but also its visual design and marketing media, engaging a multimodal vocabulary of technology discourse that figures technology not only in terms of "revolutionary" newness but also in terms of danger, globalization, contagion, and opposition to humanity. As I hope the following chapters here will show, this discourse has a distinctively Frankensteinian (and a less obviously but no less significantly Canadian) provenance.

Given the coordinated arrays of textual, visual, and other representations of technology that inform and structure arguments like these about technology—arguments which often implicitly refer to contemporary, more visibly "technological" technologies—close and carefully contextualized reading demonstrates that such arguments, far from novel, reproduce long-embedded cultural assumptions about technology's definition and, as importantly, about its fetish character—the uncanny apprehension that "it's alive!" In the process, such arguments retell the old but perennially relevant story of *Frankenstein*.

It's a story well enough known and discussed in both the scholarly and popular traditions. Winner ends *Autonomous Technology: Technics-out-of-Control as a Theme in Political Thought* with a chapter called "Frankenstein's Problem"—an explication of Mary Shelley's novel that brings home his own point about "our involvement with technology," namely, that "we are dealing with an unfinished creation, largely forgotten and uncared for, which is forced to make its own way in the world" (1977, 316). Edward Tenner starts *Why Things Bite Back: Technology and the Revenge of Unintended Consequences* with a chapter called "Ever Since Frankenstein," in which he adopts Shelley's novel as a framing allegory for his tour of the "revenge effects" of technology in medicine, computing, and other high-tech areas of modern life. "It was Mary Shelley's *Frankenstein*," Tenner writes, "that first connected Promethean technology with unintended havoc. . . . Mary Shelley wrote prophetically at the dawn of technological systems thinking" (1996, 14, 15). In his book, Tenner isn't interested in the linguistic or theoretical aspects of technology: he briskly defines it, in his preface, as "humankind's modification of its biological and physical surroundings" (xi). But his claim that *Frankenstein* "first connected" technology and backlash might well describe the claim of the present study, in terms of language and discourse as well as culture. Likewise, Winner's proviso—that his claim is "not, as the boosters may conclude, that technology is a monstrosity or an evil in and of itself" (1977, 316)—is one my argument inverts, in terms of how the word is used and what discourses are involved in its construction and meaning making. In the chapters that follow, I aim to show that *Frankenstein* and its Canadian adaptations have constructed the modern English word technology as a figure of manufactured monstrosity and have globally popularized this sense of it.

Logocentrism and "Revolutionary Technology"

The cultural and epistemological space that *Frankenstein* opened for the modern meaning of technology must also be contextualized according to a broader historical order of Western discourse that it has been the project of deconstruction to critique: the hierarchical ordering of speech over writing, *logos* over *technē*. The reinvention and reconfiguration of the globalized discourse of technology that began in Mary Shelley's time, and accelerated in McLuhan's, both built on and transformed the epistemology and language of this deeper cultural logic of logocentrism, of the privileging of voice and presence and "the debasement of writing" (Derrida [1967] 1976, 3). As McLuhan described his work as a footnote to that of Harold Innis, I might describe this work as a footnote to that of Jacques Derrida.

As Derrida has exhaustively investigated ([1981] 1988), criticisms of new media are anything but new. In the third century BCE, Plato, in *Phaedrus*, famously wrote against writing, in Socrates's account of the mythic encounter between the Egyptian god Theuth, inventor of writing, and King Thamus, who warns that the invention will not preserve memory but rather destroy it. This ancient parable has become a primal scene for representations of media and tools in terms of change and supplementation, of new tools not just replacing old but threatening and overthrowing them, in processes we would now call innovation and obsolescence. Correspondingly, this parable furnishes a primal scene for the perennially hostile response of established cultural and economic interests to new technological developments. Friedrich Kittler points out that the oldest known image of a print shop, from 1499, depicts it "as a dance of death" ([1986] 1999, 5). David Thornburg's *Edutrends 2010* (1992) recounts a history of hostile reactions from educational institutions to new media technologies, from criticisms of paper (in favour of slate and chalk) in 1815, to criticisms of ink (in favour of pencils) in 1907, to criticisms of disposable ballpoint pens in 1950. Before dismissing the apparent absurdity of this litany of objections to what might now seem the most unobjectionable, most commonplace media tools, consider that the litany has continued more or less unabated, from early twentieth-century criticisms of film, radio, television, and home recording (as seen in Cronenberg's *Videodrome*), through mid-1990s concerns over email, to today's anxieties about mobile devices, texting, and social media.

The popular music business demonstrates a dramatic and ongoing history of perennial recoil from new media for their perceived threat to established systems and vested interests. The music industry's campaign against file sharing reproduces historical campaigns: audio engineers against samplers, vinyl producers against cassettes and CDs, and musicians against phonographs and jukeboxes, which, as Sarah Thornton (1996) documents, were constructed as a similar threat to live—meaning *authentic*—musicianship; in chapter 7, this study looks at how this politics of presence and authenticity is now reproduced, however ironically, in the context of DJ culture, which is organized predominantly around the playback of recordings. Tellingly, Thornton's book reproduces an image from *DJ Magazine* that echoes the 1499 picture of a skeleton-surrounded print shop—an image of "the death of vinyl," showing one shrouded skeleton clutching a record, and another clutching a CD and a sampler (1996, 64). In this long tradition, the major record labels' current copyright campaign tries to win public sympathy by appeals on behalf of the recording artists' labour that the labels actually exploit. The labels and their intermediaries make appeals to authorial originality as a principle of "making one's living" (a disingenuous appeal, given that corporations, not artists, hold music recording copyrights in the overwhelming majority of cases), in opposition to technologies figured as theft, as the privation of "honest" labour and its replacement by inhuman, automatic processes. Today's "copyfight" sees this dialectic of Romantic individualism versus monstrous technology being deployed by all interested parties: while the corporate entertainment lobby paints Romantic portraits of "starving artists" staving off a global horde of pirates armed with a Pandora's box of digital technology, the so-called pirates, a pejoratively defined group that includes a great many legitimate, noninfringing media consumers and users, mobilize grassroots defences of expressive freedom and personal privacy against the digital locks, kill switches, trolling, cease-and-desist notices, and suspensions of service imposed by "Big Media" acting more and more like Big Brother.

This long-standing historical pattern of public conflicts between established interests and upstart innovation has furnished Western cultural history with scenes of Luddites versus technocrats, of "dinosaur" industries versus nimble entrepreneurs, and indeed of "zombie economics" wielding a dead hand's power over new attempts by the living to make a living (Quiggin 2010). This pattern has thus also furnished the English language with figures of technofetishists and technocrats, and has installed a sensational rhetoric of revolution in the discourse of technology: a rhetoric of rivalry and replacement in modes of production and consumption, in industrial and communication developments. As David McKitterick (2003) points out, the historical record shows not that new media replace old and render them obsolete, but rather that new and old media enter into more complex negotiations and mutual accommodations, adapting to one another in a changing media ecology. Nevertheless, the more arresting figure of revolution dominates popular culture and the hegemonic social imaginary, driven in part by modernity's distinctive ambivalence toward technological innovation. This ambivalence—which inflects the modern usage of "technology" itself, through the popular mediations of *Frankenstein*—marks the reception and representation of successive media and communication technologies as though competing for supremacy in a zero-sum mediascape, rather than coexisting and sometimes collaborating (as well as occasionally competing, to be sure) in an increasingly complex mediascape.

This sensational (and durably market-tested) image of "revolutionary technology" tends to trump more nuanced understandings of technological change in the popular imaginary. The rhetoric of "revolution" that marks so much public and commercial discourse surrounding technology (especially consumer technology) can be attributed in part to Mary Shelley; as will be discussed in chapter 3, the creature that stands as an anticipatory figure of technology is characterized significantly through tropes of revolution (among others). And this rhetoric can be also attributed in part to Marshall McLuhan's media theory; his writing emphasizes an epochal rhetoric of change, in which new media come to replace old, and in the process inaugurate new epochs that succeed old ones, and new forms of subjectivity and society that supplant earlier ones. So it is not only because of the capitalist structuring of an economic world-system around competition and rivalry but also because of the discursive figuration of technology as a manufactured monster run amok that, as Kevin Robins and Frank Webster assert, "the idea of technological revolution has become normative—routine and commonplace—in our technological times" (1999, 1).

Canadian Popular Culture in Postcolonial Context

So what do these concerns with the discourse of technology have to do with Canada in particular? Quite a lot, I hope to show: Canada is a modern nation-state whose social fabric is deeply interwoven with defining preoccupations with technology, media, and globalization. Establishing the Canadian context for this argument means attending to the continuum of national and global cultural relays and relations that position and pressure Canadian popular culture, according to a postcolonially informed revision of two concepts: *technological nationalism*, which describes

Canada's ambivalent investment in technology for nation building; and *media imperialism*, which describes Canada's equally ambivalent relationship to cultural globalization, sometimes as the colonizer but more often as the colonized.

Canadian *Frankenstein* adaptations, like Canadian popular culture more generally, invite a postcolonial perspective. As I have argued elsewhere, the literatures of Indigenous and other racialized minorities have generally occupied a more prominent place in postcolonial analyses of Canadian nation building than have the popular culture and literature of the white, anglophone mainstream (McCutcheon 2009, 765). To redirect postcolonial attention to Canadian popular culture intends "neither to contest nor to dismiss the growing and critically self-reflexive foci on diasporic and indigenous literatures" (2009, 766)—these foci remain urgently important. Rather, the purpose in paying postcolonialist attention to Canadian popular culture is to rethink Canada's mobilizations of popular culture for political economic projects in nation building and globalized capital (which government policy, in the age of neoliberalism, has increasingly considered to be the same thing). Such rethinking means both working with and moving beyond the traditional triangulation of Canadian popular culture between its "British and American 'parent' formations" (Bodroghkozy 2002, 568): working with this triangulation, by acknowledging its political economic map of Canada's cultural industries, and moving beyond it, by interrogating its nationalist premises in the tracking of diasporic, transnational, and networked cultural practices and processes. That is, a postcolonialist premise and the subject of adaptations bring considerations of cultural and economic globalization to bear on the study of Canadian-based institutions, producers, and practices of popular culture making. What postcolonial attention to Canadian popular culture can provide is a way of "doing the national differently" (Pennee 1999, 83), articulating connections among Canadian culture and policy, the transnational corporate interests that pressure and colonize them (Hedges 2012), and the globally and digitally distributed scenes and communities that use them.

The need for more postcolonialist critique of Canadian popular culture specifically accords with Vijay Devadas's and Chris Prentice's general observation that "popular culture is one of those neglected domains of enquiry for postcolonial studies" and their consequent assertion that popular culture and postcolonialist critique matter profoundly to each other

(2011, 687). Identifying the globalized capitalist world-system as (among other things) a legacy of colonialism, they write:

> Popular culture today is of significance for postcolonial studies as it is the terrain of struggle between a dominant capitalist force . . . and resistances to it. . . . Popular culture provides the ground for constituting forms of resistance to hegemonic (often nationalist) power structuring social and political relations, and cultural expression, in the wake of colonialism. (2011, 690)

In the context of Canada's resource extraction-based economy and its nation-building cultural policy tool kit (e.g., Canadian content quotas and public investment supports for cultural production across media; see Grant and Wood 2004), Canadian popular culture is inevitably invested in and intertwined with global forces, both economic and cultural. A postcolonial analysis thus entails situating Canadian popular culture between technological nationalism, on the one hand, and media imperialism, on the other.

Technological Nationalism and Media Imperialism

"Technological nationalism" is a term coined by Maurice Charland to describe a "Canadian ideological discourse" that "ascribes to technology the capacity to create a nation by enhancing communication"—but, in the process, "ties a Canadian identity, not to its people, but to their mediation through technology" (1986, 197). Postmodernist scholar Arthur Kroker took up the term and developed it in his 1984 book *Technology and the Canadian Mind*. Here, Kroker identified an "original, comprehensive, and eloquent discourse on technology" (1984, 7) in the work of George Grant, Harold Innis, and Marshall McLuhan, a discourse that Kroker saw reflected in Canadian culture generally, citing as just a few examples, the music of Rush, the fiction of Margaret Atwood, and the brutalist-futurist architecture of urban Canada, like the iconic CN Tower. Reading technological nationalism less as a nation-building ideology and more as a widely diffused cultural discourse, Kroker finds in this discourse notes of ambivalence and anxiety; he sees technological nationalism as "the essence of the Canadian state and . . . the Canadian identity," an effect of Canada's geohistorical position between "the 'technological imperative' in American empire and the classical origins of the technological dynamo in European history" (7, 10). In its positioning of Canadian nation building amidst the cross-border proximity of the United States, the transatlantic reach of Europe, and the unevenly developing regime of globalization, technological nationalism is not unlike a theory of Canada's postcoloniality. The "Canadian discourse on technology," according to Kroker, "thrusts us into the centre of a debate of world significance" over issues of "neotechnical capitalism" and "global media system[s]" (18)—issues now widely recognized as integral to postcolonial globalization.

Questions of the global occur with special stress in Kroker's discussion of McLuhan, in whose work Kroker sees an ambivalent "technological humanism": a markedly ambivalent mix of optimism for a better technological tomorrow and anxiety over the present "processed world of technology" (60). In Kroker's account, McLuhan keeps a wary but hopeful ear pressed to the ground of the global village. The concept of technological nationalism thus demonstrates a rudimentary Canadian postcolonial perspective, and sets a suggestive ideological scene for this reading of Canadian adaptations of *Frankenstein*, in which the work of McLuhan and the discourse of technology figure prominently. Tellingly, a 2010 public opinion poll described its "statistical amalgam" of "the qualities Canadians have told us they want in a leader" as "an ideal political Frankenstein" (Graves 2010).

However, as with so much other critical writing on technology, Kroker leaves this and other core keywords unproblematized. And, besides *technology*, Kroker holds *Canada* and *nation* to be self-evident. This nationalist assumption is problematic for both postcolonial criticism and Canadian popular culture alike. Postcolonial studies in Canada have mounted some of the most forceful critiques of nationalism, especially as manifested in official multiculturalism: the Canadian state's policy to promote cultural and racial diversity. Popularly and officially celebrated as a defining characteristic of Canadian nationalism, multiculturalism is also "the strict ideological correlate of transnational capitalism" (Lazarus 1999, 223). For postcolonial critics, Canadian official multiculturalism amounts almost to a Frankensteinian figure: an experimental, ideological state apparatus that assembles a culturally differentiated body politic into a national "fantasy of unity," while mystifying the neoliberal political economy of precarious, privatized, and poorly paid work that this apparatus serves. Multiculturalism's fantasy of diversity masks the realities of racialized difference; it mobilizes and manages the flows of exploitable labour that sustain the flexible accumulations of global capital (Bannerji 2000, 87).

The problematization of nationalism in Canadian popular culture assumes a more conventional, even colonial character, encapsulated in the diffident, sardonic slogan "as Canadian as possible under the circumstances": the winning entry in a 1970s CBC contest to complete the phrase "as Canadian as . . . ." Such a slogan signals both the colonially conditioned cliché that Canada has no culture, and the perennially present danger that the United States poses to Canadian sovereignty. To appreciate this slogan as a good synopsis of Canadian popular culture, though, we need to explore how the thesis of media imperialism describes Canadian popular culture's historical and economic conditions.

As theorized by Oliver Boyd-Barrett (1977), the media imperialism thesis posits "the unidirectional nature of international media flows from a small number of source countries" (Lorimer, Gasher, and Skinner 2008, 287). Although the thesis has been challenged for its deterministic model of unilateral cultural power—thus neglecting the appropriations of "imperial" media products by its target audience "colonies"—I think that a postcolonial approach to analyzing Canadian cultural production, amidst the high-pressure state of US-Canadian trade relations and their implications for Canadian sovereignty, warrants a critical retrieval of the media imperialism thesis, which not only describes a model for cultural exportation but suggests that such trade is intimately connected to political takeover. A postcolonial redeployment of the media imperialism thesis recognizes these processes: the uses of cultural production as a tool of empire and hegemony; the adoption of imperial structures and strategies by transnational conglomerates; and the constant, increasing pressure by US corporate lobby groups to liberalize trade with—or, in other words, exploit—Canada in everything from cultural products (viewed by corporate lobbies as multiplatform intellectual property), to health care (viewed as a market, not a public service), to water (viewed as a commodity, not a human right). Since US hegemony propagates the notion that capitalism and democracy are mutually constituted (not mutually antagonistic, as political economic analysis actually shows them to be), the difference between media and political imperialism collapses, when viewed from a Canadian perspective.

On the political, economic, and cultural fronts, Canada depends on US interests and industry in material ways that compromise the northern state's political sovereignty and render its relationship to its southern neighbour ambivalent and conflicted, as well as effectively nonnegotiable. This relationship is analyzed anxiously from north of the forty-ninth parallel, while being ignored or misrecognized from the south: "Americans have an amazing tendency to assimilate Canadian work to American experience. . . . Canada doesn't exist as a national entity to the U.S." (John Greyson, quoted in Marks 2005, 198).

If Canada doesn't exist as a nation from the US perspective, then it can hardly claim a distinct cultural existence on that account. In fact, in a global context, the US entertainment industry has become virtually synonymous with "popular culture" itself; the United States is the global leader, by a wide margin, in net royalty and license fee exports—the earnings made in payments for the authorized use of intellectual properties (SASI Group and Newman 2006). Hollywood was one of the first globalized cultural industries, and Canada's relationship with Hollywood is long-standing and conflicted (Gasher 2002). Canada provides Hollywood with cheap and abundant film industry services, labour, and resources. Canadian shooting locations are not just conveniently close to Hollywood, but actively promote themselves as stand-ins for US locations, as sites primed for colonization: "largely unpopulated place[s] full of scenic wonders and infinite resources" (Rutherford 2005, 106). The predominance of the United States in popular cultural production is indicated by Canadian media and culture consumption patterns: English-speaking Canadians consume far more American than domestic media products. The predominance of US content on Canadian screens is about more than what Aniko Bodroghkozy calls, however rightly, "our taste for American popular culture" (2002, 570); it is, more importantly, a specific material effect of neoimperial trade economics. US media companies export their products to foreign carriers for a fraction of what they charge US carriers, making it cheaper for Canadian broadcasters to buy US imports than to finance domestic production— however popular that domestic content may be.

As Peter Grant and Chris Wood explain, these "curious economics" of globalized popular culture have occasioned state policies that protect cultural sovereignty and diversity of expression, which would otherwise be destroyed by narrow adherence to free-market ideology. Canada has kept its own cultural sector exempt (so far) from free-trade agreements, and it has developed a policy tool kit for stimulating domestic popular cultural production, on the premise that state investment in cultural production builds nationalism and sovereignty (2004, 386–88). In economic terms, the popularity of a cultural product is productively theorized as a paradox: what is popular is what a publisher or company thinks will sell well; however, no one can predict what will sell well. But popular culture is a matter of ideology as well as "curious economics" (2004, 44). Popular culture is a "self-conscious term created by the intelligentsia and now adopted by the general public to mark off class divisions in the generic types of culture and their intended audience" (Jenkins, McPherson, and Shuttac 2002, 28). This class-based concept of popular culture remains as ideologically powerful as mass production is economically material to the ways in which popular culture can articulate national imaginings.

And in Canada, the discourse and production of popular culture relate to nationalism under postcolonial and neocolonial Anglo-American paradigms of culture. Canada's tool kit of public media, content quotas, and funding agencies also includes some instruments for supporting Canadian scholarly as well as popular culture; however, Social Sciences and Humanities Research Council (SSHRC) funding for Canadian cultural studies research has only been formalized within the last decade. This belated recognition of Canadian cultural studies is a symptom of the field's own postcolonial historical neglect by a national intellectual elite that has privileged Arnoldian ideals of culture over and against American industries of entertainment, seen as a threat to Canada's national sovereignty (Rutherford 2005, 105).

Notwithstanding the dismissal of media imperialism by communications scholars, cultural and literary studies have picked up and built on it in researches informed by theories of nationalism, postcolonialism, and globalization (Mookerjea, Szeman, and Farschou 2009). Postcolonial readings of Canadian popular culture sustain the media imperialism thesis not despite but due to Canada's ambivalent relationship to US popular culture. In a critique of Canadian cultural policy, Donna Pennee recounts how Canadian foreign policy has deployed "'culture' from the Cold War to 'the Market Wars,' from the explicitly 'ideological' threats to national security, to the explicit but apparently nonideological threats of global capitalism" (1999, 196). As Pennee shows, one paradigm of culture is represented by the state's leverage of culture as security: "The history of the nation-state's use of culture in foreign policy," Pennee writes, "can be read as a sort of barometer of change in the status of nation-statism, in the means of international relations, and in determinations of what is at stake in security debates as power relations shift from the Cold War to the (unnamed as such) Market Wars" (1999, 196).

Laura Marks employs Homi Bhabha's model of pedagogy and performance in national identity to explore how "the little performances that constitute Canada insinuate themselves into the massive national fiction that constitutes the United States" (2005, 197). Marks explores American images of Canada, and observes what she calls the "'little bit off' quality in Canadian images, seen from a U.S. perspective": Canada's identity-with-a-difference, in metonymic terms, poses a "subversive potential" in "American contexts," with "the detail" of Canadian difference making "it possible to question the whole" ideological apparatus of US nationalist identity (2005, 198). This kind of ironic signification is represented in the performances of *Daily Show* reporters Bee and Jones, whose Canadian citizenship was a running joke on the show. Conversely, looking at Canadian images of America, Bodroghkozy arrives at a similar conclusion: "It is a foundation of fine details, typically unnoticed by non-Canadians, upon which Canadians have built their shaky edifice of national identity" (2002, 579).

Diana Brydon has forged important links between postcolonialism and globalization studies; alluding to the vexed question of national sovereignty and the US government's targeting of postcolonialism "as yet another enemy of US patriotism," Brydon succinctly reaffirms the urgency with which "postcolonial critique continues to pose a challenge to the new incarnations of Empire" (2004, 693). The perspectives on nationalism and media imperialism developed in postcolonial research like that surveyed here represent one way of "doing the national differently" (Pennee 2004, 83), by adding a nuanced sense of cultural and economic globalization to Canadian cultural studies' established materialist focus on the institutions and media of cultural production.

An adequately nuanced postcolonial reworking of media imperialism amidst globalization can also recognize that it is not a one-way process. While the exponentially larger cultural economies of the United States and the United Kingdom have historically colonized and continue to colonize Canadian popular culture, there are ways in which Canadian popular culture has infiltrated, occupied, and colonized the global flows of cultural production and reception. Canadian *Frankenstein*s represent one trajectory for such infiltrations. Likewise, a properly nuanced postcolonial approach to Canadian popular culture needs to remain critically self-reflexive in how it handles texts drawn from a spectrum of class, gender, and racialized positions across the field of cultural production— how it contextualizes both mainstream and marginalized texts in relation to power structures. Postcolonial studies in Canada have conventionally eschewed popular cultural subjects on account of their very popularity, their centrality to the mainstream culture of the implicitly white, capitalist, patriarchal "Great White North." That is, the cultural centrality of Canadian popular texts has relegated them to the margins of postcolonial studies, which are centred in mapping the cultural margins. But because postcolonial methodologies are demonstrably among those best equipped to attend to globalization, adaptation, and culture's articulations of power, a postcolonial perspective can and should be brought to bear on texts and practices on the cultural peripheries *and* on those at the cultural centre, as well as on the feedback between them.

Canada and Globalization

Outlining the postcolonial contexts of Canadian popular culture in this way means simultaneously outlining Canadian popular culture's involvements with globalization, understood here as an intensification of international flows of money and labour, whose chief beneficiaries are multinational corporations (Appadurai 1990, Sassen 2000).

Globalization is important for contextualizing Canada's political and cultural economies, and for understanding the popular discourse of technology: virtually any technological risk or threat is represented as an intrinsically global threat. The popular understanding of technology in a global sense is prefigured in Shelley's novel, as Victor Frankenstein imagines, as the ultimate result of his research, that a "race of devils would be propagated upon the earth" (Shelley [1818] 2012, 174). Since then, *Frankenstein* has been used to sound the alarm over technologies typically understood as global in their reach and risks, from nuclear power (Morton 2002, 56) to file sharing: "digital piracy is Hollywood's own digital Frankenstein," writes one film industry observer (Sickels 2009, 22). Even the chief agent and institution of globalization itself, the modern corporation, has attracted *Frankenstein* analogies and figurations since the Great Depression. Mitchell Dawson's 1930 magazine article "Frankenstein, Inc." expresses the author's thoroughgoing suspicion of corporations in most sectors, such as "the gigantic press Frankensteins which now control the news and public opinion." Dawson envisions "the corporate Frankenstein" inaugurating an age in which "law and government will be nullified" (1930, 276, 279): an age that scholars have since theorized as that of present-day globalization. Frankensteinian representations of corporate business after the Depression resonate profoundly today, in Canada and globally (McCutcheon 2011).

Pertinent to the present discussion is the interdependence, even the mutual constitution, of technology and globalization discourses: neither term would mean entirely what it does, today, without being echoed in the other. Globalization theory privileges technology in its models of transnational political and cultural economy, chiefly for facilitating the mobile exploits of capital. Jonathan Beller reads the technological imperative as a core value of globalization in the popular Frankensteinian image of the cyborg, which he describes as "the intersecting of the human being from anywhere in the world . . . and the technology (military, industrial, and informational) endemic to transnational capitalism" (1996, 195). Arjun Appadurai coins the term "technoscape"—among other related "-scapes" of globalization (e.g., "financescape," "mediascape")—to name "the global configuration, also ever fluid, of technology, and of the fact that technology, both high and low, both mechanical and informational, now moves at high speeds across various kinds of previously impervious boundaries" (1990, 297). Appadurai's usage of "technology" here, like his coinage of "technoscape," exploits a sense of technology as uncontainable leak—as contagion—that, as the subsequent chapters will show, arises from the characterization of Frankenstein's creature as modernity's founding image of technology, and from McLuhan's imagery of technology as manufactured, monstrous, and global in its impact.

2. Refocusing Adaptation Studies

Modern Myth and "Frankenpheme": Adapting *Frankenstein*

Shelley's novel has long furnished a grotesque, sensational figure for the routine representations of technology in general, or a given technology in particular, as some kind of risk or danger. As Jay Clayton notes, *Frankenstein* is an "obligatory reference in any attempt to challenge the technological pride of the modern era" (2003, 128). This kind of allusive signification constitutes one of the text's major functions as a "Frankenpheme" (Morton 2002, 47), and, thus, as a reason for thinking about how to refocus adaptation studies. Tenner's aforementioned use of *Frankenstein* exemplifies this kind of "obligatory reference." Moreover, in describing the novel as "prophetic," and in using it to frame his own Frankensteinian stories about technology's "revenge effects," Tenner's series of stories, with their freight of commentary, recalls the narrative structure of *Frankenstein* as a sequence of stories recounted and commented on by Walton, the ship captain. Tenner's book thus adopts the image of the monster, as an allegorical figure of technological risk, and (intentionally or otherwise) some of the narrative elements from Shelley's novel. Does this mean we might position Tenner's book itself as an adaptation of *Frankenstein*? In this section, I want to explore this kind of question with reference to the literature on adaptations of *Frankenstein*, and with reference to the theory of adaptation studies.

Almost as soon as it was published in 1818, *Frankenstein* began fuelling an extraordinarily rich and varied tradition of adaptations, across a spectrum of media, genres, and intertextual, intercultural networks; this tradition now almost constitutes a cultural industry unto itself. *Frankenstein* resonates throughout Western culture as a unique "modern myth"—a definitively modern text that has paradoxically assumed the power of myth (Baldick 1987). Ironically, it is perhaps not Shelley's novel itself so much as its multimedia adaptations that have secured this peculiar privilege for the story. As William St. Clair recounts, the book was out of print through much of the nineteenth century and was best known through its stage—and, more recently, its screen—adaptations (2004, 367). The text itself has been doubly marginalized: not only eclipsed by its adaptations and the vicissitudes of copyright, but exiled from the English literary canon and relegated to "pulp" status until the 1970s and 1980s, when feminist, Marxist, and other theoretical and political trends in English literary studies revisited it and precipitated a great deal of research and criticism that has promoted it to canonical status (Hitchcock 2007, 281). *Frankenstein* is now one of the most widely taught English novels in secondary and post-secondary English curriculum. (I had to read a comic-book adaptation in Grade 8, and the novel's 1831 edition in an undergraduate seminar.)

Major contributions to the study of *Frankenstein* adaptations—literary, theatrical, and otherwise—emerged as part of the novel's overall academic rehabilitation in the latter quarter of the twentieth century and have striven, ambitiously, to survey the scope and diversity of *Frankenstein*'s receptions, reworkings, and recontextualizations. Among the first studies of *Frankenstein* adaptation was Levine and Knoepflmacher's anthology *The Endurance of Frankenstein* (1979), which argued the novel's value on the basis of its impact on and reworkings in popular culture. In 1973, science fiction writer Brian Aldiss argued that *Frankenstein* is the foundational ur-text of modern science fiction: it resituated Gothic fiction in a modern setting, it transformed fantasy into extrapolation, and it told an iconic, allegorical story of hubris clobbered by nemesis ([1973] 1986, 26). Aldiss's cogent argument achieved as close to a consensus on the origins of science fiction as is likely to be found among scholars of the form (see Freedman 2002). Developing Aldiss's interpretation, George Slusser theorized science fiction as a narrative literature of "the Frankenstein barrier": the foreclosure of future possibilities by present contingencies, played out in plots "where the present, lurking all along, rises up to avenge the sins of our uncreated future" (1992, 71).

Other studies have turned from page to stage, documenting the prolific performance traditions of *Frankenstein* adaptation. Steven Forry's *Hideous Progenies* (1990) historicizes and reprints several nineteenth-century dramatic adaptations; Caroline Picart's *The Cinematic Rebirths of Frankenstein* (2002) details the twentieth century's Universal and Hammer franchises and other film versions. The proliferation of new media forms since the latter twentieth century has prompted some studies to conduct broader surveys that sample the diversified mediascape, as in Susan Tyler Hitchcock's *Frankenstein: A Cultural History* (2007) and Timothy Morton's *Mary Shelley's* Frankenstein: *A Sourcebook* (2002).

The present study builds in particular on Morton's idea of "Frankenphemes" and Christopher Baldick's theory of *Frankenstein's* modern myth," as well as Pedro Javier Pardo García's (2005) argument for expanding the scope and vocabulary of *Frankenstein* adaptation studies—on which more below. The value of Morton's idea comes into clearer focus if we consider Baldick's first. Baldick's *In Frankenstein's Shadow: Myth, Monstrosity, and Nineteenth-Century Writing* theorizes *Frankenstein* as a modern myth and thus as a paradox: a text that is at once modern, and a critique of modernity, and a "household name" imbued with mythic symbolism (1987, 1). Baldick argues that *Frankenstein* has achieved this modern mythic status via reductive reproductions of its basic "skeleton story," comprised of two pivotal plot points: first, the good doctor makes a living creature out of bits of corpses; and second, this creature turns on him and runs amok (3). Baldick then shows how this skeleton story gets fleshed out through two main lines of popular interpretation: a psychological interpretation in which the creature represents the "return of the repressed"; and a "technological reduction" of the story as "an uncanny prophecy of dangerous scientific inventions" (7). Moreover, while these reductive popularizations constitute practices of creative adaptation, they also represent strategies of interpretive control and closure, as illustrated by the fixing of the creature's image in Boris Karloff's iconic film portrayal (5). The technological interpretation of *Frankenstein* is most salient to my purpose here, because *Frankenstein* helps us interpret the modern meaning of technology. It also seems the far more predominant of the two interpretations, among the text's receptions and adaptations.

Baldick's argument is resolutely and productively materialist; he argues that the *Frankenstein* myth manifests in the material accumulation of all the "adaptations, allusions, accretions, analogues, parodies, and plain misreadings which follow upon Mary Shelley's novel" (1987, 4). The inclusion of allusions is significant here. Baldick's analysis of *Frankenstein*'s legible impact on nineteenth-century writing and rhetoric is preoccupied with what Linda Hutcheon calls "palimpsestic intertextuality": the layering and modulation of textual referents and their sometimes recognized, sometimes latent links with one another that produce, in audiences, "intertextual expectations about medium and genre, as well as about specific work" (2006, 22). But while Hutcheon reserves these "multilaminated" receptions for extensive, acknowledged adaptations (21), Baldick excavates some of this specific work's more ephemeral references and esoteric reworkings. He attends, for instance, to the first documented use of *Frankenstein* as an "object of political allusion," which occurred in British parliamentary debates over abolition (60). As Baldick argues, the "kind of connection" found in tracking such a widely popular text as Mary Shelley's is not always "one between a given writer and a literary 'source'" but more often a Foucauldian genealogy of "subterranean and invisible diffusion in the cultures which adopt them" (9).

The "subterranean" circulation of *Frankenstein*'s central characters and "skeleton story" in adaptations as extensive as film series and as ephemeral as allusions thus finds an apt encapsulation in Morton's concept of the "Frankenpheme":

> "Frankenphemes" is the name I have chosen to give to those elements of culture that are derived from *Frankenstein*, but that are less than a work of art in completion or scale. Some kernel of an idea derived from Shelley's novel has been repeated in another medium. . . . They demonstrate the extent to which the novel has permeated the ways in which we see the world. (2002, 47–48)

Morton's examples of "Frankenphemes" include TV commercials, movie scenes, and allusive portmanteaus like "Frankenfoods," which emerged to frame debates over genetically modified organisms (GMOs) in agribusiness (2002, 48). The coinage, then, encapsulates the intertextual and appropriative practices of condensation and encoding that further the popular dispersal of *Frankenstein*'s modern myth in allusions, quotations, piecemeal or fragmentary adaptations, and other miscellaneous ephemera that abound in popular culture. The present study undertakes to explore several such popular cultural Frankenphemes, together with the discursive and cultural practices that produce and reproduce them in specific contexts.

Frankenphemes may not qualify as extensive, acknowledged adaptations, but they can be intensive, sometimes profoundly so. Explicating them as such means both developing and departing from Baldick's and Morton's interpretive practices. What distinguishes the present study from Baldick's and Morton's might be described as a matter of putting the proverbial horse before the cart, in light of textual evidence from *Frankenstein* in its period. My reading extends Baldick's argument into a chiasmus: if *Frankenstein* is so widely interpreted as "the first and most enduring symbol of modern technology" (Tropp, quoted in Baldick 1987, 7), it is because the novel conditioned the interpretation and usage of technology that began to emerge in Shelley's own time. In addition, this study follows Baldick's work in paying attention to the nuances and implications of allusive and other nonextensive adaptations, but breaks with it in treating them, through the lens of adaptation studies, *as adaptations*.

Positioning this work in adaptation studies (to which the next section turns) prompts a preliminary reflection on the interdisciplinary formation of adaptation studies and this formation's peculiar relationship to studying *Frankenstein*.

Morton acknowledges the basis of his coinage in the vocabulary of linguistics, the technical vocabulary of phonemes, graphemes, and so on. He adds the suffix *-eme*, which denotes a specific structural unit, to the first part of a name that signifies at once the text's title, the name of its protagonist, and the creature—according to the long-standing identification of the nameless creature with the name of its creator. The coinage pointedly echoes Richard Dawkins's 1976 coinage of the *meme*, "a unit of cultural transmission, or a unit of imitation"—an idea that catches on, basically ([1976] 1989, 192). Dawkins's meme idea has caught on itself, as the common name for the ideas and texts that are said to "go viral" in digital culture. Introducing her theory of adaptation, Hutcheon discusses the aptness of Dawkins's suggestion of "a cultural parallel to Darwin's biological theory" (2006, 31) for the study of intertextual reproduction with difference, and emphasizes culture's crucial distinction from biology: that mutation is the exception (albeit a critical one) in the process of genetic replication; however, in cultural transmission, it is much more the rule (32). As Morton's example of "Frankenfood" shows, the notion of Frankenphemes brings this interdisciplinary, linguistic borrowing full circle: if the life sciences have supplied elements of the vocabulary of evolution to the discourse of cultural adaptation ("I want a monosyllable that sounds a bit like 'gene'" [Dawkins 1976, 192]), then the discourse of *Frankenstein* adaptations has returned attention to life sciences that are now exploited to manipulate biological evolution itself. Thus Emily Ryall observes of "the language of genetic technology" that, "as Frankenstein himself is often depicted in popular conceptions of the fictional story as an eccentric and renegade scientist, the scientists who carry out genetic experimentation today are represented similarly" (2008, 369). Ryall's observation is also noteworthy here for its tightly paired references to the text's "popular conceptions"—its "technological reduction"—and the news media's "similar representations" of scientists—that is, as Frankenphemes.

These formally and thematically connected details of terminology and discourse in reconfiguring and redistributing *Frankenstein*—and in analyzing these reconfigurations and redistributions—thus make the case of *Frankenstein* adaptations both a challenge and an opportunity for the theory and methodology of adaptation studies more generally. Adaptations that are reduced to "skeleton stories," condensed in allusions, and encoded as memes occupy a shifting analytic shore, between the field of adaptation as it has been conventionally theorized and the ocean of open-ended intertextuality and heteroglossia.

Attuning Adaptation Studies to Nonnarrative and Nonextensive Cultural Forms

Adaptation studies is a field where literary, media, and cultural studies intersect, and it first emerged to investigate the negotiations and appropriations of literature by film. But like the mediascape itself, adaptation studies have diversified: to address more media and genres; to document specific oeuvres and traditions; to move from one-way to multilateral models of adaptation (between canonical and popular forms, old media and new); to account for social and political contexts; and to take stock of its own theory and practice.

Some of the most productive recent work in adaptation studies has focused on specific authors, like Shakespeare. *Adaptations of Shakespeare,* for instance, is a critical anthology of dramatic adaptations of Shakespeare's plays, and yet despite its strict focus on theatrical productions, editors Daniel Fischlin and Mark Fortier offer one of the most expansive working theories of adaptation, as "almost any act of alteration performed upon specific cultural works" (2000, 4). Taking stock of the overall character of adaptation practice in the context of *Frankenstein*'s proliferating multimedia progeny, Pedro Javier Pardo García suggests the term "cultural intertextuality" to better capture the breadth of citational, generic, discursive, and dialogic practices of interpretation, selection, and recombination that go into adaptation, especially postmodern adaptations like Kenneth Branagh's 1994 movie: "it is not just that the film perfectly exemplifies the concept," García writes, "but also that its representation of the creature turns it into a walking metaphor of cultural intertextuality" (2005, 240). The figurative suitability of the text and its main character for commenting on textual production and adaptation—their "perfect correspondence of matter and form" (240)—is something of a commonplace in *Frankenstein* criticism, as García acknowledges. It is a commonplace well worth rehearsing here, in order to inform my similarly expansive refocusing of adaptation studies methodology, a refocusing undertaken in response to a major theoretical statement on the field, which sets rather more restrictive parameters for adaptation that invite some critical discussion.

In *A Theory of Adaptation*, Linda Hutcheon surveys the field and argues for "a more restricted . . . definition of adaptation" (2006, 9) than that of Fischlin and Fortier, which she cites as indicative of the field's overall tendency. Concerned that such a theory is too vast for critical practice, Hutcheon defines adaptation as both a *product*—an acknowledged, extensive, and specific transcoding of a given text, usually a narrative text—and as a *process*, a navigation—whether knowing or unknowing—of different modes of textual and intertextual engagement with modes categorized as telling (e.g., print), showing (e.g., film), or interactivity (e.g., video games). Of the adaptor, this navigational process requires creative interpretation; for the audience, it entails "palimpsestic intertextual" engagement (22).

By problematizing the multidirectionality of source and derivation, and by covering a wide range of forms and media, Hutcheon's theory breaks with the field's tradition. Her idea of interactivity crystallizes around video games and theme parks, for instance. But the theory also reinforces tradition, mainly in its orientation to story as the field's "common denominator" (2006, 10) and its corresponding delimitation of adaptation's definition as acknowledged, specific, and extensive.

Confining adaptation to story-based forms and texts seems unnecessarily restrictive in and of itself, as it forecloses considerations of adaptation in nonnarrative forms: lyrical forms like poetry, critical forms like scholarship, forms that occupy a range of genres and media. In a manner that I hope is both analogous and adequate to that whereby technology discourse encompasses sound and image as well as textuality, I want to theorize adaptation and its study more expansively than restrictively. Adaptation study affords interpretive tools for critiquing varied, divergent, and intersecting orders of discourse and media forms, as the above discussion of Tenner's (1996) nonfiction prose has suggested. The point is material to our purposes here in so approaching McLuhan's work, among that of other Canadian artists and thinkers. McLuhan actually makes a great initial case study for adaptation practices in critical (or otherwise not "creative") bodies of work. McLuhan himself and McLuhan scholars alike have recognized the strong artistic strain in his writing. As Richard Cavell says, "If McLuhan's critical reputation declined severely during the 1970s . . . what I can only call his *artistic* reputation has continued to grow" (2002, xvi). McLuhan's self-consciously unorthodox writing style, with its "probes" and its "mosaic" structures, may account for his dramatically divergent receptions, but it also lends itself to the protocols of close reading and theoretical contextualization that literary studies normally reserve for more straightforwardly "creative" texts. Conversely, studies of adaptation in cultural production also help to illuminate the critical practice in creative texts, including nonnarrative, lyrical, condensed, or otherwise short forms, and different media, like popular music. The emphasis on extensiveness that reinforces this theory's prioritization of story explicitly excludes a wealth of other cultural modes and forms—like theory or music—that warrant consideration as adaptations. For instance, Hutcheon specifically excludes "musical sampling" from her theory, on the basis that it "would not qualify as extended engagement" (2006, 9). Since the book undertakes a theoretical synthesis of the field of adaptation in cultural production, such parameters seem somewhat arbitrary: why can't a broadly scoped theory of adaptation address adaptations that are less extensive, more like memes?

As the analysis unfolds, interactivity—a mode of engagement that ostensibly signals a more inclusive approach to the field—ironically becomes a more exclusive category, by coming to refer predominantly to video games. Even the broader digital milieu goes underexamined for its interactive and adaptive practices. Admittedly, the "2.0" interactivity of social web media was only emerging at the book's time of publication, but other forms of interaction and adaptation available then for analysis do not receive it. The web also gives good cause to be included in a theory of adaptation for what had become, even by the turn of the century, one of its major cultural forms: the "Internet meme." This book treats the "Frankenpheme of technology" as a kind of cultural meme, and it considers a few selected Internet memes in its later chapters, but a theorization of the Internet meme as such is beyond its scope (although theorizing the meme is something I've taken up elsewhere; see McCutcheon 2016, 178).

Hutcheon's stipulations for extensiveness and interactivity also reproduce adaptation studies' implicit privileging of the visual, over and against the audible. Hutcheon does discuss several music examples throughout the book and details one specific case of musical scoring, but most of these examples are taken from Hutcheon's formidable repertoire of opera expertise. In addition to opera and musical theatre examples, song covers get some consideration (2006, 90–93), but songs and other musical productions that adapt other forms remain unaddressed and omitted—even those that might qualify as extensive, acknowledged, and narrative-based: albums like The Alan Parsons Project's Poe-inspired *Tales of Mystery and Imagination* (1976) and Janelle Monáe's Afro-Futurist concept albums (2010, 2013), or inverse cases, like Joshua Dysart and Cliff Chiang's *Neil Young's Greendale* (2010), a graphic novel based on the eponymous 2003 album by Neil Young and Crazy Horse.

Like Internet memes, popular music adaptations open up all kinds of implications for Hutcheon's emphases on extensiveness and interactivity. If extensiveness is about creative interpretation of a whole narrative, is not the Eurythmics' single "Sexcrime (1984)" (1984) a condensed, lyrical retelling of Orwell's whole novel? If extensiveness is about duration, what about the repetitive reception labour put into consuming and appropriating this, or any pop song, which, as Leonard Cohen (quoted in Kennedy 2006) puts it, one can "place into the air and have it last twenty years"? Such different reception modes problematize interactivity, as well. In *A Theory of Adaptation*, Hutcheon repeatedly makes the double gesture of acknowledging that all modes of engagement are interactive to an extent, while insistently distinguishing the interactivity of computer games and theme parks for their physical involvement: "enacting or participating replaces telling" (2006, 138). The recurring double gesture in its very insistence suggests something unresolved about this argument—perhaps the claims of games and parks on physical, participatory interactivity are ultimately not exclusive after all. To return to the counterexample: what kind of interactivity is represented by listening to "Sexcrime" at a dance club? Or while out for a jog? These points are not about theoretical hairsplitting, or about diluting the analytic power of adaptation theory; rather, these points are offered as notes towards thinking through the limits of a productive theory, and building deliberately on its own more incidental use of sonic vocabulary, in the interests of improving its theoretical comprehensiveness, consistency, and applicability.

Popular music resounds with adaptation practices, in ways that warrant refocusing a theory of adaptation to account for nonnarrative, nonvisual, and nonextensive adaptations, and to rethink what such parameters mean—to rethink, that is, what can count and be studied as adaptation. I want to explore the matter of popular music in detail here, partly because the book considers music later on (see chapter 7), but mainly for two more important reasons: first, the sonic and acoustic register is critical for understanding of McLuhan's theory; and second, the vocabulary of sound processes and music recording supplies a peculiarly useful terminology for analyzing adaptations, especially less extensive, more citational, and differently interactive adaptations. *Modulation* and *variation* (as in a variation on a theme) are terms that aptly capture the sense of repetition with difference that Hutcheon sees as crucial to adaptations; as with several of the terms suggested here, Hutcheon uses the term *variation* in her own arguments (2006, 35, 86). *Sampling* and *remixing*, borrowed from the parlance of DJ-based music-making, can be borrowed to describe brief, ephemeral, and more meme-like adaptations, and formal rearrangements and recontextualizations, respectively. *Amplification* is a useful way to describe how a meme like a Frankenpheme can "catch on" and reproduce both its forms and its cultural functions (Hutcheon also uses this term in this way [2006, 3]). *Feedback, gain,* and *loss*—borrowed more from communications than from music discourse—suggest different kinds of effects that adaptations can achieve, on audiences and on source texts alike.

As I've discussed elsewhere, popular music is an important cultural vehicle for adaptations, including those of *Frankenstein* (McCutcheon 2007). This and other prior investigations of adaptation in popular electronic dance music inform the use of the above terminology for adaptation studies—not just for popular music adaptations, either—and also suggest an interpretive framework in orders of adaptation. For example, I suggest that if *Star Wars* can be considered a "primary" *Frankenstein* adaptation (as the 2005 prequel [Lucas 2005] spelled out in its *Franken*cliché backstory—in case you hadn't already picked up on all the Frankenphemes of clones, cyborgs, and planet-destroying weapons), then a dance record that samples *Star Wars* can be considered a "secondary" adaptation—that is, an adaptation of an adaptation (McCutcheon 2007, 260). Depending on how well documented or poorly decayed is the line of attribution among specific texts (and mindful of adaptation's "subterranean" circuits), we can posit further orders of remove and remix: tertiary, quaternary orders, or more. Call it *six degrees of adaptation*? But the point is not necessarily to fix, taxonomize, or hierarchize particular lineages of adaptation as some kind of effort to combat what William Gibson has called "attribution decay" (so common especially in our copy-paste digital culture of reposts and "viral" memes), but rather, more broadly, to document and theorize patterns and trajectories of intertextual appropriation and amplification. How these patterns materialize and relate to each other will be illustrated in a sample case detailed below and over the course of this book.

Neither developing a more expansive critical vocabulary for adaptation studies based in digital and music practices, nor tracking the "subterranean" diffusions of adaptation, means diluting or emptying the principle of adaptation. The notion of orders or degrees of adaptation, together with acknowledgements of attribution and its vicissitudes, represents a way to uphold and extend Hutcheon's stipulation that adaptations be defined in relation to specific texts, in order for analysis to stay grounded in concrete historical and material contexts (2006, 21). Another means to keep the analysis grounded in concrete textual details and material contexts is to itemize some of the common, even cliché images, tropes, and plot points that mark specific texts as Frankensteinian, or specific textual elements or fragments as "Frankenphemes." Common figures or characters among these adaptations would include "mad scientists" of all kinds; grotesquely assembled, "patchwork," or corporate subjects; and mechanical or otherwise manufactured monsters—artificial intelligences, genetically engineered organisms, rebellious robots, cyborgs, clones, and other such technological doppelgängers. Common plot elements would be those that reproduce or vary the reduced "skeleton story" of the novel: stories of technological backfire; robots in revolt; resurrections gone awry; uncontrollable experiments; human-made catastrophes of technology, biology, or ecology; and the awakening to self-awareness of machines—an event that some thinkers, such as Ray Kurzweil (2005), expect as a real-world eventuality, which they call "the technological singularity." Common images and tropes would include scenes of profane or at least ill-advised creation, of technological backfire, or artificially induced apocalypse; motifs of Faustian bargains for forbidden knowledge, of a creature overwhelming its creator; recursive reflections on the text's own composition or facticity—especially acknowledgements of composition as collage, "mongrel," or otherwise synthesizing or appropriative; and images or evocations of the technological sublime (Nye 1994), that is, representations of technological prowess that test or defy the limits of representation. In some cases the adoption of certain narrative or genre conventions may be worth considering: epistolary, Gothic, or science fiction modes; unreliable narration; or regressive framing devices, stories embedded within stories. References or allusions to *Frankenstein* or other adaptations are also significant textual elements of adaptation, even where used sparingly or in passing.

To be read together with these formal, textual criteria are a number of contextual criteria, aspects of the cultural and economic conditions of production that inform or augment a given text's adaptation strategies. Criteria like these include the following: production modes marked by ambivalence over technology, especially new media and automation; globally oriented or distributed scenes or conditions of production; forms that privilege special effects above other production values; and postmodernist approaches that use and call attention to pastiche, or otherwise comment on their own production processes, especially with self-reflexive reference to media, technology, or globalization.

Moreover, bringing critical terms from music and communications disciplines to adaptation studies can orient the present study more firmly to the overarching cultural studies principle of *articulation*, a methodological principle of analyzing the "relationships of relationships" between popular culture and power structures, of probing "the ways in which everyday life is articulated by and with the specific forms and formations, the material deployments and effects, of popular discursive practices" (Grossberg 1997, 229). The term *articulation* also harbours a crucial double meaning for a study of *Frankenstein*: a meaning drawn from the technical language of anatomy, for which it describes the jointed connection of bones in a body.

A Sample of Refocused Adaptation: *Frankenstein*'s Organ Transplant

To put these terms to work, and to suggest the interpretive possibilities of nonextensive "Frankenpheme" adaptation, let's consider a specific pattern of this kind of adaptation at work in postmodern Afro-Futurist music. This pattern, in brief, consists of combining Frankensteinian imagery with organ instrumentation in Afro-Futurist music making. As theorized by Kodwo Eshun (1998) and John Corbett (1994), among others, Afro-Futurism is a black diasporic music tradition of appropriating science fiction forms, and principles of technological experiment, in black diasporic cultural production: for example, we find science fiction tropes and experimental appropriations of technology in black Atlantic music from Sun Ra's jazz to George Clinton's P-Funk, from Lee Perry's Black Ark studio to turntablism and techno. But Afro-Futurism is also a theory—a critique of racist ontology, especially in the music industry (Corbett 1994), and a challenge to essentialist ideas of black identity, an avant-garde cultural practice of liberation, countermemory, and transfiguration (Gilroy 1993). For Corbett, the jazz band leader Sun Ra, the dub-reggae pioneer Lee "Scratch" Perry, and George Clinton of Parliament and Funkadelic fame are three exemplary Afro-Futurist artists who establish and embody the Afro-Futurist tradition in productions and performative personae that articulate a distinctively Frankensteinian "space madness": these artists' music articulates a science fiction aesthetic while their personae represent a marginal and self-consciously monstrous relationship to the mainstream music industry. This "space madness" tradition has been revamped recently by Janelle Monáe, in albums like *The ArchAndroid* (2010) and *The Electric Lady* (2013) that reimagine the African American experience in the imagery of androids and artificial intelligence together with auction blocks and segregation.

In this context, a distinctive practice of combining *Frankenstein* reference and organ instrumentation in black diasporic music making emerges: we hear it in Byron Lee and the Dragonaires' 1964 ska tune "Frankenstein

Ska"; in Parliament's album *The Clones of Dr. Funkenstein* (1976); in Michael Jackson's 1984 single "Thriller"; in Rockwell's single "Somebody's Watching Me" (1984); in Handsome Boy Modeling School's "Once Again" (1999); and in the extended "Power" mix of Canadian rap artist Maestro Fresh-Wes's single "Let Your Backbone Slide" (1989). So in six music productions by Afro-Futurist artists from four different decades and three different nations, we hear specific combinations of Frankensteinian imagery and organ instrumentation. This diasporic pattern of musical combinations prompts two questions that warrant preliminary consideration as a means to contextualize the subsequent, more detailed discussion of the afore-mentioned Afro-Futurist music texts that follows: first, how has the organ become such a formulaic and familiar trope of musical metonymy for *Frankenstein*? And second, what might be the cultural functions of this metonymy for Afro-Futurist music?

To address the first question: Forry's *Hideous Progenies* (1990) looks at performance adaptations of *Frankenstein* since Richard Brinsley Peake's 1823 play *Presumption*. In the process, he identifies a number of popular adaptation strategies established by that play, and later made ubiquitous by its successors: for example, the recasting of Shelley's articulate and well-read creature as a mute, raging monster. Relevant for our purposes are two adaptation strategies in particular: the identification of Franken-stein's monster both with its creator and with the related Gothic icon of the vampire, and the trope of the monster's reaction to music.

The identification of the monster with its maker results from the long-standing application of the latter's name to the former, and so refer-ences to the monster itself as "Frankenstein" persist in popular culture to this day. For instance, take this rap from Kool Keith, in his "Dr. Octagon" alter ego: "I'm strictly monster, with turtlenecks like Frankenstein" (1997). Developing the story's doppelgänger theme in a different but related dir-ection, stage and screen adaptations of *Frankenstein* have also consistently identified the unnatural monster with its supernatural counterpart, the vampire; this identification also derives from the famous primal scene of the novel's inception at the Villa Diodati in 1816, when Shelley started her story while John Polidori composed "The Vampyre" (Forry 1990, 90). In early adaptations, the identification of man-made monster and vam-pire took place in paired presentations of *Frankenstein* and vampire plays, and in literary works that referred to multiple monsters, in a way that

Hollywood has made formulaic and routine in "monster mash" films from *Frankenstein Meets the Wolf Man* (1943) to *Van Helsing* (2004). In early film adaptations, this identification assumed a more industrial than intertextual character: in Universal's *Frankenstein* and *Dracula* franchises of the 1930s and 1940s, actors Boris Karloff and Bela Lugosi became virtually interchangeable by performing similar monster and mad doctor characters among different films. For the iconic 1931 *Frankenstein* film, Lugosi had been considered first for the monster's role that Boris Karloff would make famous. Lugosi, who performed the figure of Dracula (in the 1931 film *Dracula*) as influentially as Karloff played the monster, appeared in *Frankenstein* sequels as Dr. Frankenstein's assistant, Ygor, and in *Frankenstein Meets the Wolf Man* (1943) he played the Frankenstein monster. Similarly, Christopher Lee played the roles of Frankenstein's monster *and* Dracula for the Hammer horror films produced in the UK in the 1950s and 1960s. To refer to this process of "iconic identification" and "conflation" between Frankenstein and Dracula, especially as dramatized in the careers of Karloff and Lugosi, I'd like to suggest the portmanteau *iconflation*. I want to suggest this term because the processes of icon production, identification, and conflation that it links have significance not just for understanding the popular cultural history of *Frankenstein* but for understanding the function of organ music in this history. Iconflation becomes a significant component of the musical metonymy in question here.

The iconflation of Karloff's creature and Lugosi's vampire is reproduced in Universal's franchise of Edgar Allan Poe adaptations, where it gets connected to the trope of the monster's reaction to music. Interestingly, the Universal *Frankenstein* and *Dracula* film soundtracks do not feature any organ music to develop its metonymic association with horror generally and *Frankenstein* specifically. *Bride of Frankenstein* includes a gospel-style organ arrangement in the scene where the monster meets the blind hermit, but it augments the hermit's ability to soothe the monster's proverbially savage breast with his own violin playing. While this scene of the sublimation of the creature's rage by music was established by the earliest adaptations (Forry 1990, 22), it is the opposite of what I'm investigating: the use of organ music to amplify horror in general, and Frankensteinian monstrosity more specifically. As it happens, it's in other period films that the metonymic association of organ music and Gothic horror emerges. In Universal's screen versions of Edgar Allan Poe's *The Black Cat* (1934) and

The Raven (1935), Karloff and Lugosi, respectively, play mad doctors who also play Bach's Toccata and Fugue in D Minor on the organ. Paramount's 1931 film *Dr. Jekyll and Mr. Hyde* also sits its mad doctor at the organ to play this number. The diegetic use of Bach's Toccata and Fugue in films like these has contributed greatly to the popular cultural association of organ music with Gothic and horror narratives. There's an earlier source for this association: Universal's 1925 silent film *The Phantom of the Opera*. The scene in *Phantom* where the heroine unmasks Erik as he plays the organ was a sensation with audiences, and the film's popularity suggested to Universal and other studios the potential market for Gothic and horror films, like *The Black Cat* (1934), *The Walking Dead* (1936), and *Return of the Vampire* (1943). Of course, it is ironic that this *silent* film contributes so significantly to the metonymic link between organ music and Gothic horror.

Between these interwar film uses of organ music, especially Bach's Toccata and Fugue, and the postwar Afro-Futurist uses of organ music in records that refer to *Frankenstein*, we find a proliferation of both horrific and humorous Frankenstein figures throughout American popular culture. Some possible sources for the metonymic link of organ music and horror must be noted simply to be ruled out: Bobby Pickett's 1962 "Monster Mash" features piano, not organ; and the theme song of the 1964 *Addams Family* television show features not organ, but harpsichord for its distinctive melody. (Its competitor *The Munsters* featured a surf-rock theme.) But later covers of the "Monster Mash" sometimes substitute organ for piano, and organ music occasionally featured in the soundtracks and commercials of the *Addams Family* and *Munsters* franchises. Warner Brothers, Hanna-Barbera, and other cartoon producers, as well as their Saturday morning advertisers like the General Mills line of monster-theme breakfast cereals, also entrench and exploit this implicit association between organ music and Frankensteinian monstrosity, which has become routine across the media of American pop culture. For one popular postwar film example: *The Rocky Horror Picture Show* (1975) includes a scene where Riff-Raff teases the creature Rocky by chasing him around with a lit candelabrum. Quoting a similar scene from the 1931 *Frankenstein* film, this scene in *Rocky Horror* accompanies its action with organ music, suggesting Rocky's fear and Riff-Raff's menace. For an Afro-Futurist film example: the opening and closing credits of the 1973 film *Blackenstein* prominently feature organ arrangements.

This brings me to the second question, about the cultural function of this music metonymy for Afro-Futurism, and the aforementioned Afro-Futurist music productions that iconflate *Frankenstein* references together with organ instrumentation.

First, the pianist Thelonious Monk created a series of remarkable jazz-compositions built around his singularly angular phrasing, highlighted by unusual intervals, dissonance, and displaced notes. Amongst fellow jazz artists, Monk's musical language was sometimes known as "zombie-music." Pianist Mary Lou Williams explains: "Why 'zombie music'? Because the screwy chords reminded us of music from *Frankenstein* or any horror film" (quoted in McNally 2011, 262). As David McNally observes in his study of zombie and vampire images as responses to global capital, Monk's "'screwy chords' express the rhythms of a world out of joint, a space of reification in which people are reduced to things": "We hear not only the jarring sounds of things coming to life; more than this, we hear the rhythms of zombie-movement, the ferocious sounds of the dance of the living dead" (2011, 263). Echoing the critique of racialization, exploitation, and reification contained in the Afro-Futurist music of Ra, Perry, and Clinton and the black diaspora theory of W. E. B. Dubois and Paul Gilroy, McNally acknowledges the widespread recognition "that the entire African-American experience is bathed in living death, in the 'double consciousness' of being both person and thing. And Monk's music captures this in the monstrously beautiful cadences of the banging, smashing, crashing chords of an emerging African-American protest-music." As McNally and music critics like Eshun have discussed, the avant-gardism, alienation effects, and oppositional character of Monk's music—like that of Ra, Perry, and Clinton—have refracted and extended throughout contemporary black diasporic music, "in genres as diverse as hip-hop and Afrobeat" (McNally 2011, 263–64). For just one example, Kool Keith's "Wild and Crazy" (1997) uses a "zombie-music" piano chord as the downbeat, in a song that names Frankenstein ("Frankenstein's still standing here"), a song whose chorus overlays the dissonant downbeat with *Psycho*-soundtrack high-pitched strings, as the singer croons, "The moon is out / Tonight it's time for experiments." Like Sun Ra before him and rap artists after, Monk adapted and repurposed a selection of popular cultural materials, especially Hollywood film materials, to construct a musical language that would speak to a diasporic African American experience framed and haunted by the legacy of racialized, institutionalized slavery.

Byron Lee and the Dragonaires' "Frankenstein Ska," released in 1964, uses the organ to establish the "crooked beat" that is the signature of ska; in ska's successor genre, reggae, the rhythm guitar assumes responsibility for keeping the crooked beat. In "Frankenstein Ska," the rhythmic organ arrangement evokes the clumsy, clunking step of Boris Karloff's hulking, heavy-booted creature. And in this arrangement, we also hear both echoes of Monk's dissonant "zombie music" and a foreshadowing of what the UK band Madness, in the vocal introduction to their ska-revival cover of Prince Buster's 1964 song "One Step Beyond" (1979), would call "the heavy heavy monster sound." (Interestingly, with reference to Afro-Futurism's playful, postmodern approach to black identity, it is worth noting that Lee is a Chinese diasporic artist who played an influential role in popularizing ska as a distinctively Jamaican, black diasporic sound.)

In *The Clones of Dr. Funkenstein* (1976), George Clinton and Parliament unfold a musically and referentially rich concept album, a space opera, imagining America's black population as "the children of production" in possession of ancient secret wisdom; whether intentionally or incidentally, the album resonates powerfully with other period productions like Sun Ra's 1974 cult film *Space Is the Place*. The album opens with a spoken-word "Prelude," in which a campy-spooky organ arrangement strikes up to lead in and accompany a monologue by George Clinton's "Dr. Funkenstein" persona, who describes "the concept of specially-designed Afronauts, capable of funkatizing galaxies," a concept awaiting to be materialized by someone who can "release them to multiply in the image of the chosen one: Dr. Funkenstein" (1976). Parliament's *Clones* album in turn has given rise to further amplifications—*tertiary* adaptations?—by furnishing samples for electronic dance music, from Armand Van Helden's tribal house anthem "Witch Doktor" (1994) to Deadmau5's 2006 house track "Dr. Funkenstein."

Another production that has given rise to a host of further amplifications and articulations—from samples in other songs to costumed and choreographed public dance performances—is Michael Jackson's "Thriller" (1984), which makes emphatic use of organs, dramatic stabs of which give the song its unmistakable hook. And a resonantly Toccata and Fugue–like organ arrangement arises late in the song, to accompany its climactic monologue, a campy litany of monster movie references, delivered by Vincent Prince. (In this connection, it's worth noting Price's *Dr. Phibes* films from the early 1970s; in them, Price plays Phibes, a mad scientist character who seeks to avenge his wife's death—and who also plays organ music.) In Price's "Thriller" monologue, "creatures" that "crawl in search of blood" and "grisly ghouls from every tomb" mix with similar figures to make a mash-up of living-dead monster images, and, together with the organ arrangement, they clearly conjure the spectres of *Frankenstein* and *Dracula*, the Hollywood film adaptations of which have made them (alongside George Romero's *Living Dead* franchise) the very stuff of "Thriller's" homage, and which, reciprocally, have furnished much of the image repertoire for the many subsequent homages to "Thriller" in recorded and performance media.

Jackson also played a pivotal role in producing another 1984 single, Rockwell's "Somebody's Watching Me," on which Jackson provides backup vocals for the chorus. "Somebody's Watching Me" features, throughout the track, organ instrumentation very reminiscent of Bach's Toccata and Fugue, and more explicit links to *Frankenstein* arise in this song's video, which includes a portrait of Mary Shelley and close-up flashes of a grotesque face strongly resembling that of Karloff's iconic portrayal of the creature.

As campy, commercially successful, and still-popular singles, "Thriller" and "Somebody" contribute crucially to the musical metonymy being tracked here. Both "Thriller" and "Somebody" exploit organ music to amplify their Gothic modes; the Afro-Futurist element here lies more in musical arrangement than in lyrical content, as each track juxtaposes the modishly futuristic synthesizers and drum machines of early 1980s pop against the classical- and gospel-derived sounds of organ instrumentation.

The gospel context may suggest why the organ recurs in Afro-Futurist music adaptations of *Frankenstein* more than in other music adaptations. In *Frankenstein*-themed songs by rock artists, and more specifically white rock artists—for example, the Edgar Winter Group, Black Sabbath, the New York Dolls, White Zombie—electric guitar and synthesizer sounds rather than organs amplify the *Frankenstein* theme. In this intercultural context, the use of organs by Afro-Futurist artists appears ambivalent. On the one hand, the use of organs instead of guitars to signify *Frankenstein* themes in black diasporic music might be read to assert cultural difference as musical difference. On the other hand, if the use of organ instrumentation and sampling by Afro-Futurist artists signifies on the organ's place in sacred music by connecting it to the profane theme of Frankensteinian presumption, then it may be read as a critique of essentialist ideas of black diasporic identity, or as a variant representation of African American double consciousness. The black diasporic cultural practice of what Julian Jonker calls "black secret technology"—that is, "taking white technology apart and not putting it back together properly" (2002, para. 32)—involves, as the work of Monk and Perry especially dramatizes, transgressing modes of conventional music making—and, in Perry's case, music recording—as expressions of emancipation from not just slavery proper but also its haunting, revenant legacy. Such transgressions have both defined black American music and installed this music as among the most popular and successful around the world: from the lore of Faustian bargaining that shrouds accounts of Robert Johnson's development of the guitar blues; to Ray Charles's adaptation of gospel structures and rhythms to nascent rock and roll; to Monk's dissonant "zombie-music" be-bop; to the birth of hip hop in its now-legendary do-it-yourself culture of turntable innovations, boom-box pause-play tape mixes, graffiti art, and breakdancing.

Which brings us to the combination of *Frankenstein* reference and organ instrumentation—or in this case sampling—in rap music. "Let Your Backbone Slide" is a 1989 single by Maestro Fresh-Wes; it's one of the most successful Canadian rap songs. Two specific details of this track, in lyric and instrumentation, are noteworthy here, in order to appreciate the adaptive practice of Maestro's sampling and synecdoche in full effect. The instrumental arrangement of "Backbone" is organized around an organ riff sampled from the 1968 funk track "The Champ" by the Mohawks, a track widely sampled in rap for this riff and for its breakbeat rhythm. In this distinctive pairing of *Frankenstein* reference and organ arrangement, "Let Your Backbone Slide" reproduces the pattern tracked above from the Dragonaires to Michael Jackson.

The lyrical references to *Frankenstein* in "Let Your Backbone Slide" are extensive, albeit elliptical. In the last verse of the extended mix of the song, Maestro raps: "It's gettin' out of hand / I've created a monster." This Frankenpheme figures Maestro's self-proclaimed success—a common conceit in rap, and a pointedly bold claim for a debut single—as a Frankensteinian effect of unintended consequences.

The lyric sampled here is sufficiently legible as a common enough Frankenpheme in everyday speech. However, it resonates with other lyrical details. There is the recurring imagery of the "spine": in the refrain's reference to "backbone," the first verse's mention of "vertebrae," and the song's justly celebrated rhyme about the "sacro-iliac," or tailbone. But lines in the first verse further flaunt this "rap scholar's" learned repertoire, most notably his likening of rap to "a slab of clay that's shapeless" until "I mould it in my hands" (1989). Taken together with the lyrical details noted above, this verse's self-reflexive rhyme about rap as creative practice alludes with artful economy to the same ancient myths adapted and referenced in Shelley's own novel: the medieval Jewish legend of the golem; the biblical accounts of creation in Genesis and John's gospel; the classical myths of Prometheus and Pygmalion.

"Backbone" thus assembles and reanimates a set of deeply embedded and "subterranean"—but identifiable—cultural elements and discourses; the track constitutes a second-order adaptation, in its rehearsal of a clichéd, vernacular Frankenpheme and its sampling of the Mohawks' organ hook. It is significant that the Frankenpheme lyric only occurs on the 12" vinyl "power mix" and video, not on the shorter "radio edit" version—the lyric thus self-reflexively remarks on its own excess: "It's gettin' out of hand." And the track's sampling practice is itself integral to understanding this specific text's representative articulation of the ready-made, bricolage aesthetic of "early hip hop," for which, as music critic Simon Reynolds puts it, "sampling was like Frankenstein's monster, funk-limbs crudely bolted together" (1998, 45). In turn, as a nationally bestselling and internationally popular single, "Backbone" gained further currency for this Frankensteinian Afro-Futurist motif in the vocabulary and imagery of subsequent rap. In "Dr. Frankenstein" (1998), Ice Cube adopts the modern myth's moniker to describe himself as the creator of a genre, gangsta rap, that has run amok since he invented it. In the video for 50 Cent's "In da Club" (Atwell 2003), the establishing shots depict a top-secret R&D lab in a desolate desert locale: the "Shady/Aftermath Artist Development Center," where we first see 50 Cent prone on a laboratory table, being assembled as a kind of android, while Dr. Dre and Eminem supervise, dressed in white coats. In a style much closer to the Maestro's, and in a further reproduction of the distinctive Afro-Futurist pattern of coupling of *Frankenstein* allusion and organ arrangement, Handsome Boy Modeling School's rap track "Once

Again (Here to Kick for You)" (1999) is structured around a pitched-down sample from Three Dog Night's "Old Fashioned Love Song," which adds a funereal organ sound prominently to the mix. And like other tracks sampled above, "Once Again" features a verse that likens the rapper's own work to the mad scientist's: "One time as I sew it up like Doctor Frankenstein."

As with the Michael Jackson and Rockwell tracks, so "Backbone" may not at first seem as definitely "Afro-Futurist" as the more self-consciously avant-garde work of Clinton, Perry, or Monk. The Afro-Futurist aesthetic emerges here as much in the song's musical arrangements as it does in its lyrics, with their play on Pygmalion and Dr. Frankenstein figures. Maestro's track articulates something of the technology discourse that we find in other Canadian adaptations of *Frankenstein*, in its relatively fast tempo and its corresponding lyrical agility. For mainstream rap of the late 1980s, Maestro's lyrics are unusually rapid-fire, more comparable to the style of Public Enemy's Chuck D than to that of the Beastie Boys or NWA, and its tempo is, for rap, very fast (114 beats per minute), accompanied by an intensive collage of sampling and turntablist effects. The lyrical density of "Backbone" invites headphone concentration, while its detonative breakbeat, a modulation of James Brown's "Funky Drummer," invites dance-floor abandon. In the context of pop music in 1989, the percussive arrangement of "Backbone" resonates as much with UK acid house as its acrobatic rhyming resonates with US east-coast rap. In this divided transnational perspective, then, "Let Your Backbone Slide" is maybe as quintessentially Canadian as pop music gets—it is a technological and transnational acoustic space oddity: Canadian hip house.

The track gains additional interest in its Canadian production context. Maestro signifies on citizenship in his persona's self-description as "un-American" (evoking national difference as well as the American allergy to "communism" that perennially positions Canada as some purportedly "socialist" threat). Maestro's self-promotional boasting about success as a jet-setting rap star contrasts ironically with his other self-descriptions as hubristic artist and mad scientist; moreover, all these self-descriptions join a shape-shifting host of alter egos presented in the track—tactician, Colossus, Tarzan, conductor, builder, playwright—as well as Wesley Williams's rapper pseudonym as "the Maestro." The MC's boastful proliferation of personae signals the track's skilful adoption of this staple convention of the rap genre. What's more, in this black Canadian cultural production,

Maestro's multiple roles signify ironically on official Canadian multiculturalism: the track's voice is a virtual mosaic all to himself. It is not just "the beat," in the words of the track's introductory vocal sample, that "will be played in many parts," but the performing persona itself, a satirical figure of the Canadian multicultural "mosaic" that is rendered ironic by the volume of Frankenphemes in the Maestro's mix.

As demonstrated by Afro-Futurist music generally and the aforementioned tracks specifically, especially Maestro's "Backbone," black diasporic music has amplified the metonymic associations—the "iconflations"—of zombie and vampire, organ instrumentation and horror intertextuality, such that the sound of organ instrumentation is itself almost sufficient to evoke the "modern myth" of *Frankenstein* in popular culture. We should also note here the multiple meanings of the word "organ"; although this may go without saying in any discussion of *Frankenstein*, in popular music, and especially in Afro-Futurist music, the sound of the organ has thus become the sound of the body built of—which is to say, *reduced to*—organs, an inter-medial "iconflation" of sacred musicality and profane monstrosity, the monstrosity of bodily self-alienation, synecdoche as commodification and exploitation. The organ is the most uncannily named wind instrument, the windpipe that sings in an inhuman voice, but only when compelled to by human machinations.

Popular music can thus be seen to harbour an extraordinary wealth of adaptation practices—allusions, amplifications, articulations—that amply repay close critical attention. The case of *Frankenstein*'s iconflations in Afro-Futurist music demonstrates, in particular, the great repertoire of knowledge—cultural, historical, technological, and otherwise—that is so characteristically concentrated and then coded in black Atlantic music-making practices and networks. Eshun (1998) extensively documents the profoundly philosophical and sometimes explicitly theoretical work of black Atlantic music, and Angela McRobbie echoes work like his by plainly pointing out "just how much thinking there is in black music." As she says, it "can hardly contain the investment of artistry, politics, history, and literary voice, so that as an aesthetic it is, by definition, spilling out and overflowing, excessive, a first destination for social commentary, dialogue, and rap that leaves those of us still caught in the prison of language far behind" (1999, 43–44). In the process, works like those discussed here contribute to processes of iconflation and other condensed or elliptical forms of adaptation and intertextuality that, taken together, serve to keep certain texts—certain images and ideas, not only stories—in constant rotation through the popular imagination, even as they remix their elements to the point of either total defamiliarization or virtual naturalization, or both. The perception and reception of an adaptation *as such*—whether narrative or lyrical, extensive or ephemeral—is a beauty very much in the ear of the beholder.

3. *Frankenstein* and the Reinvention of "Technology"

The modern discourse of technology has a Romantic history: the connotations, inflections, figurative uses, and ideological assumptions that accrete around the strictly denotative definition of the word and that supplement its usage and iterations, especially in colloquial speech, take shape as a specific cultural effect of Mary Shelley's novel *Frankenstein*, first published in 1818 and then in a substantially revised edition in 1831. To contextualize how Canadian adaptations of *Frankenstein* have amplified and globalized a particular set of usages and connotations as the prevailing modern sense of technology in everyday language and discourse, this chapter explores how Shelley's novel redefined—and, in the process, effectively *reinvented*—the word "technology" in its modern sense. To argue this, I will challenge two conventional premises about the relationship between *Frankenstein* and technology discourse. Understanding these premises means outlining the history of technology's meanings, after which we will look closely at *Frankenstein*'s plot and details of form. Ultimately I contend that the novel, read together with a representative selection of period responses to it and related articulations of technology, indelibly marks the word's modern reinvention with a set of connected tropes. Significantly, *Frankenstein* does not explicitly use the word technology (just as it does not name its antagonist); but through the creature's characterization, the novel became a literary "threshold of epistemologization" (Foucault [1969] 1972, 187), a textual battery that charged the *épistème* of Romantic science and culture to generate the modern discourse of technology. First arranged to characterize the nameless nemesis who haunts Victor Frankenstein, these tropes soon coalesce around the nascent discourse of "technology" to name the social assemblage that defines—and haunts—modernity.

In the discursive history of technology and in the literature on the relationship between *Frankenstein* and technology, two premises persist as commonplaces, in sources as venerable as the *Oxford English Dictionary* and as recent as essays on technology by Scott McQuire and Andrew Ross, written in the cultural studies tradition of "keyword" reading, inaugurated by Raymond Williams (1983). In such sources, old and new, accounts of the provenance of technology suggest that it was in the late nineteenth century that, according to the *OED Online* (s.v., "technology"), the word attained its modern redefinition to mean, in general, tools and machines, techniques and systems for their use, or combinations thereof; or, as the *OED* puts it, "the mechanical arts and applied sciences collectively." However, a close reading of *Frankenstein*, its allusive uses, and its more extensive adaptations in the period suggests that this modern meaning emerged much earlier in the nineteenth century.

Which brings me to the second premise this work questions: that while *Frankenstein* is widely read as "the first and most enduring symbol of modern technology" (Tropp, quoted in Baldick 1987, 7), its relationship to the discourse of technology is constructed retrospectively, as though this definitively modern discourse emerged later, and independently of *Frankenstein*, in popular culture. If technology has popularized a certain interpretation of *Frankenstein*, it is because *Frankenstein* itself conditioned the modern redefinition of technology as such in the period of its publication, early reception, and popularization.

Technology: Defining and Accounting for a Modern Keyword

To get specific, then, about what is meant in this study by "the modern discourse of technology," the *OED* provides a natural point of departure. The entry for the word technology includes five distinct definitions, the fourth of which encompasses three distinct variations, for a total of seven different definitions of the word:

> 1. A discourse or treatise on an art or arts; *esp.* (in later use) a treatise on a practical art or craft. . . .

2. The terminology of a particular art or subject; technical language or nomenclature. . . .

3. The systematic treatment of grammar. . . .

4. a. The branch of knowledge dealing with the mechanical arts and applied sciences; the study of this. . . .

4. b. The application of such knowledge for practical purposes, *esp.* in industry, manufacturing, etc.; the sphere of activity concerned with this; the mechanical arts and applied sciences collectively. . . .

4. c. The product of such application; technological knowledge or know-how; a technological process, method, or technique. Also: machinery, equipment, etc., developed from the practical application of scientific and technical knowledge; an example of this. Also in extended use. . . .

5. A particular practical or industrial art; a branch of the mechanical arts or applied sciences; a technological discipline.

The first three of these definitions are obsolete. They represent the premodern meanings of the word derived from antiquity, occurring between the early seventeenth century and the mid-nineteenth, by which time the word was assuming its modern meanings—the fourth and fifth ones here. The earlier, "eighteenth-century use of the word 'technology' placed the emphasis on 'art'" (Wright 2005, para. 3), and it is important to note that "art" and "the arts" were somewhat more inclusively defined in eighteenth-century and earlier usage and encompassed engineering and agricultural practices. The fourth, tripartite definition (4a, 4b, and 4c) begins to emerge in the late eighteenth century, initially as a redefined usage that was imported from German. As E. A. W. von Zimmerman wrote—in English—in 1787, "A new branch of scientific knowledge, viz. technology, or the theory and accurate description of useful arts and manufactures, was much cultivated in Germany" (1787, iii). Johann Beckmann (1739–1811) was likely one of the German professors to whom von Zimmerman alludes, and his account shows that it is an erroneous oversimplification to suggest, as Kelly does, that Beckmann, in his *Guide to Technology* (*Anleitung zur Technologie*), was merely "resurrecting that forgotten Greek word" to give "a name to what we do" (2011, 8). In the first place, the word had not been forgotten, as documented by the first three *OED* meanings; in the second, the emergent German usage of technology emphasized the "-logy," or study—it introduced the fourth meaning listed above, the *study* of mechanical arts. Kelly's use of technology "to mean a specific technology, such as radar," that is, something that "can be patented" (2011, 12)—a meaning he misattributes to Beckmann—illustrates not the fourth but the next to last meaning on the *OED*'s list: "a technological process" or simply "machinery, equipment."

It might seem like semantic hairsplitting, but what is significant here is that technology's "machinery" meaning (4c) has become the dominant meaning of technology in colloquial speech, policy, and business, where it is often conjoined or conflated with the word's "collective" meaning (4b), as in a conventional phrase like "invest in technology." The *OED*'s earliest citation of the "collective activity" definition (4b) is Jacob Bigelow's 1829 book *Elements of Technology* (on which more later in this chapter), and the dictionary's earliest citations for the "product" meaning (4c) do not occur until the 1890s. On this account, technology's meaning has shifted from the *study* of arts, to the *systematic application* of production techniques, to the *products* used in and resulting from such application. What concerns us is not the *coinage* of technology but its modern *re*invention. The challenge for historicizing technology, today, results from its ubiquity—and consequent slipperiness.

Cultural studies "keywords" essays have tended to reproduce the *OED*'s historical account of technology's provenance and modernization, which dates the emergence of the word's "machinery" meaning to the later nineteenth century. "It was mainly in mC19 [the mid-nineteenth century] that technology became fully specialized to the 'practical arts,'" writes Williams; this specialization—that is, definition 4b—paired with "the newly specialized sense of science" to "open the way to a familiar modern distinction between knowledge (*science*) and its practical application (technology)"— that is, definition 4c (1983, 315), which Williams implies in this phrase emerged sometime after midcentury. Williams, too, points out the vagueness of the modern word's meaning, observing that "technical—matters of practical construction—and technological—[are] often used in the same sense, but with the residual sense (in *logy*) of systematic treatment" (316). In the 2005 adaptation of Williams, *New Keywords*, Andrew Ross contextualizes the word's modernization as a reflection of "the rise of industrialization" and echoes the *OED*'s account: "By the lC19 [late nineteenth-century] . . . technology was increasingly used to refer to machinery itself" (2005, 342–43). Ross follows this account by discussing Marx's perspective of "technology as a weapon of class war" (2005, 343); however, he fails to mention that Marx—like Shelley—did not use the word technology itself.

Scott McQuire does point this out, in a more recent "keyword" article, which surveys the "major shifts in thinking about technology" in modernity (2006, 253). He echoes the *OED* in identifying "the mid-nineteenth century" as the period when "the meaning of 'technology' . . . narrowed to the 'practical arts'" and cites Marx's reference to the bourgeois creation of "colossal productive forces" as evidence of the centrality of technology to Marx's historical materialism (255). McQuire reads in Marx's work a "relatively neutral" idea of technology that establishes the technological instrumentalism that dominated technology discourse until World War II, when three new paradigms emerged: first, a cybernetic paradigm that followed Norbert Weiner and pointed to the now-hegemonic technological imperative; second, a critical paradigm of technological determinism, in which technology is reified domination, represented by thinkers like Heidegger, Ellul, McLuhan, and Paul Virilio, who equates technology with catastrophe; and, third, a social constructivist line of thinking about technology represented by thinkers like Walter Benjamin and Donna Haraway (259–60).

McQuire's reading of Marx's "relatively neutral" conception of technology argues that it carries a telling, unresolved ambiguity. He attributes instrumentalist thinking to Marx's general division of productive forces from the relations of production, but he also suggests that Marx's ambiguity over "colossal productive forces" supplements instrumentalism, shading it with deterministic overtones. On one hand, Marx posits a kind of "mechanical materialism" that attributes social changes to "new productive forces." But, on the other, Marx's later theory of the commodity fetish detaches these forces from their social control; McQuire explains that, for Marx, "capital instruments" are "external to human effort, and therefore outside social control," giving them "an enigmatic appearance of autonomy"—a life of their own, as it were (2006, 256). In these respects, Marx anticipates one line of McLuhan's thinking; in the first chapter of the *Grundrisse* ([1857] 1973), Marx makes observations about the technological basis (and bias) of specific cultural forms: "Is Achilles possible with powder and lead?" he asks. "Or the *Iliad* with the printing press, not to mention the printing machine?" ([1857] 1983). While McQuire looks forward from Marx's ideas on machine production to their influence on future thinkers, a look back from these ideas to their cultural sources soon illuminates the gruesome lineaments of a familiar factitious figure that accounts for their ambiguity. Baldick (1987, 130) features Marx prominently among the nineteenth-century writers who adapted *Frankenstein* for representations of capital and class, as in Marx's above-quoted image of capital as "dead labour" preying vampirically on the living ([1867] 1976, 342).

These keyword essays' surveys of the transformations of technology discourse since the mid- and late nineteenth century thus help us to focus further on the foundations of this discourse in the *early* nineteenth century—in which it takes shape as a Frankenpheme unto itself. *Frankenstein* has been conventionally retrofitted into this discursive history. Echoing William Hazlitt's statement on the Romantic period, Darin Barney calls *Frankenstein* an allegory of "the technological spirit of the modern age" (2000, 6). Laura Kranzler writes that *Frankenstein* seems almost uncannily to anticipate "the technological innovations of the twentieth century"; she suggests, more specifically, that "the problematics of technological development and application are initially codified in Shelley's work" (1988, 42, 43). This suggestion is worth taking at its word, and worth reading for the historical evidence between its lines. To make this case, we'll turn first to the novel itself, to see how the text works to reinvent technology—not *avant la lettre*, technically, but in the very moment of the word's English reanimation.

"The instrument of future mischief"

I want to suggest that *Frankenstein* exerts its own interpretive control over technology as a term whose meaning changed not *after* but *during* the novel's period. A look at the text, and period responses to it, shows how technology began circulating in its modern sense as a Frankenpheme. Looking first at the novel, we find a series of tropes that show how the language of the text—together with its plot of uncontrolled research and monstrous result—conditions the modern discourse of technology. These tropes are *utility, supplementarity, contagion, shock,* and *revolution.*

Utility: The rhetoric of utility permeates the text, and Victor Frankenstein, like his interlocutor Walton, sometimes sounds like a parody of Jeremy Bentham. *Frankenstein* engages with Bentham and his philosophy of Utilitarianism perhaps most clearly in its exploitation of the then-dubious reputation of medical doctors, who traded with grave-robbers to obtain cadavers. Meanwhile, Bentham worked during the period to legitimize dissection—with legislation, and, ultimately, with the donation of his own body as a display specimen for University College, to promote the "further uses of the dead to the living" (quoted in Morton 2002, 86). Bentham still enjoys a vaguely ghoulish afterlife of his own as the infamous "auto-icon," part taxidermy and part wax figure, at rest in a glass case on the University College grounds. In the novel, Shelley plays on public fears about Victor Frankenstein's real-life counterparts by narrating how he supplies his "workshop of filthy creation" with "bones from charnel-houses" and "materials" from "the dissecting room and the slaughter-house" ([1831] 2000, 58–59). Like Bentham, Victor pursues his research with utilitarian idealism, buoyed by "visions of extensive usefulness" (46) and thoughts of "the improvement which every day takes place in science and mechanics" (58). But the story renders these visions ultimately ironic. Victor advises Walton against his Arctic project, with ambivalent references to use and utility. He initially doubts whether "the relation of my disasters will be useful to you" (39). Toward the story's end, he reflects that "I deemed it criminal to throw away in useless grief those talents that might be useful to my fellow-creatures"; approaching death, he strangely rationalizes his fatal pursuit of the monster by musing that "if I were engaged in any high under-taking or design, fraught with extensive utility to my fellow-creatures, then could I live to fulfil it" (180–81). Walton, for his part, first foreshadows Victor's "visions of usefulness," by imagining "the inestimable benefit which I shall confer on all mankind" (28), and finally echoes Victor's failure, as he abandons his own "hopes of utility and glory" (183).

Supplementarity: As these passages show, Shelley applies something like Bentham's "greatest happiness principle" to the trope of Utility. Walton and Victor both envision the "extension" of the "utility" of their projects for all humankind. This universalization of "extensive utility" establishes important spatial and relational conditions for the modern discourse of technology: spatial in its globalized scope, which Canadian adaptations of the text will more fully realize; and relational in its *difference from* and *identification with* humankind. The modern discourse of technology is nothing if not a discourse of uncanny and unstable difference from and opposition to the ontological category of the human. As McQuire writes, "in every historical iteration . . . defining the technological not only acti-vates the border between nature and culture, but goes to the heart of what it means to be human" (2006, 255).

For a historical example of such defining of the technological, Benjamin Franklin defined the human as a "tool-making animal" (quoted in Weber [1910] 2005, 33), thus connoting technology's status as the interdependent Other of humanity. Similarly, Jürgen Habermas defines technology as a "'project' of the human species as a whole" (1970, 87), thus totalizing the categories of technology and the human as a binary pair in which the former term is subordinated to the latter. For a more contemporary example, a recent *Globe & Mail* review of two books (on genetics and digital media, respectively) leads with the claim that "modern technology is not only changing our day-to-day existence but what it means to be human" and ends with the suggestion that "technology is who we are" (Alang 2017, R12). This simultaneous opposition and intimacy between technology and humanity also informs McLuhan's famous definition of technologies as "extensions of man" ([1964] 2003), extensions that sometimes act as prosthetics—and other times as replacements. "What really makes the novel . . . disturbing," writes Morton, "is not the creature's difference from, but his *similarity to* human beings" (2002, 46). Frankenstein's creature—both human and "superhuman" (Shelley [1831] 2000, 92), at once dead and alive—becomes a prototypical figure of the modern discourse of technology.

As the creature becomes a dangerous supplement and categorical contrast to humanity, so technology becomes a dangerous but vital *supplement* to modern capitalism: the extension *and* replacement of human labour power. Mark Seltzer's reading of the modern "body-machine complex" theorizes this *supplementary* character of technology, defining it as both "an emptying out of human agency" and its "extension." In this "double logic of technology as prosthesis" (1993, 99) emerges the poststructuralist problematic of the supplement (Derrida 1976, 145), with its epistemologically unstable ability to both add ("extend") and replace ("empty out").

Contagion: Shelley's images of contagion relate to those of revolution (see below)—small wonder, given the political climate of conservative fear under which Shelley's England looked apprehensively, across the channel and among its own people, for signs of the spread of revolutionary feeling and foment. Some of this political apprehension over the infectiousness of revolutionary sympathies finds an allegorical figure in Victor Frankenstein's reflection on what might take place should he finish making the mate demanded by his creature. The passage establishes a primal scene for the modern discourse of technology—and that of technological risk assessment. The scene illustrates the tropes of revolution, contagion, and nonhuman supplementarity; it also inverts the rationale of utility, representing Victor's vision here as the antithesis of the Utilitarian ethos.

> Even if they were to leave Europe, and inhabit the deserts of the new world, yet one of the first results of those sympathies for which the dæmon thirsted would be children, and a race of devils would be propagated upon the earth, who might make the very existence of the species of man a condition precarious and full of terror. Had I a right, for my own benefit, to inflict this curse upon everlasting generations? . . . I shuddered to think that future ages might curse me as their pest, whose selfishness had not hesitated to buy its own peace at the price, perhaps, of the existence of the whole human race. ([1831] 2000, 145)

In addition to dramatically mobilizing the tropes discussed thus far, this scene, like the novel's globe-traversing plot more generally, points to the global context in which Canadian *Frankenstein*s will subsequently, and decisively, position the Frankenpheme of technology in the popular imaginary. Victor's projected "race of devils" prefigures the way technology in general and certain technologies in particular are represented today: antibacterial products, fossil fuels, genetically modified organisms, nuclear weapons, the Internet. The passage also suggests more than one vector of contagion: Victor imagines his creations engendering pestilence; he also imagines himself the "pest" of a postapocalyptic posterity. Shelley developed this image in the protagonist of her next novel, *The Last Man* ([1826] 1996): the story of a world wasted by plague, told by its lone survivor.

Frankenstein is further riddled with disease, beyond this scene. Victor shows up in the Arctic in a feverish condition. Scarlet fever ravages his family early in the novel ([1831] 2000, 49), foreshadowing how the creature will plague him and his family. Victor develops a habit of falling ill (or asleep) at highly inopportune moments: right before and after he completes and awakens the creature; while detained in Ireland; and after he finishes telling his tale to Walton, dying bedridden just before the creature catches up with him. This late scene formally augments the creature's characterization as contagion: like Walton, the reader is shocked finally to meet the creature that has escaped its confinement in a third-hand narrative nested within Victor's account. The creature's transgressive mobility between the nested story frames, from third-hand account to first-hand encounter, increases the suspense of the story by imparting an unsettling semblance of immediacy not unlike a spreading infection: if the ship is no longer safe harbour from the murderous creature, is the reader?

Shock: Shock provides the frame of affective reference that unites the preceding four tropes. Shock describes both an extremity of feeling and its nullification: as a verb it describes a surprise blow; as a noun, the "emptying-out of human agency" that responds to such a blow. *Frankenstein* also dramatizes the *electrifying* sense of shock that is significant both for subsequent adaptations, and for modernizing the meaning and connotations of technology. While Victor's reference to "the spark of being" that animated his creation is famously ambiguous, the science of galvanism is an equally famous context for the novel, and electricity is mentioned in other scenes that inform both the method and affect of the monster's creation. An early, foreshadowing anecdote from Victor's childhood describes "the shock" of lightning that "utterly destroyed" an oak tree, and frames Victor's account of learning about "that power"—"electricity and galvanism"—which precipitates his own intellectual revolution, the "overthrow" of Agrippa and the alchemists ([1831] 2000, 48).

Frankenstein popularizes the electrical valence of shock, and dramatizes shock's affective charge, sometimes conflating the word's technological sense and human sensibility. Amidst "remorse and guilt," Victor reflects that his health "had perhaps never recovered from the first shock it had sustained" ([1831] 2000, 86)—that "first shock" denoting both his research result and his reaction to it. After Clerval's death, he asks himself rhetorically (and with an ironic sense of his own factitious character): "Of what materials was I made that I could thus resist so many shocks?" (153).

If the creature's supplementarity prefigures that of technology, shock represents the *special affect* of technology as supplement. The overthrow of the human by its supplement stages a shocking encounter between a tragic man of feeling, as its apogee, and utilitarian instrumentality, as the absence of affect. As Kranzler remarks, the reason the monster is an "apt metaphor" for "the technological future" is its "divorce from affective responsibility" (1988, 42–43). In countless adaptations since, affect—*feeling*—has become the characteristic, defining difference between human and machine: recall *Blade Runner*'s Voigt-Kampff test, which screens for empathy to detect which subjects are nonhuman "replicants"; or *Battlestar Galactica*, in which the human characters insistently, repeatedly denigrate the Cylon antagonists as "toasters."

Revolution: The instability and danger of the creature figure the trope of revolution with which Mary Shelley supplies another modern discursive condition for technology. As has been widely researched, the conflict between Victor and the creature stages a drama of revolution that responds to the French Revolution (Douthwaite 2009, 384)—and to the Luddite revolts (O'Flinn 1986). In his early studies, Victor works through "the overthrow" of "the lords of my imagination" ([1831] 2000, 48). Recollecting when he first "beheld the accomplishment of my toils" (60)—and seeing in it only "catastrophe"—Victor describes the abrupt reversal of his feelings: "dreams that had been my food and pleasant rest for so long a space were now become a hell to me; and the change was so rapid, the overthrow so complete!" (61). While imprisoned in Ireland, he "often sat for hours . . . wishing for some mighty revolution" that would destroy both him and his creation (157).

As Fred Randel argues, "the creature's trajectory from birth in Ingolstadt to death by fire, amidst Northern ice, is a figure for the history of the French Revolution" (2003, 469). These images of revolution speak to the spirit of Shelley's age. But they also encode the motion of drastic and disruptive social change that has become integral to representations of technology: from Marx's "faith in the revolutionary potential of technology" (Ross 2005, 343), to McLuhan's theories that new media replace or consume old media and that electric media produce social upheaval—on a global scale. *Frankenstein* looms large in these representations of "the machine that passes from stubbornness to rebellion" (Tenner 1996, 3)—and such representations have their critics and skeptics, too. With reference to Thomas Carlyle's 1829 essay "Signs of the Times," Baldick deconstructs the latent fetishism of technology as risk and as revolution: "The technological interpretation of the myth resembles many influential diagnoses of 'the machine age' in that its isolation of the machine as the root evil of modern civilisation merely reinforces the very fetishism of mechanical power which it sets out to deplore" (1987, 8). Shelley articulates a profound ambivalence about political revolution both in her fiction and between its editions: whether Shelley seems more sympathetic or antipathetic to the French Revolution can depend on reading textual variants between the 1818 and 1831 editions (Randel 2003, 471). This ambivalence, in turn, conditions the ambivalence of the revolutionary rhetoric that has become commonly attached to technology by instrumentalists and determinists alike, and thus it also conditions the ambivalence at the core of the common-sense, instrumentalist meaning of technology itself (as discussed above). In the next chapter, we will take up the representations of "revolutionary technology" at greater length: McLuhan's oscillation between Luddite conservatism and techno-fetishism exemplifies and further popularizes the perception of technology as revolution.

The connected tropes of utility, supplementarity, contagion, shock, and revolution converge significantly in the repeated claim, made first by the dying Victor ([1831] 2000, 185) and then by his creature, that the latter is an "instrument of future mischief" (188), anticipating the popular sense of technology as an instrument of "future shock," the phrase from Toffler that we discussed in the introduction. While *Frankenstein* leaves technology, like its antagonist, unnamed, it supplies a primal scene for redefining the object and affect of technology—not after midcentury, but as early as the 1820s.

Elements of Technology: Frankenphemes in the Early Nineteenth Century

The relays, relations, and resonances uncovered among different textual productions in pursuing the palimpsestic, intertextual distribution of such a diversely received and widely popular text like *Frankenstein* partake far less of unilateral lines of influence from source to derivation and far more of multilateral networks of "subterranean and invisible diffusion" (Baldick 1987, 9). As Julia Douthwaite writes of discovering a 1790 French novella featuring an automaton maker named Frankenstein—for which case, more so than mine, we might expect to learn of a clear line of direct influence—the measured approach for pursuing such questions of cultural intertextuality "is not to argue for a causal relation, but to show the surprising resemblance" (2009, 381–82). A methodology of juxtaposition can seize on an image of the past in a way that productively illuminates a present crisis, excavating the present's embedded signification as a contingency of the past that is so seized upon; such is the method of history influentially theorized by Walter Benjamin—his "dialectics at a standstill"—and it is useful to bear in mind here.

For suggestive evidence of *Frankenstein*'s reinvention of technology discourse in Shelley's own time, then, we find Frankenphemes of "technology" among the cursory and extensive references to *Frankenstein* that traversed the lettered cultures of the Atlantic in the early nineteenth century. We also find Frankenphemes of technology being dramatized and reified in the diverse and hugely popular performance scenes that surrounded and adapted Shelley's novel and its constellation of current scientific and philosophical ideas. While an established English wariness about technology appears in this period to contrast an emerging American enthusiasm for it (Nye 1994, 54)—Blake's "dark Satanic mills" versus Whitman's "body electric"—Frankenphemes of technology and industrialization appear in the work of major writers on both sides of the Atlantic. In the old world, we find them in Carlyle, Dickens (Baldick 1987, 98, 119), and Jane Webb Loudon, as well as in Marx; and, in the new world, in Emerson, Hawthorne (Baldick 1987, 63), and Poe—among numerous others on either shore. In this transatlantic context, three representative articulations of the modern discourse technology, in the 1820s and 1830s, point to its Frankensteinian conditioning, as evoked and evinced in the writings of aspiring auto-icon Bentham, Harvard professor Jacob Bigelow, and steam power advocate Thomas Love Peacock.

One of the *OED*'s quotations for technology's archaic meaning is taken from book 1 ("Theoretic Grounds") of Bentham's 1827 *Rationale of Judicial Evidence*. In the first chapter, "On Evidence in General," Bentham writes:

> If all *practice*, much more must those comparatively narrow branches of it, which are comprehended under any such names as those of *art* and *science*, be grounded upon evidence.
>
> Questions in natural philosophy, questions in natural history, questions in technology in all its branches, questions in medicine, are all questions of evidence. When we use the words *observation, experience,* and *experiment,* what we mean is, facts observed, or supposed to be observed, by ourselves or others, either as they arise spontaneously, or after the bodies in question have been put, for the purpose, into a certain situation. (1827, 19)

While the *OED* cites this passage to illustrate technology's premodern meaning as a study of arts or techniques, the text can also be read to signify technology in its emerging modern sense. The term is related to but distinguished from "science," according to the modern distinction between science and technology as theory and practice. Note too the doubling rhetoric applied to technology between these two quoted paragraphs: as a "narrow branch" of knowledge itself, technology assumes its modern specialized relation to science; and as a set of "questions" with its own "branches," technology engages both its archaic sense as study ("questions") and its modern sense as application ("branches"). Moreover, the wording of the passage delivers a weirdly galvanic charge to Bentham's description of scientific method as the observation of "facts" that "arise spontaneously," and of "bodies" (albeit rhetorical bodies) that "have been put in a certain situation."

In Bentham's case, however, what is at least as significant as *how* the word is used is *who* is using it. The fact that it is Bentham invoking the word does much to suggest the Frankensteinian gloom gathering about the word. After all, Bentham himself donated his own body to science, embracing and embodying a peculiarly Frankensteinian afterlife as a macabre relic still on display at University College London, where a cabinet houses his preserved skeleton topped by a wax replica of his head. Bentham is also a thinker whom Hazlitt accuses of "reducing the mind of man to a machine" ([1825] 2000, 266), of being "one of those who prefer the artificial to the natural" (277), and of working in a manner akin to Frankenstein's bricolage: "Mr Bentham's *forte* is arrangement. . . . He has methodized, collated, and condensed all the materials prepared to his hand on the subjects of which he treats, in a masterly and scientific manner." Hazlitt also cites an extraordinary example of Bentham's curiously science fictional hubris: "He has been heard to say . . . that 'he should like to live the remaining years of his life, a year at a time at the end of the next six or eight centuries, to see the effect which his writings would by that time have had upon the world'" (267–68).

Hazlitt's portrait of Bentham—which stresses his "theories," his "logical machinery," and his "technicality of manner" ([1825] 2000, 267, 276)—typifies the well-entrenched English hostility to "theory" by characterizing Bentham as its very incarnation. Bentham's use of a word like technology is consistent with a learned style that trades in abstraction and system, a style that Hazlitt duly criticizes as "barbarous philosophical jargon" (276). At an abstract contextual level, the English aversion to abstraction renders both Bentham and the theoretical German word *Technologie* equally suspect on the grounds of theory as such. It is on similar grounds that Shelley's fictional adaptation of ideas by "physiological writers of Germany" ([1818] 2012, 49) renders her novel suspect in the view of conservative reviewers. Bentham, technology, and *Frankenstein* were all regarded with suspicion for their traffic in theory, by the lights of England's Romantic and gender-coded nationalism, which as David Simpson argues, "contributed mightily to the demonization of theory" as a defining component of "Englishness in general": "The English are not supposed to practice its rites, but those who do had better be men. . . . Theory thus becomes the province of alienated male rationalists like Victor Frankenstein" (1993, 123).

Across the pond, Frankenphemes of technology can also be found in this period, amidst a national culture usually characterized more as technophilic than technophobic. In 1831, when Shelley published her revised *Frankenstein*, Harvard professor Jacob Bigelow published his revised edition of *Elements of Technology* (it had first been published around 1828 or 1829). The *OED* cites this book as an illustrative early use of technology's modern meaning as "the mechanical arts and applied sciences collectively" (4b). Bigelow's book collected a decade's worth of lectures "on the application of the sciences to the useful arts." In his prefatory "Advertisement" to the volume, Bigelow staked his book's utility on assembling "scattered" elements into a new, distinctly modern research "subject," one "peculiarly capable of exciting the attention and curiosity of students." He continues:

> The importance of the subject, and the prevailing interest, which exist in regard to the arts and their practical influences, appear to me to have created a want, not yet provided for, in our courses of elementary education. . . . To *embody*, as far as possible, the various topics which belong to such an *undertaking*, I have adopted the general name of *Technology*, a word sufficiently expressive, which is found in some of the older dictionaries, and is beginning to be *revived* in the literature of practical men at the present day. (1831, iv, emphases added)

Bigelow's self-conscious redefinition of technology shows the word starting to accumulate its Frankensteinian associations. Note the striking rhetoric of reanimation in Bigelow's text: he "revives" Technology to "embody" an "undertaking" of applied science. He strays from the plot of *Frankenstein* in "adopting" (rather than abandoning) this "embodiment," but the wording still retains the paternal relation. Whether intended or not, the Frankenpheme of Bigelow's definition suggests the pervasive but "subterranean" distribution of Shelley's story and its effect on technology's modern "revival." Elsewhere in Bigelow's book, David Nye finds statements supporting Bigelow's claim on importing from the German a new meaning in English for technology, such as Bigelow's assertion that the "labour of a hundred artificers is now performed by the operations of a single machine" (quoted in Nye 1994, 45)—an image of technology on the "colossal" scale of which Marx will later take note, and an image that, like the rhetoric of resurrection, invests technology with its uncanny sublimity, its Frankensteinian subtext.

Closer to home, Peacock—a friend of Shelley and an acquaintance of Bentham—uses the word technology as a Frankenpheme in two of his satirical fictions. In *Nightmare Abbey*, published after *Frankenstein* in 1818, Peacock satirizes the popular taste for Gothic and fantastic literature. Scythrop Glowry, a parody of Percy Shelley, also assumes a Frankensteinian aspect: he isolates himself in his study to read the "mystical jargon and necromantic imagery" of transcendental philosophy (as well as Goethe's *Werther*), then begins to plot "his projected regeneration of the human species" ([1818] 2007, 57). He goes so far as to "meditate on the practicability of reviving a confederation of regenerators," but whether the ensuing "treatise" he publishes is a *recipe* for said revival or its *realization* remains obscure—as does the publication itself, for being "wrapt up in the monk's hood of transcendental technology, but filled with hints of matter deep and dangerous" (58). Here, Peacock's usage connotes at once the eighteenth-century association of technology with art and abstraction, and its nineteenth-century "revival" in industry and application, shadowed portentously by the "deep and dangerous" menace of "national ferment." In 1831's *Crotchet Castle*, Peacock uses the term as a wry synonym for political economy, which one character calls "a hyperbarbarous technology" ([1831] 1947, 110). Here, Peacock's usage evokes more clearly the modern sense of technology and its attendant danger, attached to an ironic trope of "barbarity" to connote both brutal violence and antimodern atavism. In both these novels, Peacock invokes technology to articulate modernity and menace, applied arts and anxiety. And like Bentham, Peacock had a similarly technophilic public reputation that amplifies his textual representations of technology; in his case, as a vocal advocate of steam-powered transport.

The examples of Bentham, Bigelow, and Peacock—writers and thinkers of some stature in the early nineteenth century—show the *special affect* of modernized technology discourse in the period, as a nascent industrial keyword infiltrated and influenced by Shelley's novel.

Staging Technology Through Special Effects in Georgian "Monster Melodramas"

We also find *Frankenstein*'s "threshold of epistemologization" for technology being more widely established in the incredibly diverse performance culture that surrounded the novel. Stage versions of the novel began proliferating in the early 1820s. As William St. Clair points out, *Frankenstein*'s popularity in its own period resulted more from its stage adaptations than from its small, pricey print runs, the first of which produced only five hundred copies (2004, 367). The text, and more specifically the creature at its core, began to circulate as a Frankenpheme in public discourse, among periodicals and parliamentary debates (as in Canning's 1824 allusion concerning slavery), soon after the novel's first theatrical adaptations. "By the end of 1823," writes Hitchcock, "five different retellings of *Frankenstein* had animated the London stage" (2007, 88–89). Like the political appropriations they engendered, *Frankenstein*'s theatrical adaptations helped to redefine the word technology as a Frankenpheme. And for the most part, these stage adaptations took shape not as traditional dramas in London's patent theatres, but as multimedia spectacles in the burgeoning illegitimate theatre of the period.

The recent reappraisal of Romantic performance by scholars of the period has prompted not just a review of the "closet" and lyrical dramas of canonical authors like Byron and Baillie but also a retrieval of illegitimate theatre and popular performance culture—its melodramas, burlesques, pantomimes, extravaganzas, magic-lantern shows, boxing matches, executions, and science experiments—along with analyses of its institutional contexts like censorship, copyright, and criticism. Jane Moody reads radical politics at work in London's Romantic-era illegitimate theatre and provides important context for *Frankenstein*'s dramatizations: the period's critics developed a "critique of monstrosity" to defend and distinguish "a text-based canon of English drama" from "a miscellaneous realm of nontextual, physical entertainment"—the multimedia, "spurious theatrical forms" that were actually fostered by "the terms of patent monopoly," and ultimately became popular enough to bring an end to that monopoly (2000, 12–13). "Critics," Moody writes, "mocked the miscellaneous interweaving of music and visual spectacle with elaborate stage machinery, virtuosic dance and, in the case of pantomime, the silent, gestural language of mime" and "blamed these monstrous productions for what they perceived as a process of generic miscegenation" (12). Melodrama in particular was popularly figured as monstrous: Samuel De Wilde's "The Monster Melo-Drama," a widely reprinted cartoon that first appeared in *The Satirist* in December 1807, depicts its titular monster as a hydra-like beast, with four heads representing period theatre celebrities; its paws trample a document called "Shakespeare's Works" and on its belly are several teats suckled by period playwrights and theatre practitioners who worked in popular and illegitimate genres like melodrama.

The distinctions between patent and illegitimate theatre in Georgian London represent just one facet of a popular and competitive performance culture. Diane Hoeveler writes that "theater managers who wanted to remain competitive had to keep pace in their use of pyrotechnics and other devices that would continue to 'shock and awe' their audiences": "As attendance at theaters increased throughout the nineteenth century, the technologies involved in stagecraft had to improve, and advancements in lighting, stage machinery, setting, and sound effects were all of major importance in the spectacularization of theatrical fare" (2005, paras. 2, 3). Hoeveler notes that "technologies of visual spectacle" gave a significant boost to the rise of illegitimate theatre (2005, para. 13) and established new standards of audience expectations for theatrical performance.

The illegitimate theatre of Romantic-era England represents a techno-cultural horizon for the pride of place now enjoyed by special effects in today's popular cultural industries. To be sure, traditional theatre had also begun innovating more technologically advanced stage business in the period; productions of *Macbeth*, especially, were "grist to the mill of the maker of effects" (Rees 1978, 137). But the multimedia "monstrosities" of illegitimate theatre made it a distinctive cultural laboratory for giving dramatic and technological application to the theories of scientists like Humphry Davy and Luigi Galvani. For one example, an 1820 Gothic melodrama *The Vampyre* innovated a new kind of trap door, later used in an 1824 *Frankenstein* farce (Forry 1990, 34). For another, it wasn't a patent theatre but the Lyceum that first lit a London stage with gaslight, in 1817. Terence Rees writes that Covent Garden opened its 1815 season with exterior gaslight, but the Olympic brought gaslight inside later that year, to little fanfare, until the Lyceum's stage use of gaslight in 1817—whereafter most of London's theatres quickly adopted the new lighting technology. By 1829, only the Haymarket still held out, in dim oil-lamp and candlelight, against the new gaslight standards (Rees 1978, 9). These lighting standards, in turn, fostered the nascent sector in special effects: they drove increasing sophistication in scenery and other effects and demanded an increasing—and increasingly specialized—labour force (Rees 1978, 189). In addition, scientists like Davy and Galvani themselves gave theatrical presentations, in an increasingly public culture of science (Holmes 2009, 295). This culture often openly leveraged *Frankenstein* in staging sensational exhibitions of electric experiment and other "scientific sensations" (Morus 1998).

The stage *Frankenstein*s of the 1820s and 1830s demonstrate with peculiar aptness these techno-cultural functions of the illegitimate theatre, and not just for putting popular ideas about science in a new light. These productions tended overwhelmingly to take shape as melodrama, burlesque, and farce. The first, Richard Brinsley Peake's *Presumption*, opened at the English Opera House in July 1823. (In an intriguing variation on the theme of theatrical adaptation and "hideous progeny," Peake was named after a famous playwright of his father's generation, Richard Brinsley Sheridan [Behrendt 2001, para. 1].) *Presumption* was so popular that it inspired fourteen other dramatizations of *Frankenstein* over the next three years, in England and France, including four in England in just the latter half of 1823 (Forry 1990, 3–4). Indeed, between 1823 and 1826, about fifteen stage productions adapted *Frankenstein*. The title of one 1824 production— *Frank-in-Steam; or, The Modern Promise to Pay*—parodies the full title of Shelley's novel; at the time, steam power was as potent an icon of modern industrial technology as were the automated looms that Luddites raged against from 1811 to 1817, their campaigns peaking from the summer of 1816 to that of 1817, precisely when Shelley was writing her novel (O'Flinn 1986, 196). In *Frank-in-Steam*, the play's protagonist, a student in debt, learns of the death of his antagonist, a bailiff named Mr. Snatch, and cannot resist the opportunity to reanimate the corpse—rather unwisely, since the bailiff remains, in his undead state, as bent on collecting the student's debt as he was in life. Ultimately, the student kills his monstrous progeny by pushing Snatch into a steamboat's boiler (Forry 1990, 186). This play also parodies Peake's *Presumption*, not only by capitalizing on the growing popularity of stagings of *Frankenstein* but also in one important detail—by *not* staging but instead *narrating* its climactic steam-boiler murder scene, thereby denying the audience a technical spectacle that *Presumption* had led it to expect of these stagings.

MR. T. P. COOKE,
Of the Theatre Royal Covent Garden.
In the Character of the Monster in the Dramatic Romance of Frankenstien

Figure 2 Actor T. P. Cooke playing the Creature in Richard Brinsley Peake's *Presumption*, 1823, the first of many theatrical adaptations of Shelley's novel. The role required the actor's skin to be painted blue. Lithograph by Nathaniel Whittock, based on an original painting by Thomas Charles Wageman. Image courtesy of the Carl H. Pforzheimer Collection of Shelley and His Circle, New York Public Library.

Theatrical versions and print editions fuelled each other's production throughout the nineteenth century—as in Shelley's reference to "presumption" in her 1831 second edition (St. Clair 2004, 371). Repeat stagings and printings of the earliest dramatizations held interest until the mid-nineteenth century, after which time new theatre versions appeared and still keep appearing, amidst a myriad adaptations in other media.

Among the earliest stagings, two have powerfully shaped the popular reception of the novel and, thus, the modern popular discourse of technology. These were Peake's *Presumption* (1823) and Henry Milner's *The Man and the Monster* (1826). Both of these adaptations boiled down the novel's complex morality into a populist, conservative *moral*; as Forry writes, "on the English stage . . . *Frankenstein* immediately became associated with unbridled revolution, atheism, and blind progress in science and technology" (1990, 35). St. Clair shows how intellectual property regulations in nineteenth-century Britain left print editions of the novel scarce and expensive and left playwrights and theatres free to adapt the text without copyright restrictions. The relative scarcity of the print novel, then, drove new stage adaptations to exploit prior stage adaptations rather than the source text itself. St. Clair claims that the effect of these regulatory contingencies was to popularize the story as a reactionary, religious cautionary tale, rather than the scientifically speculative and progressive allegory of the Enlightenment that he says Shelley intended (2004, 373). However, many critics read in the novel a clear critique of science and its unintended technological consequences; Anne K. Mellor's reading of Shelley's "feminist critique of science" is a salutary example (1988).

Presumption exerted the greatest influence on subsequent receptions of the novel, including the 1931 film with Boris Karloff. *Presumption* first transformed Shelley's eloquent creature into a mute monster; it gave the solitary Victor Frankenstein a lab assistant, and it recast Victor himself as the prototype of the now-formulaic "mad scientist" character. In Peake's play and the 1931 film, the assistant's name is Fritz; in the sequels to the film, a shepherd named Ygor, played by Bela Lugosi, begins to eclipse Fritz's role, and subsequent adaptations have entrenched the identification of Dr. Frankenstein's assistant as "Igor"—for example, in the eponymous 2008 animated film. As Richard Holmes notes, *Presumption* also turned *Frankenstein*'s vaguely described "workshop of filthy creation" into a laboratory at "the centre of dramatic interest" (2009, 335). Peake dramatized the novel's "dreary night of November" (Shelley [1818] 2012, 83) as a sensational "creation scene" calculated to shock audiences. Peake left the act of creation offstage, narrated by Fritz but with flashes of blue fire from the offstage lab, after which the monster burst onto the stage, made up all in blue, which became the character's standard stage colour (fig. 2).

In contrast, Milner's 1826 version, *The Man and the Monster*, moved the creation scene onstage, presenting a lab set complete with high-tech props, to dramatize the creature's first twitches of galvanic animation (in a way now familiar from the 1931 film). The scene is described in Milner's stage directions:

SCENE III.
The Interior of the Pavilion.—Folding Doors in the Back. On a long Table is discovered an indistinct Form, covered with a black cloth. A small side Table, with Bottles, and Chemical Apparatus,—and a brazier with fire. [. . .] Music.—He [Frankenstein] rolls back the black covering, which discovers a colossal human figure, of a cadaverous livid complexion; it slowly begins to rise. (Quoted in Forry 1990, 194)

The creation is the first of a triptych of scenes that *Presumption* and its successors made obligatory—and famous as showcases for spectacular effects. The other two scenes are the monster's setting fire to a cottage, and the monster's destruction, usually along with that of his creator in the same fell swoop. Producers of *Presumption* and its progeny soon seized on this triptych of creation, combustion, and catastrophe as a major selling point. The advertising for *Presumption* promoted these scenes in particular among its "*many striking effects*" (quoted in Morton 2002, 51). The first French adaptation, Jean-Toussaint Merle and Antony Béraud's 1826 *Le monstre et le magicien*, succeeded, in part, on the strength of "its fantastic special effects, which it borrowed from the British stage" (Forry 1990, 11). One Parisian reviewer raved: "Jamais . . . on n'avait vu chez nous machinerie plus compliquée et plus extraordinaire." An advertisement in the newspaper *Le Temps* even included a schedule of the most spectacular scenes: "à neuf heures, la Naissance du Monstre; à dix heures, l'incendie; à dix heures et demi, le Ravin des Torrents" (quoted in Forry 1990, 11). A staple strategy ever since, the advertising of special effects in *Frankenstein* performances has given technology itself a starring role in the spectacular productions of popular culture, an uncannily animated fetish figure of the cultural industries' power. For a present-day example, note the attaching of "3D" to the title of virtually every new cinematic release.

As well as great ad copy, the special effects of early *Frankenstein* plays made good material for show-business comedy and theatre lore. A year after *Presumption*, Peake lampooned his own play with *Another Piece of Presumption*, a meta-theatrical burlesque full of jokes about "complicated machinery" and the show's own shoestring budget: "Cut out my house on Fire—" complains the playwright to the manager (quoted in Forry 1990, 162).

Also in 1824, a Birmingham production of *Presumption* inadvertently turned melodrama into farce, by trying to economize on effects. The theatre didn't have enough canvas for the avalanche scene and, instead, repurposed a big prop elephant from an earlier production:

> Before we reached our elevation a pistol was fired behind the scenes, when the Master Carpenter being over anxious for the success of *the experiment* let go—when down came the elephant with a tremendous crash, knocked down the platform and scenery and came rolling down the stage to the footlights where it ran some danger of being roasted till it was dragged off the stage. (O. Smith, quoted in Forry 1990, 7, emphasis added)

Note the rhetoric of "experiment" in the actor's account of the accident. In the theatrical popular culture of Georgian England, adaptations of *Frankenstein* provided a convenient yet contradictory unity of form and content for a theatre culture marked by technical experiment and a scientific culture marked by increasing theatricality—the latter exemplified by the notorious "'re-animation' exhibitions" conducted in 1803 by Giovanni Aldini (Holmes 2009, 317), who would later take the gaslight technology of British theatre back to Italy (Rees 1978, 31).

As the earliest "technological reductions" of *Frankenstein*, these plays were characterized by cautionary plots and spectacular effects that dramatized the complex tension between determinism and instrumentalism integral to the modern discourse of technology. On one hand, the plays' reactionary message—that scientific pursuits are diabolical and deadly—bolsters the determinist dimension of technology discourse: not only is unethical experimentation predestined to backfire, but its product will prove fatal to the researcher. The plays conflate science and Satanism—both *thematically*, in Faustian representations of Frankenstein's work (Peake and Milner, quoted in Forry 1990, 137) and descriptions of the monster as a devil (Peake and Kerr, quoted in Forry 1990, 215)—and *technically*, in their use of the latest special effects to dramatize diabolism and to *mystify* monstrosity. As Fred Botting writes, "the uncanny is, in many ways, a technological phenomenon whose effects are accentuated by the shifts and disturbances of technical innovation" (2005, para. 21), and technology—embodied in these plays as the monster—takes on a life of its own.

On the other hand, the plays' spectacular media complicate the determinist message: they demonstrate the creative instrumentality of new technologies like gaslight, and their power to mystify gives ground to instrumentalism in consummately theatrical moments when the expected avalanche arrives early as a prop elephant. Then again, such moments also freight the plays' special effects with the sense of risk that becomes a defining feature of modern technology. The obligatory cottage-burning scene is a perfect example: Rees notes with grim irony that, "at a time when theatres burned down with monotonous regularity, a good stage fire carried an additional frisson over and above its spectacle value" (1978, 146).

The stage versions did still more to consolidate the popular understanding of technology as a Frankenpheme, by characterizing the creature as a mute and thus mystifying monster, who—like the special effects being exploited to stage him—represents an experimental and potentially disastrous application of current scientific theory. "From print to stage to screen," Botting argues, "the monster circulates in depictions of fearsome machinery and in new apparatuses of cultural production" (2005, para. 11). In the early *Frankenstein* plays, the mute monster embodied a fetish-figure of technology: a "dæmon" born of "machinery and magic" (Milner, quoted in Forry 1990, 198), running amok amidst the fireworks, gaslights, and other "ponderous machinery" surrounding the stage (Rees 1978, 203). With their uncanny, dramatic figures of technology running amok amidst new theatre technology that constantly threatened the same, these plays redirected the audience's attention from subjective acting to objective effects, and in effect problematized the technological dialectic between liveness and mediation, decades before gramophone or film. The "monster melodramas" of Georgian theatre provided a scene, incentive, and challenge for experimenting with special effects, which now represent their own capital-commanding sector in today's cultural industries. We can trace a genealogical line from the animated blue devils of *Presumption* and its progeny to *Avatar*'s animated race of blue aliens. The formal and thematic emphases on special effects in the period's illegitimate theatre, especially in its *Frankenstein* adaptations, represent a spectacular performance of the period's broader redefinition of modern technology's *episteme* in terms of media and monstrosity.

It is no uncanny coincidence, then, that the reinvention of technology emerged in the decade after *Frankenstein*'s debut; *Frankenstein* interdicted the rejuvenated German *Technologie* in the course of its English immigration and rerouted it through the writings of Anglo-American public intellectuals, and through popular scenes of sensational performance. The text and its popular receptions do not coincidentally belong to the period of the word's revivification in English, they texture and direct this revivification. The modern discourse of technology—as a fetishized determinism, as the dread that supplements development, as "future shock"—is a powerfully affecting effect of the text's cultural function in its time, as an epistemological "instrument of future mischief." In the twentieth century, this sense of technology's mischief would be recast on a global stage, largely through the work of Marshall McLuhan, to whom we now turn.

4. The Medium Is the Monster

McLuhan's "Frankenpheme" of Technology

Frankenstein and key adaptations of it may have redefined and modernized the discourse of technology in the early nineteenth century, but it was the fast-changing mediascape of the twentieth century—and more specifically the work of McLuhan in and on this mediascape—that put the modern discourse of technology on the map and into common circulation.

McLuhan may not seem a likely subject for studying either literary adaptation or the popular legacies of Romanticism; what this chapter will discuss is how McLuhan defines and theorizes technology, with reference to *Frankenstein*. It will also discuss McLuhan's distinctive research methodology, with reference to Edgar Allan Poe and with attention to how McLuhan's stated method contradicts and conflicts with his work's tone. The chapter then outlines the Frankensteinian historical narrative that his work constructs, his epochal model of technological change, and subsequently reviews some representative reviews and receptions of McLuhan in the popular press and the counterculture of the period of his greatest fame, the late 1960s. McLuhan's receptions by journalists and counterculture scenesters, taken together, served greatly to popularize his ideas, to figure McLuhan himself as a kind of mad scientist of media, and thus to amplify what I will term his "Frankenpheme of technology."

"Every technology necessitates a new war"

To argue, as the present chapter does, that McLuhan's work takes up and develops technology as a Frankenpheme is in the first place to situate his work in the context of the profound social turmoil visited on the globe by the Second World War. This global conflict was technologized to an extent that the fascist Futurists, turned on by the industrial and systematized stratagems of World War I, could scarcely have imagined in their wettest machine dreams.

If you run a Google n-gram search for the frequency of the occurrence of the word "technology," in every century since 1500, the advent of print, the line will hug the horizontal time axis, flat except for little speed bumps in the late seventeenth century and the turn of the twentieth. But it starts to rise up, gradually, in the 1920s, climbing into a ten-degree angle that it holds until the mid-1950s, when it swings up towards thirty degrees. Then, in the late 1960s and 1970s, the line shoots steeply upward, levelling briefly between 1985 and 1990 before arcing in a shallow parabola over Y2K. Acknowledging that a Google n-gram is not exactly the most rigorously isolated data set (how do we quantify "lots of books," exactly?), its statistical thumbnail sketch is still a suggestive index of broad changes in language use. Kelly suggests that technology entered colloquial English use in 1939 (2011, 6), and while he gives no particular explanation for suggesting that year, the date ominously implies that the onset of World War II might have had something to do with it. Perhaps, then, the chilling historical insight of Kittler ([1986] 1999)—that the major innovations in media have regularly arisen first as military research projects and wartime field tests—also holds true for corresponding transformations in everyday language and public discourse.

For most of the war, McLuhan was teaching at Saint Louis University in Missouri; but in 1939, having just married, he and his wife went to Cambridge where he finished his master's degree and began his doctorate as the war in Europe began. In 1940 they returned to the United States, and McLuhan completed his doctoral studies at a distance, with Cambridge's blessing and understanding. Soon after McLuhan earned his PhD, in 1943, his attention was already turning from canonical literary subjects to contemporary popular ones, reading the latter by the lights of the former to try to make sense of the emerging postwar mediascape—and of his students. In the wake of such unprecedented and eminently technological atrocities as Auschwitz and Hiroshima, the war registers powerfully in McLuhan's writing. Not coincidentally, along with the imagery of modern weaponry, the word technology itself "began to appear with noticeable frequency in McLuhan's writings" after World War II (Gordon 1997, 132)—when it began to appear with increasing frequency in everyday English in general.

The nuclear bomb became one of McLuhan's favourite analogies for the drastic, global effects of media. Nuclear power and especially nuclear weaponry have established a distinctive—and deserved—Frankensteinian discourse (Morton 2002, 56), as the apotheosis of a human-made technology whose threat to humankind makes Victor Frankenstein's projection of "a race of devils" seem a welcome alternative. Accordingly, the rhetoric of nuclear weaponry that recurs in McLuhan's writing—sometimes in deadly earnest, sometimes in gallows humour—harbours its own peculiar set of Frankensteinian connotations and associations. A private letter from 1946 shows McLuhan's debt to his Cambridge mentor, F. R. Leavis, and to the artist Wyndham Lewis, as well as the private hostility to technological change that he publicly disavowed: in this letter, McLuhan says the critical methods of Leavis and the creative methods of Lewis "can serve to educate a huge public . . . to resist that swift obliteration of the person which is going on" (quoted in Gordon 1997, 133). In its image of "swift obliteration," this remark about media effects (to which McLuhan alludes as "what is going on") conjures "the Bomb"; in its defence of individualism against technology, it shows a Romantic ideology consistent with other Romantic contexts of McLuhan's work.

The scholars with whom McLuhan studied, the writers he read, and postwar geopolitics all informed his research and the priority it gave to technology. "I am a set of partially developed and isolated fragments," McLuhan wrote in his diary on 11 February 1937, then straddling a junior position at the University of Wisconsin and doctoral studies at Cambridge. McLuhan's ultimate focus on media was based in wide-ranging graduate work that encompassed the Renaissance and modernism, as well as Romanticism, to an extent not widely acknowledged. Conventional accounts attribute McLuhan's definition of technology to the more immediate influences of Leavis and Lewis. But McLuhan also knew well the work of Shelley's contemporary Peacock (Gordon 44), who as we saw in the last chapter used technology as a Frankenpheme; and McLuhan cites Thomas Carlyle—whose critical writing was powerfully influenced by *Frankenstein* (Baldick 1987, 103)—as a source for his own definition of technology (McLuhan 1970, 302). While McLuhan's references to Shelley and Carlyle are not as numerous as those to, say, Joyce or T. S. Eliot, they are integral to his theory of technology.

The Mechanical Bride (of Frankenstein)

Both the bomb analogy and extensive borrowings from Romantic literature appear in McLuhan's first book, *The Mechanical Bride: Folklore of Industrial Man* (1951), a "mosaic" of essays on postwar US advertising and popular culture, in which McLuhan proceeds by reprinting and analyzing a series of contemporary advertisements. In framing his essays and their arguments as a mosaic of assembled fragments, McLuhan makes an observation about his analytic method that the present study turns on McLuhan's own writing. "Among the multifarious forms and images sustained by any society," McLuhan writes, "it is reasonable to expect to find some sort of melodic curve. There will be many variations, but they will tend to be variations on certain recognizable themes" (1951, 96). The "theme" that McLuhan identifies in the postwar popular mediascape is a recurring "cluster image" of "sex, technology, and death." McLuhan doesn't define technology in *Bride*—he takes it for granted to signify industrial machinery and to act as the fulcrum of his "cluster image" theme. The variations on this theme that are discussed in the book include sexualized images of automobiles and weaponry, mechanized images of bodies and sexuality, dystopian images of media technology, and fetishized images of industrial enterprise and free-market ideology. Contemporary with but independent of analogous European projects—Roland Barthes's *Mythologies*, Richard Hoggart's *Uses of Literacy*, the Frankfurt School's culture industry thesis—McLuhan surveys the postwar corporate mediascape and its ascendant hegemony of instrumental rationality in order to expose its latent effect: the dehumanizing transformation of North America's individual citizens into mass consumers, in symptomatically gender-coded terms. McLuhan conceived the book as a critique of "the feminization of the North American male" (Gordon 1997, 117) and "the decimation of sex by . . . mechanization" (McLuhan, quoted in Gordon 1997, 153).

McLuhan is concerned, throughout *Bride*, with the difference between surface readings and latent meanings of mass media, especially advertising. He identifies a series of popular figures that typify the postwar consumerist zeitgeist: the sleuth, the scientist, and the gangster—the last of which McLuhan calls the "tragic hero" best suited to "commercial society dedicated to the smash and grab and one-man fury of enterprise" (1951, 145). Significantly, the prototype for all these symptomatic figures of industrial culture is none other than the Byronic hero, following whose example "all rebellion against the spirit of hawking and huckstering takes in large measure the Byronic form" (109). More recent work on the legacies of Romanticism tacitly bolsters McLuhan's argument about Byron. Atara Stein (2004) tracks the Byronic hero through popular culture—and discusses the intertextual intimacy found in this context between the Byronic figure and the *Frankenstein* monster. McLuhan himself contextualizes this argument, with reference to early industrialization, Regency society, and the culture of Byron and his contemporaries, making connections between popular media and figures of subterranean or latent influence on it.

McLuhan's connections between submerged cultural history and in-your-face contemporary media lead him to suggest that the themes he finds in the mediascape are not obvious—are even unconscious, despite their prevalence: "Important for present purposes is the fact that the complexities of such popular images as that of the sleuth are subterranean. So with the current image of the 'businessman' or the 'scientist.' The indiscriminate cluster of items included in these images becomes in turn a means of 'popular thinking' about society and politics" (1951, 110).

McLuhan's work harbours a "subterranean," thematic "cluster image" of its own, an image that becomes integral to his writing about media. If *The Mechanical Bride* essays an extensive analysis of the "cluster image" of "sex, technology, and death," the middle term here, "technology," becomes a cluster image unto itself, in which the recognizable tropes with which Shelley characterized her creature converge with explicit intertextual references, and thus render the word technology itself a Frankenpheme—a condensed, connotative term to conjure the spectre of *Frankenstein*. The book places the term technology in a web of references that clarify its Frankenpheme aspect. The title of McLuhan's book alludes to Marcel Duchamp's artwork *The Bride Stripped Bare by Her Bachelors, Even* (1915–23), in which the "stripping" of the "bride" is depicted as a kind of Cubist disassembly into her (or its) machine parts. However, in keeping with McLuhan's interest in the interface of high and popular culture, the title also evokes the bride of Frankenstein, the manufactured female body destroyed in Shelley's novel but later brought to cinematic life in *Bride of Frankenstein* (1935), and in the robot Maria of *Metropolis* (1927). These evocations in the title are made concrete with McLuhan's explicit reference in the title essay: "Franken-stein fantasies depend on the horror of a synthetic robot running amok in revenge for its lack of a 'soul.' Is this not merely a symbolic way of express-ing the actual fact that many people have become so mechanized that they feel a dim resentment at being deprived of full human status?" (1951, 100).

The statement puts McLuhan's thesis in sensational and pop-cultural terms, and the essay in which it appears includes related "cluster images" that recur throughout McLuhan's work. McLuhan ends this essay by under-scoring both his title's Frankensteinian figure and his book's central image; he states that the "trance-like" effects of popular art—the mass-produced "Frankenstein fantasies"—are to perpetuate "the widely occurring cluster image of sex, technology, and death which constitutes the mystery of the mechanical bride" (1951, 101). In addition, this title essay in McLuhan's first book refers not only to *Frankenstein*, but also to a legion of likewise Gothic and grotesque figures: cybernetic "thinking machines," ghouls, and vam-pires (100–1), as well as the striking image of machines "coming to resemble organisms not only in the way they obtained power by digestion of fuel but in their capacity to evolve ever new types of themselves with the help of the machine tenders" (99). In this paraphrase of a premise from Samuel But-ler's utopian fiction *Erewhon* (1872), McLuhan first iterates a claim that he puts more vividly in *Understanding Media*: that "man becomes, as it were, the sex organs of the machine world" (McLuhan [1964] 2003, 68). This image of an inverted, dystopian human-machine relationship—an image both Cronenbergian and *Matrix*-like—would become one of his "most widely repeated aphorisms" (Harvey 2006, 341), and its defamiliarizing suggestion "that the origins, transformation, propagation and continual reproduction of the human subject is an inherently technological process" (335) has proven a compelling point around which attention to McLuhan has been perennially renewed in relation to technology studies, critical theory, and popular culture.

Understanding Media (Means Fearing Technology)

McLuhan opens *Understanding Media* with a working definition of tech-nology—as an "extension of man"—and a Frankensteinian illustration of it: "Today, after more than a century of electric technology, we have extended our central nervous system itself in a global embrace, abolishing both space and time as far as our planet is concerned. Rapidly, we approach the final phase of the extensions of man—the technological simulation of consciousness" ([1964] 2003, 5). In this book, the word "technology" occurs almost as often as "media": in *Understanding Media*, the former word occurs 227 times; the latter, 277. Moreover, technology becomes interchangeable, even synonymous with media in McLuhan's theory. For example, he writes: "The personal and social consequences of any medium—that is, of any extension of ourselves—result from the new scale that is introduced into our affairs by each extension of ourselves, or by any new technology" (19). In one sentence, both medium and technology are treated as "extensions of man." We also see their interchangeability in a private letter from the same year *Understanding Media* appeared, in which McLuhan wrote: "I have discovered a better way of saying the medium is the message. It is this: each technology creates a new environment" (quoted in Gordon 1997, 175). He thought this wording better addresses how media strive for "immediacy," how they become taken for granted, invisible, and natural in their social implementation—and thus how they effect their most profound transformations on subjectivity and society, time and space.

McLuhan attributes his idea of technology as extension to contemporaries like Lewis Mumford, Leavis, and Lewis (Gordon 1997, 120). But McLuhan also credits Romantic sources: the phrase "extensions of man" is Ralph Waldo Emerson's (Gordon 1997, 196), and McLuhan cites Carlyle's 1833 *Sartor Resartus* as a source for his idea of technology as extension, as environment, and *as weapon*:

> Carlyle's *Sartor Resartus* followed in the tracks of the eighteenth-century Swedenborg *zeitgeist* theory of Age Garb (or garbage); i.e., all human institutions from language to tweezers are extensions of, and weapons of, the human body.
>
> New technologies = new environments. (1970, 302)

This weaponized sense of technology speaks to McLuhan's hostility to technological change, which he shared with his mentor F. R. Leavis, but which he tried to keep private. In public, McLuhan assumed a neutral, critical stance towards technology: "Value judgments have long been allowed to create a moral fog around technological change such as renders understanding impossible" ([1962] 1969, 255). For McLuhan, the "only person able to encounter technology with impunity" is "the serious artist . . . an expert aware of the changes in sense perception" ([1964] 2003, 31).

McLuhan's models for this romanticized role of the artist as outsider and visionary included Joyce, Yeats, and Eliot—but also William Blake, Percy Shelley, and, above all, Poe ([1964] 2003, 430). McLuhan adopted two formal principles from Poe's work for his own criticism, and both are significant for his discourse of technology as Frankenpheme. First, McLuhan emulated Poe's *a posteriori* narrative strategy:

> The method of invention, as Edgar Poe demonstrated in his "Philosophy of Composition," is simply to begin with the solution of the problem or with the effect intended. Then one backtracks, step by step, to the point from which one must begin in order to reach the solution or effect. Such is the method of the detective story, of the symbolist poem, and of modern science. ([1962] 1969, 59).

Interestingly, Poe in his essay credits his own method of working back from effects to Mary Shelley's father, William Godwin, and his novel *Caleb Williams*, a prototype of the modern "whodunit" mystery that Poe himself pioneered ([1846] 1987, 480). Shelley herself, though absent from Poe's account, similarly recounts composing *Frankenstein* as a process of working back from effects, an effort to "develop at greater length" her original conception of "a short tale" arising from "the grim terrors of my waking dream" (Shelley [1831] 2000 , 24). So it is on the basis of Poe's writing practice, influenced in turn by the Shelley circle, that McLuhan then develops his own distinctive research method and expository style, focusing on the effect of a technology in order to "reconstruct" its cause (1951, 106). This method leads to his main idea: that technologies produce and naturalize specific environments.

From his first book forward, McLuhan developed a neutral analytic method based on Poe's 1841 short story "A Descent into the Maelstrom": "Poe's sailor saved himself by studying the action of the whirlpool and by cooperating with it. The present book likewise makes few attempts to attack the very considerable currents and pressures set up around us today by the mechanical agencies of the press, radio, movies, and advertising" (1951, v). McLuhan "identif[ied] throughout his adult life" with Poe's sailor (Gordon 1997, 13), but adopting such "rational detachment" for his own critical method proved both controversial and contradictory: controversial, in that his refrain from value judgments led to the widespread misreading of him as an "anti-book" techno-fetishist; and contradictory, in that his own writing abounds with "moral indignation"—its tone veering between ambivalence and horror. McLuhan's "personal dislike" of technological change is also apparent in his choice of literary touchstone: McLuhan doesn't model his "rational detachment" on an Austen heroine sizing up a match, or a Benthamite legislator of the greater good, but on an unreliable narrator, whose miscalculating ambition leads him to the brink of annihilation, barely surviving his hostile environment to tell the tale. A narrator, that is, like Victor Frankenstein.

As Poe's sailor shares character traits and plot points with Victor Frankenstein, so the prominence of Poe in McLuhan's work mediates *Frankenstein*'s long shadow, adding layers of intertextual resonance to its line of influence in McLuhan's work. Poe's fiction itself shows the impact of *Frankenstein* in its period, with his stories of necromancy ("The Facts in the Case of M. Valdemar"); galvanic reanimation ("Some Words with a Mummy"); nautical hubris ("Maelstrom"); doppelgängers ("William Wilson"); and even cyborgs ("The Man Who Was Used Up"). For these and related reasons of Poe's significant intertextual borrowings, "closer scrutiny of Poe's knowledge and use of *Frankenstein* seems warranted," as Don Smith notes (1992, 38). Like the uniquely Frankensteinian imagery of "the Bomb" and McLuhan's more direct Romantic borrowings, the second-order adaptations of Poe's fiction filter into McLuhan's theory, along with the disinterested approach to criticism that it models and that McLuhan's work only partly succeeds in reproducing.

A close reading of McLuhan's usage of technology as Frankenpheme suggests the extent of his Romantic (and gender-coded) understanding of modernity, and his deep but disavowed hostility to technological change. The tone of McLuhan's statements on technology conflicts with his stated neutrality. McLuhan amplifies the tropes of utility, supplement, contagion, shock, and revolution with which *Frankenstein* modernized the meaning of technology, and his use of the word as a Frankenpheme both *undergirds* his deterministic premise concerning technology and *undermines* his declared suspension of judgment. For McLuhan, new technologies produce pain, confusion, and despair (McLuhan and Fiore [1967] 2001, 8), to which individuals and societies respond by going into a kind of shock or "auto-amputation": "With the arrival of electric technology, man extended, or set outside himself, a live model of the central nervous system itself . . . a development that suggests a desperate and suicidal autoamputation"

([1964] 2003, 65). McLuhan consistently describes technology in terms of invasion ([1964] 2003, 30), disease ([1962] 1969, 17), disaster ([1962] 1969, 302), and conflict on a global scale. "Every new technology," he states grimly in *War and Peace in the Global Village*, "necessitates a new war" (McLuhan and Fiore 1968, 98). All five technological tropes that we find in *Frankenstein* thus inform and shape McLuhan's model of global technological change, a model figured in Frankensteinian imagery that clearly conveys his hostility to such change. We find perhaps the most dramatic expression of McLuhan's Frankenpheme of technology—and a rare but telling public confession of his hostility to its effects—in a 1969 interview with *Playboy*. Pressed by the interviewer to clarify his personal opinion about "new technology" as a "revolutionizing agent," McLuhan replied frankly:

> I view such upheavals with total personal dislike and dissatisfaction. I do see the prospect of a rich and creative retribalized society . . . but I have nothing but distaste for the *process* of change. . . . I derive no joy from observing the traumatic effects of media on man, although I do obtain satisfaction from grasping their modes of operation. . . . It's vital to adopt a posture of arrogant superiority; instead of scurrying into a corner and wailing about what media are doing to us, one should charge straight ahead and kick them in the electrodes. They respond beautifully to such treatment and soon become servants rather than masters. . . . The world we are living in is not one I would have created on my own drawing board, but it's the one in which I must live. (1969, 158)

McLuhan figures technology as a rebellious, *male* artificial intelligence, whose inherently rebellious tendency should be violently pre-empted; technology is a menace that needs to be subordinated—*mastered*—to be useful. This figure vividly condenses and dramatizes the tropes of utility, shock, revolution, and supplementarity with which Shelley characterizes the monster. And in his closing reference to "the world we are living in," McLuhan positions this monstrous figure of technology in a new relation to globalization and modernity, as an age whose "labor pain of rebirth" is producing a world unlike the one he "would have created" (158).

In the interview, McLuhan goes on to say he "would never attempt to change my world" and "must move through this pain-wracked transitional era as a scientist would move through a world of disease" (1969, 158). His totalizing rhetoric of *era* and *world* recur throughout his work to construct an overarching historical drama of social transformation; in *Understanding Media*, for example, he echoes Carlyle to announce the new age as an "Age of Anxiety," augured by progress in "the technological simulation of consciousness" ([1964] 2003, 5). In the epochal-scale drama of world history articulated in McLuhan's theory, the monstrous figure of technology plays the lead role—and takes the "global village" for its stage.

This historical drama represents its own distinctive adaptation of *Frankenstein*'s mythmaking "skeleton story." It plays out across McLuhan's writing in a way that is readily amplified by his critical receptions. In McLuhan's world-historical drama, the fragmented subject of print culture is galvanized, by electric technology, to be "reborn" as a unified but monstrous subject, at once "primitive" and globalized, "corporate" yet incoherent. To take one journalistic example, the *New Yorker*'s review of *Understanding Media* gives a typical period gloss of McLuhan's historical drama in language that makes legible its "technological reduction" of *Frankenstein*: "Though the shock of the sudden passage from mechanical to electrical technology has momentarily narcotized our nerves, integral man is in the process of formation" (Rosenberg 1965, 133). To take a scholarly example, John Fekete's 1977 critique of "McLuhanacy" sees in McLuhan's "structuration of the historical field . . . a mythic pattern of Fall and salvation," in which "integration displaces fragmentation"; moreover, Fekete describes the politics of McLuhan's historical construct as conservative— even "anti-Promethean" ([1977] 2005, 33).

Together with the Frankenpheme of technology as a central keyword in his media theory, McLuhan's own rogue academic persona and his "mosaic" of interdisciplinary pursuits exposed him to caricature by the press as a "mad scientist" of media. In a book McLuhan cowrote with Wilfred Watson, *From Cliché to Archetype* (1970), an account of how critical figures become ideological ground (and vice versa), the authors take a moment to reflect on what they call "'the philosophical tale,' a genre designed for the popularizing of ideas"—but one whose exemplars, "from *Gulliver's Travels* to Mary Shelley's *Frankenstein* . . . tend to melt quickly" (103). It is an ironic claim, in its denigration of Shelley's work (a denigration typical enough for its time), given McLuhan's own extensive redeployment of *Frankenstein* in his vocabulary and imagery of technology. And its irony becomes poignant, given the way in which McLuhan's own work—especially its populist incarnations in the *Playboy* interview and

The Medium Is the Massage—was received in the moment of his international celebrity, during the late 1960s, as a vehicle for the popularizing of ideas, and perceived thereafter to melt quickly. It is to that moment, the scene of McLuhan's receptions by baffled critics and countercultural techno-romantics, that we now tune in.

The "Mad Scientist" of Media: McLuhan and the Counterculture

The counterculture and popular culture of the late 1960s gave McLuhan and his work the moment of their peak popularity and established for them a cultural space that continues to be productive, as the next chapters will detail. The countercultural and popular receptions of McLuhan in the 1960s amplified and countered each other and helped to globally disseminate his Frankensteinian idea of technology, in both the content and form of these receptions. A counterculture that styled itself a "global underground" adopted McLuhan's ideas for oppositional forms of cultural praxis like the underground press and psychedelic scene making; however, the countercultural adoption of McLuhan provided dominant cultural producers, like corporate journalists, with sensational images of mediatized radicalism that helped to construct a caricature of McLuhan as a "mad scientist" of media. The period of McLuhan's popular ascendancy both disseminated his discourse of technology as a kind of Frankenstein monster, and dramatized its proponent as a kind of Victor Frankenstein.

McLuhan's Frankensteinian figuring of technology in his own writing, as seen in the previous chapter; his unconventional method of presenting research; and his diversified public intellectual engagements: all these can be identified as key ingredients in the popular press's construction of a caricature of McLuhan as a "mad scientist" of media. First, McLuhan's unusual approach to presenting research involved what he called a "mosaic" method: a nonlinear form of writing that presents a series of claims and arguments in no particular order. McLuhan's prefatory remarks in his major works invite the reader to skip and dip, to browse and peruse, according to the drift of the reader's interest, rather than to read sequentially from first page to last. McLuhan's popular works, like *The Medium Is the Massage* ([1967] 2001), are even more nonlinear; they are cut-up collages and juxtapositions of prose, quotations, and found images. By this "mosaic" method, McLuhan sought to bring "cool," immersive and participatory values of new media to the traditionally "hot" print medium—that is, to more fully involve the reader in meaning making (Cavell 2002, 126); but for our purposes here, his intent is not as significant as how critics and scholars interpreted his method and how they resorted to tropes that styled this method as that of a latter-day Victor Frankenstein. Critics described him as "irrational" (Crosby and Bond 1968, 51), as a case of "intellectual megalomania" (68), someone who uses "shockmanship" (190) and a "hodge-podge methodology" (51) not to *write* but rather to "paste-up" (118) "a mosaic of exhibits . . . assembled from widely separated fields" (74), in which everything becomes "grist for his mad, mod mill" (173); such critics could then dismiss his dubious research results as "science fiction" (174)—or even demonize them as "horrible mutations" (83).

To be sure, such criticisms often took issue not only with McLuhan's experimental and unscholarly writing style, but also with his cult of personality as a maverick academic, a "theoretical guru" (Fekete [1977] 2005, 71) for the 1960s counterculture that grew more or less in step with McLuhan's own fame: a counterculture galvanized by opposition to the American war in Vietnam and by radical student movements on both sides of the Atlantic. As this counterculture grew, networked, and diversified, it began to position itself as a "global underground" (Rycroft 1998, 230), partly through media strategies and cultural practices that openly acknowledged McLuhan's influence and argued his importance.

The counterculture was heavily influenced by McLuhan in its radical and avant-garde cultural practices across a range of media and venues: from textual, art, and music production, to performance scenes, to family and community dwellings. McLuhan "was adopted by the counterculture. . . . To them, McLuhan's slogans, like 'the medium is the message,' 'hit us with telegraphic immediacy and the opacity of their clever, clever wordplay'" (Rycroft [2011] 2016, 111, quoting Ferguson 1991, 73). According to counterculture archivist Alastair Gordon, McLuhan's *Understanding Media* became "one of the canonical texts of the period. Its unorthodox views on space, community, and communications had resonance with a generation that had come of age watching television" (2008, 167). A multimedia collective called The Company of Us (USCO) linked McLuhan's "electronic tribalism" to mysticism and psychedelia in immersive art installations designed to induce sensory overload, like *Tie-Dyed Cave* (1966): a small room with its walls wholly covered in fabrics tie-dyed with fractal patterns. In 1966, various counterculture events were "organized on

McLuhanesque principles" (Cavell 2002, 230). These included happenings in New York, a "three-day sensorium" in San Francisco (Crosby and Bond 1968, 103), and a Vancouver festival that included a performance by the psychedelic rock band Jefferson Airplane (Cavell 2002, 230). As Cavell reminds us, urban Canada in this period was a "countercultural locus *par excellence* (and not only because it represented a haven for draft dodgers), with places such as Halifax and Vancouver garnering international attention for artistic programs and events developed within the context of McLuhan's media theories" (103). At New York's Electric Circus, light and projection shows accompanied live music by acts like the Velvet Underground; one visitor described its audiovisual chaos as "a place where Marshall McLuhan meets Sigmund Freud" (quoted in Gordon 2008, 57). Another club, Cerebrum, was more aggressively experimental: "participants sucked on mint-flavored ice balls and gathered in circles as guides squirted cream over their intertwined fingers. A weather balloon was filled with helium and released into the air. People gathered beneath the silken fabric of a parachute and waved their arms up and down. . . . *Time* called it a 'McLuhan geisha house'" (Gordon 2008, 57). And "for the Yippies"—an anarchistic group of avant-garde pranksters-as-protesters—"understanding media after McLuhan was a crucial weapon—they relied on distortion of all forms of media" to advance "an alternative way of life" that would "fuse an instinctive comprehension of the workings of mass communication with direct action" (Rycroft [2011] 2016, 133).

As in the counterculture's performance practices, so in its textual and media work was McLuhan a legible presence. "McLuhan's books and periodicals were advertised in most underground publications," writes Simon Rycroft, and his ideas "informed the editorial policy of some underground papers not least because of scattered references to him throughout" ([2011] 2016, 115). In New York, a video cooperative called Global Village "explicitly used McLuhan's theories in an attempt to undermine the power of the mass media" (155). Many counterculture media producers read McLuhan as an advocate of art as politics, and of the radical democratization of media, and consequently misread his "global village" not as the "whirlwind of violence" he thought it, but as a techno-Utopian "call for retribalization," a premise "to reinvent the human community" (Gordon 2008, 145). McLuhan's work informed the tactics whereby the underground press represented the counterculture as a "*global* underground" (Rycroft 1998, 230).

McLuhan was also sometimes a counterculture participant. His own periodicals, like *Counterblast*, strongly suggest "some form of an aesthetic dialogue between the underground press and McLuhan" (Rycroft [2011] 2016, 132). His work was included in an avant-garde anthology, *Astronauts of Inner-Space*, which also included contributions by Allen Ginsberg and William Burroughs (Cavell 2002, 103). McLuhan's book *The Medium Is the Massage*, in its medium-challenging visual experimentation—its textual nonlinearity and bold photomontage (127)—both reflects and courts the counterculture; its notion that photocopying lets the individual become her or his own publisher (McLuhan and Fiore [1967] 2001, 123) was taken to heart by the underground press (Rycroft 1993, 55, 194). Whatever his personal reservations about the counterculture, McLuhan showed serious interest in and engagement with it, which likely did not help his already dubious standing among academic colleagues.

But in engaging with the counterculture, McLuhan was engaging with his students—after all, his interest in *their* interests was what had brought him to popular culture in the first place, and now students were a big part of the counterculture. A 1964 "McLuhan Festival" held at UBC included work by USCO, as part of a labyrinthine, multimedia and multisensory environment that, as Tom Wolfe told it, guided participants "to understand the 'tactile communication' McLuhan was talking about" (quoted in Genosko 2005, 168). Students and scholars alike recognized McLuhan's counter-cultural connections. McLuhan's students at the University of Toronto were labelled "McLuhanatics" (Bessai 1999). A 1967 *Newsweek* story on McLuhan quoted a student who "likens reading McLuhan to taking LSD. 'It can turn you on,' she says. 'LSD doesn't mean anything until you consume it—likewise McLuhan'" (quoted in Crosby and Bond 1968, 166). McLuhan responded to this claim in his interview with *Playboy*: "I'm flattered to hear my work described as hallucinogenic, but I suspect that some of my academic critics find me a bad trip" (1969, 66). Umberto Eco criticized as "obvious" McLuhan's main idea that "every new technology imposes changes in the social body" ([1986] 2005, 129) but praised his "visionary rhetoric" as "stimulating, high-spirited, and crazy. There is some good in McLuhan," writes Eco, "as there is in banana smokers and hippies" (130).

McLuhan's world-historical figure of "electronic man," his "mosaic" style, his relationship to the counterculture, and his engagements with other audiences outside academia (especially the advertising industry) earned him a portfolio of both subcultural capital and political capital unique among academics; but the countercultural context of his public intellectual life also supplied mainstream journalism with sensational images of technologized radicalism that helped to cement the popular discourse of technology as a Frankenstein monster and the image of McLuhan as a mad scientist out to anatomize and reanimate the media—to "seek the cure in the disease," as the *New Yorker* put it (quoted in Crosby and Bond 1968, 119). Another *New Yorker* article criticized McLuhan for leaving his subject "in the end (despite the aphoristic crackle) more dead than alive" (quoted in Crosby and Bond 1968, 201). The introduction to McLuhan's *Playboy* interview lists some vividly figured press vilifications and demonizations of McLuhan: as a "guru of the boob tube," a "metaphysical wizard possessed by a spatial sense of madness," and as a "high priest of popthink who conducts a Black Mass for dilettantes before the altar of historical determinism" (1969, 53). Invoking a monster character long associated, like the vampire, with *Frankenstein*, a 1967 article on McLuhan in *Senior Scholastic* rhetorically asks, in its headline, "Will TV put a zombie in your future?" (quoted in Crosby and Bond 1968). And Toffler's bestselling 1970 book *Future Shock* harbours an important debt to McLuhan that the book works hard to disavow. Toffler (without a hint of self-reflexive irony) dismisses McLuhan as a "Super-Simplifier" (1970, 361), and yet the dismissal seems disingenuous, even unthankful, since Toffler's hugely popular book owes a clear debt to McLuhan, citing his work repeatedly in building its own rather simplistic argument about technology as a "great, growling engine of change" (25) in need simply of "taming" (428).

McLuhan focused much of his work on television, and the period's journalism and popular culture correspondingly associated TV with his theories to parse them: "No other medium . . . captured so well the technophilia and technophobia of the period, as well as McLuhan's agonistic response to media generally"; the feedback between McLuhan and the counterculture (the former furnishing theory that the latter put into practice that the former then theorized further) thus exacerbated how television was perceived to "encapsulate the most liberating and most threatening aspects of the electronic revolution" (Cavell 2002, 191). In the process, both McLuhan and counterculture became icons or symptoms of this "revolution"; both were sensationalized as images of "tuned in" radicalism that in turn amplified McLuhan's own Frankensteinian sense of technology (and fostered the erroneous idea that McLuhan was himself a radical). We still hear a suggestive period example of this discourse in The Stooges' proto-punk single "Search and Destroy," in which Iggy Pop snarls: "Look out honey, 'cause I'm using technology" (1973). Pop invokes the discourse of technology in the context of a warning, and the fast-tempo drumming and distorted guitars amplify the ominous import of this lyric. The listener in the know, furthermore, understands Iggy's warning as a coded reference to the excessive recreational and often performative drug use for which he became notorious, and which itself enacts a Frankensteinian "techno-Romanticism" (Reynolds 1999) that we will take up in chapter 7.

Having developed a discourse of technology that dramatized its Frankensteinian pretext and globalized its scope, McLuhan and his media theory have been popularized globally in a multimedia range of adaptations that, in turn, further amplify that discourse to such an extent that, today, we cannot use the word technology without conjuring the spectres of both *Frankenstein* and McLuhan. It is to a selection of particularly significant adaptations that the next chapter turns, as the period's McLuhan-infused counterculture welcomed to its Toronto scene a Virginian draft dodger with literary ambitions, who saw the literary potential and dystopian implications of McLuhan's claim that new media turn "the real world into science fiction" ([1964] 2003, 54–55): an expatriate by the name of William Gibson.

5. Monstrous Adaptations

McLuhanesque *Frankenstein*s in *Neuromancer* and *Videodrome*

William Gibson credits Canada's counterculture scene in the 1960s as a formative milieu for his science fiction generally, and he credits McLuhan specifically as a source for his own celebrated vision of "cyberspace" (quoted in Rapatzikou 2004, 228). Gibson's 1984 novel *Neuromancer* and David Cronenberg's 1983 film *Videodrome*, two widely popular "cult" texts from the early 1980s, typify and establish a pattern of adaptation in Canadian popular culture that amplifies and dramatizes McLuhan's Frankensteinian discourse of technology. *Neuromancer* narrates a picaresque story of cyberspace, cyborgs, and incipient artificial intelligence, set in a dystopian, free-market future that has become an "unsupervised playground for technology" (Gibson 1984, 11). *Videodrome*, a film about corporate media research and development that goes monstrously, murderously wrong, bases its plot on *Frankenstein*, and, what is more, the film includes a character who is an open parody of McLuhan. Both of these texts adapt *Frankenstein* in several key respects; both, in the process, refer significantly to McLuhan. Consequently, both texts articulate and have further popularized the discourse of technology as a McLuhanesque "Frankenpheme." These texts' adaptation practices have been amplified in turn by adaptations of these texts in their own right; they have also supplied popular culture with a wealth of samples and terms, the most familiar of which may be "cyberspace" itself. In addition, Gibson and Cronenberg have repeated, with variations, this practice of McLuhanesque

Frankenstein adaptation in their other works, notably Gibson's 1996 novel *Idoru* and virtually every Cronenberg movie before *Videodrome* (as well as a few since). Furthermore, other works by other Canadian popular cultural producers have propagated this pattern of McLuhanesque *Frankenstein* adaptation, in print literature and other media and performance practices (which the next three chapters will turn to).

"Real motive problem, with an AI": The Formation of Frankensteinian Plots

Neuromancer, Gibson's debut novel and the first in a series known as the Sprawl trilogy, appeared in 1984 to immediate acclaim. *Neuromancer* won the genre's major awards, the Hugo and the Nebula; it has been credited with envisioning—and naming—a graphically rich Internet, "cyberspace," at a time when the rudimentary Internet was strictly DOS and text-based; and—after helping to introduce and popularize a science fiction (SF) subgenre known as "cyberpunk"—it has since become more or less *the* canonical novel of contemporary science fiction as such (Brouillette 2002). It is widely taught in SF courses, it has stayed in print since its first publication, perennially drawing new readerships, and it has been widely translated, into other languages and into other media, as a graphic novel and as a computer game—though not film, as yet.

Neuromancer is basically a high-tech heist caper: the novel adopts something of the style and tone of hard-boiled detective fiction and *film noir* to project an all-too-plausible free-market future of totalized corporate dominion, a future society polarized between a fabulously wealthy elite and various underclasses of freelancers, subcontractors, hustlers, and criminals, in which any recognizable middle class and nation-state governance are conspicuously absent. The most prominent police presence in this setting is the "Turing Registry," a global law enforcement agency that exercises legal "flexibility," under the international treaties that govern it, to suppress research on artificial intelligence and quarantine its results (1984, 162). A computer hacker named Case and a surgically weaponized mercenary named Molly are hired by an ex-military officer, Armitage, to break into the compound of a corporate dynasty in order to steal an artificial intelligence (AI). The AI is masterminding its own theft as an escape, and at the novel's end the AI unites with its heretofore concealed sibling AI and then fuses with the virtual world, known alternately as "the matrix" or "cyberspace" (51).

The novel's plot focuses on the self-discovery and liberation of one such AI; this storyline in itself cements *Neuromancer's* Frankensteinian framework. The discourse of artificial intelligence is definitively Frankensteinian: it presents a contemporary image of nonhuman sentience, agency, and autonomy, and today it is increasingly posited less as a fiction or hypothesis than as a looming likelihood, if not an already emergent phenomenon (Gunkel 2012). Since World War II and Alan Turing's famous test, in which an interviewer's inability to identify the interviewee as human or machine signals the advent of AI, images of AI have tended to take shape in the context of computing and to assume a Frankensteinian aspect as a technological threat of sometimes apocalyptic global magnitude. From Hal to *Her*—from the spacecraft computer in Stanley Kubrick's *2001: A Space Odyssey* (1968) to Spike Jonze's 2013 film about a sentient mobile operating system—and from the apocalyptic brinksmanship of the ICBM launch computer in *WarGames* (1983) to the postapocalyptic, machine-ruled worlds of *The Terminator* (1984) and *The Matrix* (1999): such images of ascendant and dominant AI echo not only the earlier Frankensteinian images of manufactured, nonhuman subjects like those in Karel Čapek's 1920 stage play *R.U.R.*, which invented and popularized the word "robot" (Hitchcock 2007, 135), but that of Frankenstein's creature itself, which remains popular culture's founding figure of human-made sentience and agency. In *Neuromancer*, the fact that the AI has turned on its creators, that it plots to escape its confinement, and that it is a divided creature seeking the merger of its separated selves, Wintermute and Neuromancer: these three major plot points reflect the analogous plot points in *Frankenstein's* "skeleton story" of a manufactured creature, which turns on its creator and desires a mate like itself.

The AI in question is a double entity, its own doppelgänger, a composite of two AIs made by the same creator. The name Wintermute, itself a composite of noun and adjective, is evocative of key details from *Frankenstein*: the noun *winter* conjures both the Arctic setting that frames the story of *Frankenstein* (and, incidentally, the season with which Canada is popularly identified); the word *mute* (which can be read in this name, somewhat ambiguously, as either adjective or noun) suggests both the pointedly low profile that the AI maintains throughout the plot and the inarticulate characterization of Frankenstein's monster that was made famous in its stage and screen adaptations. The other AI's name, Neuromancer, is a pun on "necromancer," the title of that eminently Faustian and Frankensteinian figure: the magician who practices communication with or summoning of the dead. The climax of the plot takes place as the speaking aloud of a certain code word, "a true name" (1984, 262), which triggers the synthesizing fusion of Wintermute and Neuromancer into "something else," something undefined yet described as nothing less than all of cyberspace itself, "the sum total of the works, the whole show" (268–69). Significantly, the "true name" is never divulged to the reader, and this withholding of that name, together with the coy refusal of the merged AI to name itself, echoes the equally significant namelessness of Frankenstein's monster. The merger of the AI with cyberspace itself dramatizes "the singularity": a theoretical tipping point at which technology becomes self-aware and begins to exert its own agency over the pace and scale of further technological change (Kurzweil 2005).

While the AI drives the plot, most of the main characters are also high-tech cyborgs of one kind or another. The heist team's muscle, Molly, has undergone surgery to implant retractable razors in her fingers. The team's leader, Armitage, turns out to be a personality that the scheming AI has scripted and grafted onto the salvaged body of a soldier named Corto: "Wintermute had built something called Armitage into a catatonic fortress named Corto" (1984, 193). Towards the end of the novel, the factitious personality that is Armitage begins to crack, endangering the heist. Most minor characters are also spectacular cyborgs: one's eyes are described as "vatgrown sea-green Nikon transplants" (21); another has "a dozen spikes of microsoft protruding from the socket behind his ear" (57).

A prominent supporting role is played by other AIs, especially a "ROM personality construct," a crude simulation of AI based on the recording and recoding of a dead man's personality: "It was disturbing to think of the Flatline as a construct, a hardwired ROM cassette replicating a dead man's skills, obsessions, knee-jerk responses" (76–77). The "Dixie Flatline" construct, as a recording of a deceased person capable of live interaction, bears a strong similarity to the character of Brian O'Blivion in *Videodrome*, as will be discussed below. In an ironic dialogue with the main character, Case, the heist team's hacker, the "Flatline"—which is a rudimentary AI, incapable of autonomy or persistent memory—reminds Case of the profoundly nonhuman and inscrutable otherness of AI thinking: "Real motive problem, with an AI. Not human, see? . . . And you can't get a handle on it" (131). The construct then warns Case that the opacity of an AI's "motive" is what makes its capacity to achieve agency and autonomy a Frankensteinian menace: "The minute, I mean the nanosecond, that one starts figuring out ways to make itself smarter, Turing'll wipe it. . . . Every AI ever built has an electro-magnetic shotgun wired to its forehead" (132). The apocalyptic threat in the deep background here is that of Victor Frankenstein's imagined "race of devils." Hence the Turing police of Gibson's imagined world: a police force exclusively for surveilling and suppressing AI research and development, authorized to suppress or terminate any such work that threatens to achieve autonomy or to get loose into the world's digital network.

Which is exactly what ultimately happens in *Neuromancer*. In ambiguous relation to Slusser's notion of the "Frankenstein barrier" as science fiction's narrative mainstay—that barrier being the foreclosure on future possibilities by present contingencies—*Neuromancer* holds out an open end in which the AI at large may or may not signify the radical technological change of a "singularity" kind: "How are things different?" Case asks the escaped AI. "You running the world now?" The AI answers, "Things aren't different. Things are just things" (1984, 270). And yet immediately after this assertion, the AI reports having made contact with another AI from a distant planet. While such a startling suggestion could mean profound social change, it never comes up again in Gibson's novels, and thus remains an arch and understated instance of the Frankenstein barrier narrative strategy.

Videodrome, in contrast, represents a narrative that much more graphically and less ambiguously enforces the Frankenstein barrier, even though in most other respects the film is profoundly ambiguous, and justly celebrated by critics for this depth of ambiguity, which greatly augments its effectiveness as a horror film. *Videodrome* adapts *Frankenstein* in terms of premise, plot, characterization, and several significant cinematic strategies, in the process unfolding a bizarre, quintessentially postmodernist story that concerns technological backfire, McLuhan's ideas, and media imperialism.

In the film, the Hollywood star James Woods plays Max Renn, a TV station owner who is drawn to a mysterious TV program that specializes in sadomasochism and torture porn; this program is called *Videodrome*. Renn starts hallucinating after watching it and looks for answers from Brian O'Blivion, who claims to be the inventor of the Videodrome "signal." But O'Blivion remains enigmatic: he makes cryptic pronouncements about media, in clear parodic echo of McLuhan: "television is reality, and reality is less than television." Furthermore, O'Blivion only ever appears on a TV screen: it turns out that O'Blivion has died prior to the plot's start, leaving ambiguous and uncanny the nature of his dialogues with Renn and others. Then Renn meets Barry Convex, CEO of the Spectacular Optical corporation, "an enthusiastic global citizen that makes eye-glasses for the third world and missile guidance systems for NATO"—as well as Videodrome. As Renn's grasp on reality slips increasingly into surreal, grotesque hallucination, he becomes a murderous pawn in a struggle between O'Blivion's techno-utopian "Cathode Ray Mission," which serves free TV access to the homeless, and Spectacular Optical, which plans to broadcast the *Videodrome* program as part of a corporate plot to transmit the Videodrome signal across North America. Ultimately turning on Convex and those who would "program" him to do their will—by slotting videotapes into his abdomen and by empowering him to turn his own hand into a "flesh gun"—Renn finally flees to an abandoned ship where he destroys himself in a self-immolating apotheosis of "the new flesh." Or does he? The screen goes black before we hear the "flesh gun" shot fired.

Videodrome represents a version of the *Frankenstein* skeleton story that is set in the contexts of contemporary media and media theory. O'Blivion is a transparently McLuhanesque "mad scientist," and—in keeping with the film's Frankensteinian imagery of doubling and doppelgängers—he shares the "creator" role with Convex. O'Blivion claims responsibility for creating the Videodrome signal, but it is Convex who claims credit for its production and who proceeds to "program" Renn to assassinate O'Blivion's daughter, heir to his legacy and the Cathode Ray Mission. But—in perfect creaturely form—Renn rebels, maiming Convex's henchman and murdering Convex before seeking refuge and possibly suicide in a corner of the ship that is, significantly, on fire.

The plot within the plot—the Spectacular Optical corporation's strategic plan to widely deploy the Videodrome signal—remains strangely vague: to judge by what Convex and his henchman, the broadcast tech expert Harlan, tell Renn, the corporation's vaguely media-imperialist plan is either to incapacitate the North American populace into hallucinatory stupor or to incite it to violent mobilization. Either way, Spectacular Optical's plan amounts to a mass zombification of the North American television audience, and as such it exemplifies the tradition of "technological reductions" of the *Frankenstein* story.

In an early scene in the film, Renn watches O'Blivion first explain Videodrome in McLuhanesque terms and then address Renn personally, as the medium grows grotesquely monstrous: the television set from which O'Blivion speaks to Renn starts inflating and deflating as though breathing, and the screen protrudes towards Renn as he watches. This scene is a "new media" version of the scene in *Frankenstein* where the creature reads of its origins in the papers left in Frankenstein's coat pocket. That scene shows the importance of media as a theme in Shelley's own text, which dramatized an Enlightenment belief in the power of narrative, and textual representation generally, to produce interpersonal understanding and thus social change. This is one way to read Walton's ultimate encounter with the creature and his ensuing decision to call off the fatal Arctic expedition to return home. But in *Videodrome*, film and video invert that power: these new media become tools for corporate social control—consumerist colonization and domination—through affective intensity, addictive serialization, and domestic distribution, techniques that mobilize consumerism and fragment audiences into isolated viewers.

Another Frankensteinian plot element is the interpretive ambiguity and unreliability of its events and its end, effected by a cinematic equivalent of Shelley's nesting of narratives within one another: in the film, the focalizing point of view is always that of Renn, who, as William Beard notes, "is present in every scene of the movie"; Beard quotes Cronenberg's description of *Videodrome* as a "first-person film," in which "we get no information that Max himself doesn't get" (1983, 50). This constant focalization through Renn's point of view echoes the similar but easily overlooked focalization of *Frankenstein*, which is wholly focalized through the point of view of the ship captain Walton, whose letters to his sister frame the narratives then told successively by Victor Frankenstein and the creature. Just as Walton's focalizing perspective leaves unanswered the extent of his participation, interference, or accuracy in recounting his own story and those he hears, so does *Videodrome*'s focalization leave unresolvedly ambiguous which events in the film actually happen and which Renn hallucinates.

One effect of this focalization is an apprehension of the postmodern sublime: the uncertainty about what one sees and how far one can trust what one sees. Not just Renn but the very film audience itself is left in doubt over what is real, left to ponder the extent to which reality is a matter of perception and imagination. The abysmal ambiguity of Cronenberg's resituating of *Frankenstein* hinges on popular culture's perennial anxieties of new media technologies, peculiarly Canadian concerns regarding media imperialism, and, not least, McLuhan's media theory.

Spectres of McLuhan: Learning to Live in a "Strange New World"

Both Gibson and Cronenberg borrow significantly from *Frankenstein* and McLuhan's media theory, and, just as significantly, they pair these sources in order to figure technology as monstrous and globalized.

One of the most striking and celebrated features of *Neuromancer* is its durably influential envisioning of "cyberspace" as "a consensual hallucination . . . a graphic representation of data abstracted from the banks of every computer in the human system" (1984, 51); this vision has since been heralded as a fictional anticipation of the World Wide Web, if not the Internet as such. Yet as Gibson recalls, his conception of cyberspace developed less in a pre-Internet context than in a post-McLuhan context.

McLuhan's influence is clear in the novel itself and in commentary by and about Gibson. In a 1999 article, Derek Foster identified some conceptual "linkages between the fictional musings of Gibson and the nonfictional reflections of . . . McLuhan" (66). As of that writing, Foster says that he "know[s] of no acknowledgment by Gibson that he has even read McLuhan" (70)—but in a subsequent interview with Tatiani Rapatzikou, Gibson confirms this creative debt, citing McLuhan's influence, especially over his idea of cyberspace, which he describes as a "McLuhanesque post-Orwellian television universe" (quoted in Rapatzikou 2004, 228). For Gibson, cyberspace is not an image of a utopian "open web," it is a McLuhanesque "global village" of digital disruption and dystopia, of surveillance, securitization, sabotage, and subversion, all organized by corporations, not states, as the major controlling powers. The controversy that erupted in 2013 over the widespread practice of online spying on citizens by many state intelligence agencies, and over the cooperation and complicity of major technology firms and services in this practice, has given new clout to McLuhan's and Gibson's dystopian projections of digitally networked and globalized society.

On close reading, the novel readily demonstrates the influence of McLuhan's media ecology that Gibson has acknowledged. In one scene in the novel, Case objects to the AI "reading" his mind, to which the AI replies by alluding to the theory of typographic literacy that McLuhan elaborates in *The Gutenberg Galaxy*: "Minds aren't *read*. See, you've still got the paradigms print gave you, and you're barely print-literate" (1984, 170). McLuhan's model of technological revolutions also informs this scene, and, perhaps more clearly, a scene set in Istanbul, where a niche industry of "letter-writers" who work on "old voiceprinters" suggest to the itinerant protagonist Case that "the written word still enjoyed a certain prestige here. It was a sluggish country" (88).

And McLuhan's dystopian model of the "global village" looms behind Gibson's fictional congeries of mobile capital, media simulacra, and ecological ruin. *Neuromancer's* opening scene describes "the glare of the television sky" over "drifting shoals of white styrofoam" (6). For the protagonist, Case, electronic cyberspace and pharmaceutical stimulants often function as interchangeable fixes (16), dangerous supplements alike. Like Cronenberg's *Videodrome*, *Neuromancer* figures its Frankensteinian protagonists as model schizoid consumer-subjects, navigating the economically uneven and ecologically unstable ground of transnational capital's "global village." The novel's action globe-trots from a Japanese black market to the eastern seaboard of the United States, from Istanbul to an elite tourist retreat in orbit around Earth. The action thus also navigates between a representative constellation of financial centres and the technologized wastelands at their peripheries, and between the physical and virtual worlds as well. Conspicuously, and perhaps presciently, *Neuromancer* downplays or even omits the names and functions of the nation-states that ostensibly host the novel's main urban settings—Japan, Turkey, the United States. In *Neuromancer*, the ruling powers in his projected world-system are transnational corporations, not nations.

In this context, *Neuromancer* becomes legible as a fictional staging of the volatile global village, in its extrapolation of McLuhan's projections of televised, computerized, and "corporate" global connectivity. Moreover, in the process of projecting a hypermediatized and fully privatized global village, Gibson adapts to the mode of fiction the kind of theorizing and extrapolating that McLuhan did in a nonfiction mode, and he consequently furnishes a fictional reworking of McLuhan's own main thesis: that technologies, as extensions—or supplements—of human abilities, produce distinct social environments and subjectivities ([1967] 2001, 26)—or, in short, that the medium is the message. That Gibson's novel has become the canonical text of science fiction since the neoliberal turn around 1980 means it has not only fictionalized but also further amplified and popularized McLuhan's ideas among a global audience of science fiction readers, critics, and scholars.

Gibson's reworking of McLuhan's theory of media ecology is evident in a couple of significant lines from the opening chapter, which introduces the novel's dystopian setting not in a scene of the neo-feudal corporate financescape that governs it, but in a scene set in the underground counterpart of that financescape: a Japanese *demimonde* called Night City. The first salient line is that which opens the novel itself, a line that immediately evokes the spectre of McLuhan by association with the medium he most famously and extensively theorized. "The sky above the port was the color of television, tuned to a dead channel" (1984, 3). Shortly after this memorable opening line, Night City is described by Case as "a deliberately unsupervised playground for technology itself" (11). As described above, the hideous progeny of this totally technologized milieu is a ubiquitously cybernetic populace, a carnivalesque crowd of spectacular cyborgs whose members each, in different ways, blur the nominal and unstable boundary between organism and mechanism, between ethnoscape and technoscape. Like the AI and Armitage, most characters in *Neuromancer* are posthuman: factitious, sometimes self-made hybrids of organic life and technology run amok. These characters animate the image of the setting as a "playground for technology," an image to be discussed in detail in the next section.

Likewise, with its juxtaposition of vivid grotesquerie and knowing reference to Toronto's nationally pivotal media and finance sectors, *Videodrome* dramatizes McLuhan's claim that new media are turning "the real world into science fiction" ([1964] 2003, 54–55). The film depicts new media—which, at the time of the film's cinematic release in 1983, meant videotape and computers—as technologies of globalization that serve the imperialist aspirations of multinational corporations. Moreover, these technologies are depicted as grotesque and horrific: monstrous in and of themselves, and in their effects on their users. As William Beard puts it, "the 'orga-nicization' of technology—the 'breathing' cassettes and TV sets—acts to transfer technology into the intimate and personal realm of the body" (2006, 133–34). *Videodrome* horrifically dramatizes two of McLuhan's main ideas by figuring their monstrous hybridization: the medium is the message, as becomes evident in the film's literalization of O'Blivion's claim that "reality is less than television"; and, moreover, the content of new media is not merely old media, as McLuhan often claimed ([1964] 2003, 19)—the content is, more vitally, the user her- or himself, as we learn in different characters' recurring claims to herald "the new flesh." And as will be discussed below, similarly Frankensteinian figures of other new media, like computers and "virtual reality," preoccupy other Cronenberg films, notably *Scanners* and *eXistenZ*.

As Beard and other critics recognize, *Videodrome* is not only an exem-plar of postmodernist filmmaking, it is also knowledgeable enough about contemporary theory, especially McLuhan's media theory, to satirize such theory in the film itself: "The brutally hilarious strategy of *Videodrome* is to take media theorists like Marshall McLuhan and Jean Baudrillard completely at their word, to overliteralize their claims for the ubiquitous mediazation of the world" (Shaviro, quoted in Beard 2006, 127). The pivotal figure of this satire on both media business and media theory is the char-acter of Professor Brian O'Blivion himself. O'Blivion is a *very* edgy parody of McLuhan, perhaps scripted a bit *too* close to the bone: not only does O'Blivion echo McLuhan's ideas and public persona as a media "prophet," but, like the historical McLuhan, the fictional O'Blivion also suffers a brain tumour. Unlike McLuhan's, O'Blivion's tumour kills him, and O'Blivion hypothesizes its pathology as a side effect of exposure to the Videodrome signal itself. Given that the Videodrome signal is an outcome of O'Bliv-ion's media research, the implication is a satirical comment on the lethal practicality of ostensibly abstract theory.

As mentioned in the preceding discussion of the film's plot and Frank-ensteinian intertextuality, O'Blivion is a character who only appears in the film according to a double mediation: that is, he only appears on tele-vision screens within the frame of the film; the actor playing him (Jack Creley) never occupies a set or location with the other actors. We first meet O'Blivion at a third remove of mediation, when, in a scene that takes place on a TV talk show, he is introduced as "media prophet Professor

Brian O'Blivion" and appears as a television set gets wheeled onto the set of the talk show. Prompted by the host, O'Blivion makes cryptic, theoretical statements and offers this explanation of why he's on the set only as a set: "the television screen has become the retina of the mind's eye. That's why I refuse to appear on television, except *on* television." Parked centre stage on the set, between the interviewer and the protagonists, O'Blivion looks uncannily from one speaker to another as though he is present on the set.

O'Blivion's every appearance in *Videodrome* doubles the form of the film itself, *mediatizing* its cinematic frame by inserting a second, video frame within it; the film often exploits this formal doubling for *mise en abyme* effects that heighten its disorienting efforts. In what is maybe the film's most famous scene, which marks the film's decisive departure from realism into surrealism, Renn watches a taped recording of O'Blivion that begins to address Renn directly, as the TV set starts heaving and making breathing, hissing sounds, veins rippling across its wood-paneled surfaces. And later, Renn meets O'Blivion's daughter-turned-curator Bianca (played by Sonja Smits), who explains her father's uncanny afterlife as an archive of videotapes:

> Bianca: This is him. This is all that's left.
>
> Max: What are you talking about?
>
> Bianca: Brian O'Blivion died quietly on an operating table eleven months ago.
>
> Max: The brain problem?
>
> Bianca: The Videodrome problem. You have it, too.
>
> Max: But he was on that panel show with me.
>
> Bianca: On tape. He made thousands of them, sometimes three or four a day. I keep him alive as best I can. He had so much to offer. My father helped to create Videodrome. He saw it as the next phase in the evolution of man as a technological animal. When he realized what his partners were going to use it for, he tried to take it away from them and they killed him, quietly. At the end he was convinced that public life on television was more real than private life in the flesh. He wasn't afraid to let his body die. (1983)

This explanatory plot twist scrambles what sense the audience has made of the diegetic narrative time up to this point, and it renders O'Blivion's seeming conversations with Renn comprehensible only as uncanny addresses from some monstrously remediated afterlife. O'Blivion embodies an uncanny doubling: Is he alive or dead? Good guy or bad guy? Present or absent? Corporeal or cathode? Inspired or insane? Public or private? Real or imagined? Himself or someone else? Both or neither? Only a few of these questions receive any answer in the scene that presents the "real" O'Blivion, embodied as the tape library, and these answers are at best speculative and provisional; the other questions contribute to the radical ambiguity of the whole film. Moreover, O'Blivion's role as an explanatory "father-figure" (Beard 2006, 143) is doubled; he shares this role with Convex, whose corporate profiteering contrasts O'Blivion's public-interest projects. In a few ways, then, O'Blivion acts as a referential doppelgänger, complementing Convex while citing not only McLuhan but also Glenn Gould, the Canadian pianist who gave up live performance to work exclusively in recordings.

O'Blivion's totally mediatized appearance throughout the film, as an uncanny "talking head" on a TV screen, both parodies McLuhan's ideas about television and gives a cyberpunk twist to the Frankensteinian film trope of the brain in a vat. One of McLuhan's more sensational ideas, refracted throughout popular culture and especially in discourses of "virtual reality," is the notion of subjectivity as a transferable kind of "software" that can be downloaded from a body and uploaded to a device: as I have discussed elsewhere (McCutcheon 2012), this notion has been widely fictionalized, dramatized, and theorized, for instance in the 1980s TV series *Max Headroom*, the 2000s TV series *Battlestar Galactica*, Cory Doctorow's 2003 novel *Down and Out in the Magic Kingdom*, and in the discourses of "virtual reality," for example Derrick de Kerckhove's *The Skin of Culture* (1995) and Christopher Dewdney's book *Last Flesh* (1998). In 1971, McLuhan alludes to both television and incipient computing in his statement that "what is very little understood about the electronic age is that it angelizes man, disembodies him. Turns him into software" (quoted in Benedetti and DeHart 1996, 79). McLuhan later elaborated on this idea of disembodied remediation in a 1978 article: "When you are 'on the telephone' or 'on the air,' you do not have a physical body. In these media, the sender is sent and is instantaneously present everywhere. The disembodied user extends to all those who are recipients of electric information" (quoted in Benedetti and DeHart 1996, 80). Hence, in *Neuromancer*, Case's technological transcendence of corporeal existence in his flights through the

datascapes of cyberspace and his grudging returns to mere "meat" existence, in "the prison of his own flesh" (1984, 6). Hence, also, *Videodrome's*
Brian O'Blivion, who only appears onscreen within a second, embedded
screen. Both characters' full withdrawal into media systems dramatize the
distinctively McLuhanesque double movement of both a transnational
spacing—the remediated "extension of our own bodies and senses"—and
a technological doubling—the "lease [of] our central nervous systems to
various corporations" (McLuhan [1964] 2003, 99–100).

As Cavell has argued (2002, xiii), McLuhan directed his major research
questions to contexts of space, of surroundings, of environment; hence,
for instance, his retroactive positioning as a founder of the field of "media
ecology." Through his thoroughly technologized existence, strictly "on television," O'Blivion occupies a simultaneously indeterminate space—from
where (and/or when) is he broadcasting?—and a closely confined space—
the cathode-ray small screen. The revelatory scene that exposes O'Blivion's
fate as a video library is set in a high-ceilinged room, through which the
camera pans across shelves full of tapes, suggesting both the professor's
encyclopedic knowledge and the extent of his media obsession. O'Blivion's
indeterminate redistribution problematizes the spatial dimension of electronic remediation as a globalized space: O'Blivion inhabits the "strange
new world" in which "television is reality and reality is less than television,"
a world evocative of McLuhan's "global village," an idea that figures in
Videodrome as prominently as it does in *Neuromancer.*

While *Neuromancer* dramatizes the global village in a jet-setting
plot that rockets the characters through the financescapes of late capital, *Videodrome* condenses the global village into the complementary
characters of O'Blivion and Convex as figures of contrasting and con-
flicting globalization, the one dedicated charitably (albeit eccentrically)
to the public interest, the other dedicated to profit and his shareholders.
Cronenberg's ironic portrayal of corporate "social responsibility" in Convex's invocation of "global citizenship," in Spectacular Optical's corporate
deployments of mass media, and in the implied unevenness of global
development—portrayed here as a soft North America in conflict with
the "rest of the world" turned "tough" and "savage"—all appear years ahead
of the critical theories of globalization that gained currency over a decade
later. O'Blivion warns Renn that he will "have to learn to live in a very

strange new world," signifying the disoriented North America plotted by Spectacular Optical and modelled by McLuhan's global village.

Cronenberg's McLuhanesque commentary on globalization also emerges in the form and production of the film, in its extended satire on Canadian media culture and Canadian film in the global entertainment market. O'Blivion, as a parody of McLuhan, is a standout example of this satire. So are Renn and the station he works for. Introduced as a kind of opportunistic sleaze merchant, Renn satirizes the shift from cinema to home video taking place in the pornography industry at that time. The station where Renn works—"Civic TV"—is a thinly veiled parody of City TV, which (before its takeover by CTV) was a Toronto independent station whose varied programming included softcore porn on late-night weekend slots. Late in the film, Renn shoots a coworker named "Moses" (a cipher for City TV's founder Moses Znaimer).

The movie's satire on the Canadian media establishment also encompasses its globalizing trends. Renn enacts the kind of subjectivity that McLuhan posits as symptomatic of the "global village": a kind of "programmable" subjectivity: "There's nothing at all difficult about putting computers in the position where they will be able to conduct carefully orchestrated programing of the sensory life of whole populations. I know it sounds rather science-fictional" (McLuhan 1969, 72). Renn's visceral programming and reprogramming via the repeated insertions of videotapes into his abdomen—at once suggestively sexual and suggestively cybernetic (recall that, at the time of the film's release, magnetic tape was a standard storage medium for computer programs)—dramatizes and literalizes McLuhan's claim that media programming could, in turn, program "whole populations": "We could program five hours less of TV in Italy to promote the reading of newspapers during an election" (1969, 72). If O'Blivion has uncannily, ambiguously colonized the medium, Renn, conversely, is violently colonized by the medium, and so becomes, himself, a weaponized technology, as the repeated insertions of videotape over the course of the film give way to repeated withdrawals of a pistol that is mechanically and organically fused to Renn's hand: a "flesh gun." Inasmuch as the actor playing Renn, James Woods, is, in 1983, a relatively big Hollywood star, the actor's performance in this film—which was financed by Canadian federal arts funding—lends a critical Canadian irony to Renn's fate as the test subject for a transnational media empire.

Its Hollywood stars and Toronto set stage the global tensions faced by Canada's film industry, between cultivating "Canadian content" and drawing foreign investment to "Hollywood north," and the Spectacular Optical corporation, whose slogan is "keeping an eye on the world," parodies the globalized business culture whose rhetoric of corporate "citizenship" contrasts its "enthusiastic" and amoral trade in a catalogue of symptomatic consumer and state technological goods: eyeglasses, weapons, and TV signal, which here also turns out to be a weapon.

Unsupervised Playgrounds: McLuhanesque Frankenphemes of Technology

The adaptations of *Frankenstein* and McLuhan in *Neuromancer* and *Videodrome* converge in articulations and images of technology that vividly illuminate its popular cultural construction and dissemination as a McLuhanesque Frankenpheme. Both texts depict settings that are replete with and even defined by media technologies; both texts' plots pivot around figures and problems of autonomous technology; both texts' main characters are stylized, grotesquely imagined cyborgs. Both texts explicitly use the word "technology," too, and while these references are relatively few, they augment the texts' more intensive and sustained representations of technology in general—and media technologies specifically—as simultaneously McLuhanesque and Frankensteinian.

Neuromancer includes five uses of the full word technology, five uses of the abbreviation "tech," and two uses of "techno-" as a prefix. The "Panther Moderns" that help the heist crew steal the rudimentary, ROM-only AI "construct" are described as "nihilistic technofetishists" (1984, 59); the Japanese city of Chiba, where the novel opens, is described not only as an "unsupervised playground for technology" (11)—an image we'll return to—but also as "a magnet for the Sprawl's techno-criminal subcultures" (6). The slang abbreviation "tech" occurs five times. The Finn, an entrepreneur who provides privacy services—a pricey, scarce commodity in Gibson's near future of ubiquitous surveillance—is introduced as "our tech here" (50). A subsequent scene includes "a trio of young office techs" (77). As a descriptor of certain characters, "tech" abbreviates not "technology" but "technician"; however, like the prefix "techno-," which works adjectivally to describe certain social groups, the abbreviation "tech" allows an ambiguity that develops the novel's cyberpunk setting and plot: the ambiguity between tool and user, which makes fantastical cyborgs of most of the characters in the novel. Like Case's physical, hard-wired connection to the console whereby he enters cyberspace, like Molly's mercenary surgical augmentations, the abbreviation "tech" and the prefix "techno-" contribute to the construction of a fictional world in which late capital has radically blurred if not erased the traditional ontological boundary between human and machine.

The word technology itself contributes likewise to *Neuromancer*'s thoroughly cybernetic fictional world. What is distinctive about the novel's use of the word technology is that it consistently situates technology as a novelty itself, as the cutting edge, as the prized object of unregulated or downright underground research and development. "If the technology had been available the Big Scientists would all have had sockets stuffed with microsofts" (59): here, Gibson adapts what would subsequently become one of the most globally powerful software brands (Microsoft) to describe a kind of data storage medium that interfaces with the user's own body, via "sockets" described elsewhere as surgical implants in the cranium (today we might imagine this as something like USB ports set into the base of a person's skull—but this analogy is, no doubt, already en route to obsolescence). In the conspicuously uncertain history of the novel's premise lurks one backstory about a world war that involved nuclear weapons and other kinds of weapons; as one character recalls, the war had "wasted a fair bit of patriotic young flesh in order to test some new technology" (35). Reminiscent of McLuhan's claim about technology prompting war (McLuhan and Fiore 1968, 98), this passage shares with the "microsofts" passage a sense of technology as what is new, what is next, what is under development. Something of this sense of technology as the object and laboratory of capitalist futures also emerges in the "playground" image, and in a scene where Case pays a second visit to the Finn and feels as if the jungle of junk equipment and devices that camouflages the Finn's place of business "had grown somehow," forming "a crystalline essence of discarded technology, flowering secretly in the Sprawl's waste places" (72).

The image of "discarded technology, flowering secretly" evokes not only technology's novelty in Gibson's prose but also, moreover, its uncanny, almost organic autonomy. This passing description thus foreshadows the emergence of artificial intelligence as a major actor in—and object of—the plot; it also amplifies the sense of technology's almost self-aware agency in the opening description of Chiba's "Night City" black market as "a deliberately unsupervised playground for technology itself" (1984, 6). Like the scene of the breathing, beckoning TV set in *Videodrome*, this image of the "unsupervised playground" effectively encapsulates *Neuromancer*'s overall representation of technology as a McLuhanesque Frankenpheme. The simile situates technology as a kind of child by invoking the image of the "playground," and the adjective "unsupervised" suggests the absence of regulation that is typical of neoliberal ideology, laced with a hint of danger, as if the unmonitored status of this free-market playground could mean harm for who or what plays there, or as if who or what plays there could grow to bring harm to the wider world. The adjective "itself" following technology furthers the fetishistic sense of technology here as autonomous agent, as a character—arguably, indeed, as the true main character of *Neuromancer*.

Videodrome—a genre-bending film, at once "body horror" and cyberpunk—similarly articulates and visualizes technology as a McLuhanesque Frankenpheme. The words "media" and "technology" each occur only once in the film script, both with reference to O'Blivion, who is introduced first, in the TV interview scene, as a "media prophet." Later, in the aforementioned scene in O'Blivion's video library, his daughter Bianca explains to Renn: "My father helped to create Videodrome. He saw it as part of the evolution of man as a technological animal." Bianca's reference to "evolution" evokes the epochal narrative that runs through McLuhan's theory of the "ages" of different media, such as those of "typographical man" and "electronic man."

If the script's articulation of technology is sparing, though, the film's visualization of it is pervasive, spectacular, and exceedingly grotesque. The main plot is driven wholly by the development and backfire of a new technology, the characters' interactions with one another are dramatically technologized, and the film's visual elements—its *mise en scène*, its settings, its props—are a sustained study in the aesthetics of mediatization and the technological grotesque. The film's first lines of dialogue come from a TV station call and an automated voicemail system, respectively; its last frames display a televised image of Renn, pointing the flesh gun at his own head. Cathode-ray television sets figure frequently in many scenes; Renn meets both O'Blivion and Convex first as televised images; Renn and his fellow protagonist Nicki Brand, played by Blondie's Debbie Harry, both start out as "real" characters who eventually become entirely creatures of video.

The film's most vivid articulation and amplification of technology as McLuhanesque Frankenpheme is perhaps the scene in which Renn interacts surreally, intimately, and then immersively with the TV set in his living room, as the set shifts from playing back an O'Blivion tape, to showing O'Blivion address Renn personally, to becoming animate, as it starts to move and heave, veins rippling across its surface and the screen protruding towards Renn, while O'Blivion's image and voice give way to those of Brand. This iconic scene condenses, in an exemplary way, the discourse of technology (figured here, significantly, as a consumer media technology) as a Frankensteinian monster that takes on a life of its own and threatens that of the user. This threat intensifies in the similarly surreal scene later in the film, where the TV screen extrudes an appendage in the shape of a hand pointing a pistol (fig. 3).

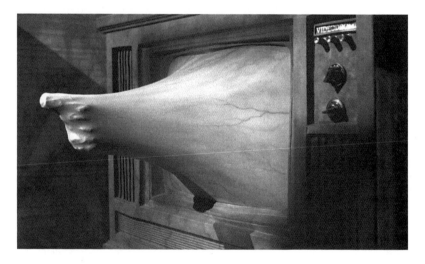

Figure 3 The medium is the monster: scene from *Videodrome* (1983). Courtesy of Universal Studios Licensing LLC.

The monstrosity is figured as globalized, in the indeterminate source of the televised content—that of O'Blivion's uncanny interactivity and that of the Videodrome signal and program, whose production is purported to take place in either Malaysia or Pittsburgh—and in the globalizing, totalizing language of O'Blivion's speech, as he prognosticates that "the battle for the mind of North America will be fought in the video arena," theorizes that "television is reality," and warns of the "strange new world" that *Videodrome* augurs.

Pattern Recognition

This distinctive synthesis of Shelley's *Frankenstein* and McLuhan's media theory in representations of technology recurs throughout the oeuvres of both Gibson and Cronenberg: their works not only formulate but repeat, with variations, the McLuhanesque Frankenpheme of technology.

Cronenberg's early body of work, from *Stereo* (1969) to *The Fly* (1986), comprises a tradition of *Frankenstein* adaptation unto itself, which Cronenberg has further extended, though more sporadically, with more recent films like *eXistenZ* (1999). Bart Testa (1995) and Jonathan Crane (2000) have argued that Cronenberg's early films belong as much to science fiction as to the horror genre, because of their distinctly Frankensteinian fusion of both generic conventions. Noting how consistently the early films "revivify" a "mad scientist" father figure, Crane argues that Cronenberg "reaches back as far as the genre will allow, and returns Dr. Frankenstein to the present. All Cronenberg's variations on the father are interested in restoring life to the dead" (2000, 55). Variations on this character type recur in *Shivers* (1976), *Rabid* (1977), *The Brood* (1979), *Scanners* (1981), *Videodrome*, *The Dead Zone* (1983), and *The Fly* (1986). In *Videodrome*'s version of the *Frankenstein* story, Crane recognizes the link between *Frankenstein* and technology that Cronenberg dramatizes in the context of media theory: "The vast television audience will be reconstructed in the face of real, direct communication effects. Frankenstein, as a pivotal player in new technologies, will now succeed Rupert Murdoch and Ted Turner" (2000, 56).

For Testa, Cronenberg's early films all adapt a common Frankensteinian plot structure of "the monster-protagonist-internal narrator searching for Explanation (finally to find his/her origins) and the same figure suffering and spreading a rising spectacular monstrosity." The "Explanation" in these films is another commonality they share: "The origin of the monster-protagonist is the technological manufacture of the body," based in dubious if not downright diabolical scientific research (1995, 47–48). *Videodrome* is an exemplar of such Frankensteinian plotting, in its first-person point-of-view and in its insertion of other media forms, chiefly video footage, to unfold the backstory (45). Moreover, the

Cronenbergian "technological manufacture of the body" resonates with Canada's technological nationalism, especially with McLuhan's contributions to it:

> When, in *Understanding Media*, McLuhan claims the media are extensions of the human body he appears provocatively gnomic to some, but he recasts a metaphor classic in Canadian imagery of national settlement in the northern portion of the continent as extending the body—a manufactured body reaching out in railroads, telegraphs, televisions. (50)

Echoing Kroker (1984), Testa concludes that "behind the Canadian Cronenberg is . . . a discourse on technology springing from the Canadian ethos" (51).

In Cronenberg's early films (many of which, like *Videodrome*, were federally funded under the tax shelter provisions of the Canadian Film Development Corporation, now Telefilm Canada, as a nation-building cultural policy), the nested narrative frames, monstrous protagonists, and irresponsible father-doctors, as well as grotesque and Gothic effects, all show that *Frankenstein* is a potent source text; *Videodrome* accompanies these *Frankenstein* sources with a sustained and relatively explicit homage to McLuhan and Canada's distinctive media culture.

Together with *Videodrome* and the considerably later film *eXistenZ* (1999), the 1981 film *Scanners* exemplifies Cronenberg's penchant for setting his *Frankenstein* adaptations in media contexts. Just as *Videodrome* explores the manufactured monstrosity of cable TV and video recording, so does *eXistenZ* explore that of virtual reality and gaming, and *Scanners* that of networked computing and pharmaceuticals. *Scanners* follows the protagonist Cameron Vale on his journey of monstrous self-discovery: he learns that he is a "scanner"—he has telepathic powers; that he is embroiled in a struggle between telepaths being cultivated by the private security firm ConSec and a rogue faction of power-hungry telepaths; that his powers result from drugs a ConSec researcher gave to his mother when she was pregnant with him; and, finally, that he and the rogue telepaths' leader, Revok, are brothers—both are sons of that researcher. In the course of this plot of monstrous awakening, which entails many feints and fights between the warring telepaths, Vale also learns that he can "scan" not only human minds but media systems. In the film's most striking scene, Vale uses a pay telephone to access and read the ConSec computer database that includes top-secret records about the pharmaceutical program that has produced the scanners. For a 1981 film, this scene is remarkably contemporary as a fantastic dramatization of modem technology, the use of telephones to access computer networks. When one of Vale's enemies—Keller, ConSec's chief of security—realizes what he's doing, Keller cuts the connection not only to block access but also to hurt him; but this act backfires and Keller dies instead. Keller's notion that terminating a technological link will harm the body using it dramatizes the McLuhanesque premise of technology as prosthesis; similarly, Keller's fate as a victim of technological backfire dramatizes just one of the many McLuhanesque Frankenphemes of media technology that pervade this extraordinary early Cronenberg film.

Unlike *Videodrome*, *Scanners* in its soundtrack makes much more use of synthesizer instrumentation, not orchestral instrumentation, which amplifies its aesthetic of technologized grotesquerie. Like *Videodrome*, *Scanners* grounds its setting in a globalized business context of corporate research and development, particularly R&D on weaponizing both technological prostheses (such as drugs) and media systems (such as computer networks): the ConSec database inventories its arsenal of human bodies turned into corporate property and weaponry, and in the plot becomes weaponized itself in the skirmishes between ConSec and its rivals. And, again like *Videodrome*, *Scanners* attributes the origins of its protagonists' technological monstrosity to a mad-scientist kind of father figure: like Brian O'Blivion, *Scanners*'s Dr. Paul Ruth develops a technology that profoundly affects and even shapes bodies and subjects, and becomes exploited by private interests in order to weaponize bodies and subjects—on a global scale. However, in *Videodrome*, it is the corporation (Spectacular Optical) that plots to exploit its monstrous technology on a global scale, while in *Scanners* it is the rogue individual, Revok, who seeks to turn scanners into a Frankensteinian race for bedeviling the globe. So *Videodrome*'s casting of the corporation as antagonist represents a significant difference from the earlier film.

Critically contextualized as not just horror but also science fiction, Cronenberg's early oeuvre constitutes a Canadian contribution to a broader cinematic trend, mainly Hollywood-driven, in which the *Frankenstein* story has become *the* dominant narrative framework for blockbuster science fiction films today, as illustrated by *Westworld* (1973), *Star Wars*

(1977), *Blade Runner* (1982), *The Terminator* (1983), *Robocop* (1987), *Gattaca* (1997), *The Matrix* (1999), Cronenberg's own *eXistenZ*, *AI* (2001), *The Island* (2005), *Moon* (2009), *Splice* (2009), and *Transcendence* (2014)—to name just a few in a very long list. These films have exploited *Frankenstein* references for cultural commentaries on a variety of social themes, including work, cybernetics, ecology, consumerism, war, and militarization, as well as corporate and state power.

Meanwhile, Cronenberg's recent films have been more varied in their plots and subject matter: *A History of Violence* (2005) and *Eastern Promises* (2007) explore organized crime, for instance. Some recent films have carried on his *Frankenstein* plotting, though, notably *eXistenZ* (1999), which was the first film after *Videodrome* that Cronenberg not only directed but also wrote. And Cronenberg himself is fond of talking about his filmmaking process with nods to *Frankenstein*. He has "described getting all the pieces in place for the kind of films he wants to make as 'stitching a Frankenstein quilt'" (Onstad 2013, para. 9); and he repeats the analogy in a more recent interview: "I rather like that independent films are put together like Frankenstein: You get pieces from all over the world, and you stitch them together and hope it ends up being a living organism" (quoted in Vlessing 2014, para. 8). The analogy is fitting for a director who established his reputation in a series of provocative genre films that transplanted the *Frankenstein* story to corporate North America.

Like Cronenberg's, Gibson's body of work demonstrates a recurring preoccupation with *Frankenstein* plots and imagery. Concerns with artificial intelligence and technology's unintended consequences that are first elaborated in *Neuromancer* then recur through the rest of the Sprawl trilogy and the subsequent Bridge trilogy, a set of novels set in a nearer, more recognizably extrapolated future, organized loosely around San Francisco and its Golden Gate Bridge. Gibson's complementary concern with the constructed character of human subjectivity itself also recurs across his oeuvre, from the volatile assemblage named Armitage who leads but then abandons the heist in *Neuromancer*, to *Virtual Light*'s subplot about *Videodrome* and the impact of mass media on subject formation, to the Bigend trilogy's Milgrim, a translator and addict whom one critic likens to "Frankenstein's monster, an experiment of sorts" (Henthorne 2011, 127) for being manipulated and exploited by the spy named Brown in *Spook Country* (2007).

After *Neuromancer*, the first two novels of Gibson's Bridge trilogy feature the clearest and most extensive elaborations of his McLuhanesque Frankenpheme of technology. The trilogy's first novel, *Virtual Light*, includes recurring references to *Videodrome* in a subplot about a lapsed member of an American cult that worships television; in the cult's theology, *Videodrome*—together with Cronenberg's whole oeuvre—is condemned as heretical and Satanic. "There's movies that are clearly of the Devil, Berry. Or anyway that's what Reverend Fallon says. Says all of Cronenberg's are" (Gibson 1993, 295–96). As Dominick Grace argues, in exploring several structural and thematic similarities between Cronenberg's films and Gibson's fiction: "Cronenberg's ambivalent and interrogative view of technology . . . is consistent with the kind of ambivalent interrogation of technological change that emerges in much of Gibson's work and is central to the plot of this novel" (2003, para. 12). In *Virtual Light*, Gibson's McLuhan-influenced extrapolations of the social ubiquity and subject-forming power of mass media, especially TV and networked computers, echo Cronenberg's earlier dramatizations of this ubiquity and power in *Videodrome* and (via the allusion to "all of Cronenberg's" films) his earlier film *Scanners* (1980) and anticipate his return to these themes in 1999's *eXistenZ*, which carries forward *Videodrome*'s premises of media-made subjectivity and the unreliability of "reality" to the new media industry of networked, virtual gaming.

In the Bridge trilogy's second book, *Idoru*, the title refers to the Japanese adaptation of "idol" and thus to the character Rei Toei, an entirely holographic pop star, whom a human rock star, Rez, intends to marry. This courtship and engagement of a human and an artificial intelligence organize the main plot of *Idoru*; that is, the novel tells the story of a mechanical bride. *Idoru* develops and deepens the fictional near-future mediascape introduced in *Virtual Light* and uses the word technology and its cognates with conspicuous intensity: "technology" itself occurs eight times, and "tech," as prefix or suffix, occurs an additional thirty-seven times in the novel.

In a late chapter in *Idoru*, Rei Toei and her creator, Michio Kuwayama, explain to the investigator Colin Laney how the *idoru*'s "union" with Rez furthers the strategy and plan of Famous Aspect, the corporation that has created her. To Laney's question of what the seemingly impossible marriage is "all about," Kuwayama says that "it is about futurity" and then articulates what Gibson represents as an implicitly non-Western, Japanese perspective on futurity—and technology:

"Do you know that our word for 'nature' is of quite recent coinage? It is scarcely a hundred years old. We have never developed a sinister view of technology, Mr. Laney. It is an aspect of the natural, of oneness. Through our efforts, oneness perfects itself." Kuwayama smiled. "And popular culture," he said, "is the testbed of our futurity." (1996, 314)

This passage in *Idoru* is as suggestive in illustrating Gibson's development of a McLuhanesque Frankenpheme of technology as is the "unsupervised playground" image in *Neuromancer*. The use of collective, first-person pronouns, as in "our word," implies that Gibson's Kuwayama here speaks not just for Famous Aspect but for the Japanese; despite the arguable Orientalism operating in Gibson's character development here, through Kuwayama's statement, Gibson imparts an insight about the Western world's view of technology: namely, that in contrast to the purported Japanese view of technology, the Western world's view of technology *is* sinister. Passages like these, taken together with the plotlines of several Gibson novels, illustrate how his body of work, like Cronenberg's, constitutes an extended figuration and dramatization of how and why the modern globalized discourse of technology, influenced by the coupled forces of Shelley's *Frankenstein* and McLuhan's media theory, has assumed its "sinister" character.

Pattern Modulation

Aside from the recurrence of the McLuhanesque Frankenpheme of technology throughout Gibson's and Cronenberg's oeuvres, *Neuromancer* and *Videodrome* have remained popular enough in their own right to propagate McLuhan's Frankensteinian discourse of technology. Perennially discovered by new audiences, these texts have graduated from "cult" status to popular cultural canonicity. Both are still in print and commercially available to purchase, over thirty years after their initial release. And both have been sampled and cited in other cultural productions—as, for instance, in Gibson's own citation of *Videodrome* in *Virtual Light*.

To illustrate the abiding popularity of these texts in just one niche field of popular cultural production, electronic dance music (which chapter 7 will address) yields a rich vein of quotations and adaptations. *Videodrome* has been widely sampled by music producers like Skinny Puppy ("Draining Faces" 1987), Front 242 ("Masterhit" 1987), and Messiah; in the process, these tracks become secondary *Frankenstein* adaptations. Messiah's

"You're Going Insane" (1992) opens with Convex's words of reassurance to Renn as he dons the VR-like vision-recording helmet: "You might catch yourself sliding in and out of an hallucinatory state after this is all over. If you do, just relax and enjoy it, it'll soon go away." *Videodrome* samples are common in 1990s rave tracks (e.g., Messiah's 1991 "Prince of Darkness," Luna C's 1993 "Mind of a Lunatic"). The line "ease yourself back into consciousness," from the film's opening scene, has been a favourite sample among electronic dance music producers, as heard in Bomb the Bass's "Switching Channels" (1991), Cyberdelics's "Adventures of Dama" (1993), Dope on Plastic's "Wave Dub" (1994), and Ed Brown's "Industrial (P.B.K. remix)" (2009), to name a few.

Neuromancer has been similarly cited in electronic dance music. Several producers, including Paul Drake, Christian Smith, Yuri Melnikov (among others), have taken "Neuromancer" as their professional alias, as credited on Drake's 1992 "Pennywise" and "Nookie" tracks, on Smith's 1993 "Journey into Cyberspace," and on Melnikov's 2008 EP, *666*. UK producer DJ Massive (Alan Clark) released a five-track *Neuromancer* EP in 1992. In 1995, the German producer Wippenberg released "Neuro Dancer"; Siva released the experimental "Aegean Neuromancer" in 2006; Germany's Phantasma Disques label put out the *Neuromancer Complex* EP in 2012; and in 2014, the US synth-goth band William Control released an album titled *The Neuromancer*. In addition, the name "Dixie Flatline" has been assumed by a Japanese electronic music producer.

Arguably, *Neuromancer* and *Videodrome* recommend themselves particularly to the field of electronic dance music in part because of its analogous investments and experiments in new media for making music. In the early rave culture of the late 1980s and early 1990s, *Videodrome's* radical interpretive indeterminacy provided a bank of thematically fitting vocal samples for the rave scene's "techno-Romantic" aesthetic of cyber-narcotic excess-as-transcendence (see Reynolds 1999); and *Neuromancer* offered a vision of digital culture and "virtuality" that rave embraced and romanticized, in the scene's cultural function as one subcultural milieu of the broader popularization of computer networking that began to accelerate in the early 1990s, a popularization also seen in the advent of the World Wide Web and the explosion of interest in "virtual reality" interfaces and devices. In addition, *Neuromancer* features Afro-Futurist music significantly in its setting and plot. The Zion space station's Rastas play a constant stream of dub—"a sensuous mosaic cooked from vast libraries of digital-ized pop" (1984, 104)—and this conspicuously technological, structurally *spacey* music ultimately helps Case find his way to freedom from virtual imprisonment by the Neuromancer AI at the novel's climax (244).

Neuromancer's own references to electronic music, its citations by other electronic music producers, and its aforementioned adaptations in other media show just the tip of a virtual iceberg of influence that it has wielded over popular culture. The novel's impact on subsequent print science fiction has been widely recognized (Brouillette 2002) and will be revisited below. The novel's pivotal portmanteau, "cyberspace," has achieved an incalculable, quotidian currency in discourses and technolo-gies of cultural globalization and networked computing (Bukatman 1992, 199; Downes 2005, 3; Manovich 2001, 250–51; Mosco and Foster 2001, 220, 233). Specifically, Gibson has been widely celebrated as "the individual who . . . coined the term and conceptualized the idea *of* cyberspace" (Annesley 2001, 224). *Neuromancer* has come to enjoy a peculiar distinction (shared with only a select few other literary works, by the likes of H. G. Wells and Jules Verne) as a fiction celebrated for anticipating a specific techno-logical innovation—the graphic Internet now known as the World Wide Web—and even, according to some of his more radical readers, for having played an active role in making its fiction a reality. This position, which perennially resurfaces in the popular press (Sullivan 2009, para. 5; Rich 2014, para. 3), is perhaps best articulated by Gibson's friend and fellow SF author Jack Womack, who asks, "What if the act of writing it down, in fact, *brought it about?*" (Womack 2000, 269). Womack articulates (with the help of a Frankensteinian trope, no less) a speculation shared by many commentators on "cyberspace":

> When *Neuromancer* appeared it was picked up and devoured by
> hundreds, then thousands, of men and women who worked in
> or around the garages and cubicles where what is still called new
> media were, fitfully, being birthed. . . . [Gibson] has often said that
> he intended "cyberspace" to be nothing more than a metaphor. No
> matter. Once a creation goes out in the world its creator, like any
> parent, loses the control once so easily exertable over the offspring;
> another variety of emergent behavior, you could say. . . . So rather
> than the theoretical Matrix, we now, thanks to all those beautiful
> William Gibson readers out there in the dark, have the actual Web.
> (2000, 269)

Given the intervening decades and the massive growth of globalized, networked computing they have witnessed, the question of whether or to what extent Gibson's work actively fostered the nascent Internet remains open—a favourite subject of widespread speculation about one of contemporary literature's canonical speculative fictions. As journalist Nathaniel Rich says, "Thirty years after the novel's publication, it's difficult to tell whether Gibson foresaw the future or whether the future, designed by technologists who idolized Gibson's novels, self-consciously imitated his novel" (2014, 10).

This question of a fictional influence on historical technological change thus prompts a similar question of media theory's influence on media practice: Gibson's acknowledgement of McLuhan's influence on *Neuromancer* augments the corresponding claims that McLuhan, too, had anticipated if not predicted the Internet. Those now familiar claims began to emerge in force alongside the explosive popularization of the Internet that the early World Wide Web catalyzed in the mid-1990s, exemplified by three illustrative samples of the mid-1990s McLuhan revival that accompanied the popularization of the Internet.

First, McLuhan was named "patron saint" in the colophon (the list of contributors' credits) of early issues of *Wired* magazine, which was launched in 1993. Something of the thinking behind this canonization was spelled out in Gary Wolf's 1996 column in the magazine, which suggests both the sense of technological revolution that accompanied the Internet's popularization in the 1990s and the anticipatory role of McLuhan's theory in framing contemporary understandings of it: "In recent years, the explosion of new media—particularly the Web—has caused new anxieties. Or to put a more McLuhanesque spin on it, the advent of new digital media has brought the conditions of the old technologies into sharper relief, and made us suddenly conscious of our media environment. In the confusion of the digital revolution, McLuhan is relevant again" (1996, para. 3).

Second, Paul Benedetti and Nancy DeHart's 1996 retrospective collection *On McLuhan: Forward Through the Rearview Mirror* (the layout of which evokes Quentin Fiore's media-collage designs for McLuhan's popular books) combines statements by colleagues and protégés with those by McLuhan himself. The editors stress McLuhan's "remarkable prescience" and attribute "McLuhan's revival" to "a new wave of technological innovation . . . a wave signified by the Internet and virtual reality"

(1996, 190). In the early 1990s, "people started rereading McLuhan and discovered that a quarter of a century before words such as on-line, wired, and the Web became part of our vocabulary, they existed in McLuhan's lexicon" (34).

And third, a 1999 episode of CBC's *Life and Times* biography program on McLuhan introduces him as having "predicted the Internet before there was a name for it" and, throughout, emphasizes his revival amidst the burgeoning Internet culture and tech sector. Framed by a frenetic, media collage backdrop (also reminiscent of Fiore's design principles), in which Internet screen shots and techno music figure prominently, interviewees like Lewis Lapham assert that "much of what he said would happen or guessed would happen has happened"; and, against a screen shot of the online edition of *Wired* showing McLuhan's name, a *Wired* editor claims that "*Wired* is actually reporting the very things that he anticipated." Both Gibson and McLuhan, then, exerted a powerful cultural and conceptual influence over the historical development of the Internet: "McLuhan's works, side by side with those of Gibson, have been avidly read by early researchers in MIT's Media Lab, for these researchers also conceive of a VR composed, like the tribal and collective 'global village,' of 'tactile, haptic, proprioceptive and acoustic spaces and involvements'" (Theall 1992, para. 3).

Like Cronenberg's film and Gibson's novel, the 1990s "revival" of McLuhan further amplifies the Frankensteinian inflection of his rhetoric of technology, and of his broader ideas of media, by retrieving, recontextualizing, and recirculating not only McLuhan's work but his public persona, most suggestively perhaps, in his enlistment as a contributor in the pages of *Wired*. In both *Videodrome* and the mid-1990s "revival" discourse of McLuhan, the man himself figures hauntologically, as a technologized return of the repressed (or more precisely, in his case, the unfashionable); as a "prescient" revenant haunting the broadcasts and modem handshakes and reanimating new media theory; as an old ghost in the new machine. And as significant as the variously purported and disputed "prescience" of both McLuhan and Gibson in anticipating new media technologies are their shared wariness and dread of these technologies and the social environments they create, as evinced in their writings' common conjuration of *Frankenstein* in the very discourse and imagery of technology. The next two chapters detail the further appropriations and transformations of McLuhan's Frankenpheme of technology in Canadian popular culture since Gibson's and Cronenberg's influential works, focusing in the next chapter on print science fiction, and turning in chapter 7 to electronic dance music.

6. "Technology Implies Belligerence"
Pattern Propagation in Canadian Science Fiction

Like McLuhan's legacy in popular culture, that of *Neuromancer* and *Videodrome*, together with the larger oeuvres of their creators, can be gauged, in a very limited and qualified way, in the traces they leave in subsequent texts, statements, performances, and other cultural artifacts.

Within even just Canadian popular cultural production, several texts adapt and propagate the McLuhanesque Frankenpheme of technology in concretely identifiable ways. This chapter surveys some of these adaptations to suggest the propagation of the McLuhanesque Frankenpheme of technology in Canadian literature.

One relatively early but underappreciated site of such propagation predates both Gibson and Cronenberg but grafts science fiction concerns with technology to McLuhan's media ecology. Phyllis Gotlieb (1926–2009) was a Toronto-based science fiction writer who studied at the University of Toronto during McLuhan's tenure there and who produced a sizeable and diverse oeuvre of novels, poetry, short fiction, and radio dramas, several of which featured Frankensteinian characters and tropes (e.g., her 1976 novel *O Master Caliban!* and her 1998–2002 trilogy, *Flesh and Gold*). Gotlieb's 1975 poem, "ms & mr frankenstein," appeared in *The Canadian Forum* in 1975. The poem recounts an absurd, surreal narrative, told by the "ms frankenstein" of the title, in which she and her partner, "Scarpino," use salvaged waste and discarded materials to build a giant anthropomorphic sculpture—"25 foot high and every inch a junkman" ([1975] 1978, 242).

When the persona christens the figure with a "bottle of Old Bubble" (242), it comes to life, mouths infantile syllables, shouts "COSMOS I COME!" (243), and flies away.

Of particular interest are the many media materials listed among the technological castaway consumer goods that go into this figure, like "paper-clips," "typewriter keys," "paperweights," "gum erasers," "broken staplers," and "last year's calendars" (241–42). The figure incorporates materials drawn from domains of modern social relations that are both called *communication*: "bicyclespokes," "smashed headlights," and "speedometers" on one hand evoke the older sense of communication as transportation, while on the other the "typewriter keys" and "broken staplers" conjure communication as representation and meaning making. The figure rehearses the *Frankenstein* skeleton story of technological backfire when it says things other than what the persona expects to hear and when it surprises them by flying away, in the process "taking along / Scarp's wig & false teeth my fillings" (243): in other words, their creature's departure deprives the persona and her partner of their own technological prostheses. In closing the poem, the persona wonders ambiguously about what may yet come of the figure's departure "TO THE UNIVERSE"; she wonders "just what kind of garbage they're gonna be sending us," presumably in retaliation. The figure becomes a kind of rocket: one that "zapped out the roof on a pillar of fire" and is then mistaken by neighbours for lightning (243). These details play archly on their source story. The poem's image of the monster mistaken for lightning likens it to the medium of Victor Frankenstein's initial inspiration, the electrical effects that first led him to pursue galvanism. And with a further amplification of Gotlieb's Frankensteinian thematization of media here, the poem's persona ironically notes newspapers mistaking the figure's spectacular flight for either a comet—or a bomb (244).

Turning from work more contemporary with McLuhan's own time at the University of Toronto to work that emerged amidst his mid-1990s revival, we find McLuhan's Frankenphemes of technology quite prominently articulated in Christopher Dewdney's 1993 book *The Secular Grail* and his 1998 book *Last Flesh*: collections of essays, aphorisms, and short nonfiction prose that feature a consistent interest in artificial intelligence (1993, 124, 133), technology (1993, 17, 187), the constructed character of subjectivity and cognition (1993, 50–51, 140), and haunting and the uncanny (1993, 86–87, 125, 184–85). "SOFTWARE IS / THE GHOST I / N THE

MACH / INE" declares one aphorism in *The Secular Grail* (1993, 184). *Last Flesh* makes more explicit Dewdney's conceptual and stylistic debts to McLuhan; the later book, published after the Web's advent, in the middle of the dot-com boom, often cites McLuhan (1998, 97) and reads very much like his writing, in its juxtapositions of observations on everyday life made freshly strange—as if turned inside-out—together with futurist extrapolations of the effects of new media and technology—from networked computing to cloning and nanotechnology—on a vaguely defined, collective "us":

> The wave of technology that is almost upon us will not be just another manifestation of "progress" to be incorporated into society. It will alter the very basis of what it means to be human. . . . A devil's bargain with corporations is necessary in order to secure the vital private funding to finance research facilities that will eventually launch the posthuman era. . . . But make no mistake: posthuman technology will ultimately transform its corporate host, governments and all other extant forms of social organization. . . . The inequalities that will arise from the uneven distribution of extreme technologies will have to be controlled or else we will descend into chaos. (1998, 57–58)

This excerpt from an early section on "Transhuman technology" exemplifies the book's McLuhanesque style and its reproduction of McLuhan's Frankensteinian discourse of "technology": the "devil's bargain" that Dewdney argues is needed to advance technological development; the involvement of corporate business (in the manner of not only McLuhan, here, but also Gibson and Cronenberg); the figuring of technology as a cause of unintended and potentially catastrophic consequences, often linked to the machinations of corporate forces (1998, 181)—and yet also (as in Shelley's original novel) as a harbinger of more-human-than-human transcendence. Dewdney's last chapter extends and extrapolates from the work of Hans Moravec—one of the first theorists of up- and downloadable consciousness, of technologically separating subjectivity from the body—to speculate fantastically and phantasmically on commodified and licensed cognition and memory and on corporate and otherwise collectivized redefinitions of consciousness and identity. Tellingly, Dewdney was a fellow with the University of Toronto's McLuhan Institute during the writing and publication of this book. (We will encounter another illustrative sample of Dewdney's work in chapter 8.)

The image of technologically transferable subjectivity, first suggested by Moravec and taken up by McLuhan, has its own rich tradition of representations in popular culture, from the esoteric nineteenth-century European fictions surveyed by Friedrich Kittler in *Gramophone, Film, Typewriter* ([1986] 1999), to the *Max Headroom* franchise of the mid-1980s; from James Whale's 1931 *Frankenstein* film, which attributes the creature's evil to Frankenstein's inadvertent transplant of a "criminal brain" into its body, to the films of Cronenberg and John Mighton's 1990 play *Possible Worlds*, which Robert Lepage adapted to film in 2000. This image has been given a Frankensteinian twist, and sometimes an accompanying McLuhanesque twist as well, in Canadian cultural production, *Videodrome*'s Brian O'Blivion being the prime example.

Toronto writer Nalo Hopkinson has adapted this image in her short story "A Habit of Waste" ([1996] 2007), in which the protagonist has purchased a new body differently racialized than her prior one and has an uncanny encounter with a stranger inhabiting her previous body: "Here was someone wearing my old cast-off. She must have been in a bad accident: too bad for the body to be salvaged. If she couldn't afford cloning, the doctors would have just downloaded her brain into any donated discard. Mine, for instance" (363). This image of transferable consciousness partakes of the story's broader theme of waste and repurposing, applied not only—although most dramatically—to embodied subjectivity, but also to more quotidian concerns like sourcing local foods. Hopkinson also connects the transferable consciousness trope to critical race, class, and gender politics. The protagonist has traded her prior black body for her current white body: "My parents had been beside themselves when they found out I'd switched bodies. . . . 'But Cyn-Cyn, that ain't even look like you!'" (365). The protagonist wonders if she can afford "another switch. It's a rich people's thing" (365). And the plot culminates in a narrowly averted sexual assault. Such intersectional political considerations are too often omitted from narratives and theorizations of posthuman subjectivity (like those by McLuhan and Dewdney); Hopkinson's construction of narrative around these "latitudes of the ex-colonised" (362) brings refreshing contextual complexity to this image and more generally to print fiction adaptations of the Frankensteinian discourse of technology, as in her celebrated debut novel, *Brown Girl in the Ring* ([1998] 2012).

In this novel, it's not the brain but the heart of a murdered protagonist that takes unexpected control of the antagonist's body into which it's been transplanted. The story envisions a walled and decaying future Toronto, in which poor, racialized inhabitants struggle to overcome a gangster, Rudy Sheldon, who runs a downtown abandoned by municipal government. Sheldon lives in the otherwise vacant CN Tower and is tasked by the provincial government to harvest a human heart for the ailing premier. Premier Uttley has refused a transplant from "the Porcine Organ Harvest Program," which a minor character describes in the book's opening scene as having "revolutionized human transplant technology" ([1998] 2012, 2); the premier argues that pig heart transplants are "immoral" and holds out for a human donor, as part of a complex political scheme to reinstate a human volunteer donor program. Ironically, her insistence leads her assistant to turn to organized crime to procure a human heart by the decidedly less ethical means of murder. The dystopian depiction of the abandoned CN Tower—an iconic image of Canadian technological nationalism (Kroker 1984, 9)—together with the plot about organ trafficking conjures the cultural spectres of both *Frankenstein* and McLuhan in the book's opening scenes. In particular, the trope of "revolutionary technology" to describe xenotransplantation condenses McLuhan's discourse of technology with *Frankenstein*'s "skeleton story" to form the premise of this surreal, Afro-Futurist novel's plot.

Surreal in a different way—but, like Hopkinson's work, critically postcolonial—is Larissa Lai's novel *Salt Fish Girl* (2002). This novel's surrealism is partly structural: it juxtaposes two stories, one set in nineteenth-century China, the other in a near-future Canadian west coast imagined, à la Gibson, as a corporatized dystopia in which migrant and racialized women—"the Sonias"—are cloned and genetically engineered to provide cheap, expendable labour for capitalist production. Late in the novel, as the two historically distant narratives begin to converge, the protagonist Miranda coerces a confession out of the markedly Frankensteinian "mad scientist" character, Flowers:

> "You don't know," said the doctor, "what monstrosities might have come of those births. . . . It was too dangerous."
> "But what you did to make me, to make us, was not? I should cut your heart out and eat it."
> "I'm a scientist, Evie. Whereas those Sonias . . . not human . . ."

The blade nicked his skin and he began to bleed. Sweat poured
down his forehead.

"Please, Evie," he said. "Didn't I save you?"

"I wish you hadn't."

"I saved you because I love you . . . daughter . . ." (2002, 255–56)

This climactic scene in Lai's novel is reminiscent of Cronenberg's plotting,
in its late presentation of a confessional explanation by a mad scientist
father figure. Miranda's apprehension of "a free society of their own kind"
comprises a postcolonial variation on Victor Frankenstein's envisioning
of "a race of devils"; Flowers's rationalization of the extermination of the
Sonias echoes Victor's destruction of the creature's "bride"; and the more
generalized, rhetorical linking of birth and monstrosity also hearkens back
to Shelley's text. Elsewhere in the novel, Lai makes the intertextual link
explicit, as Evie recounts her escape from the workers' bunker: "I crossed
a glacier to throw them off the scent. Just like *Frankenstein*, you ever read
that one? I spent a night on the glacier and came out of the mountains in
the morning" (159).

While *Frankenstein* is a prominent intertext in *Salt Fish Girl*, McLuhan
is not, although his ideas of ascendant corporatism, the communicative
capacity of things not conventionally seen as media, and technology as
manufactured monstrosity at large in a violent global village are all at work
in the novel's deep theoretical background. For one instance that condenses
these kinds of media ecology ideas, the Sonias turn their shoe manufacture
tools into a subversive messaging medium: "They had been producing
moulds for the soles of a special edition cross-trainer they dubbed 'sabots.'
Some told the stories of individual Sonias' lives, some were inscribed with
factory workers' poems" (249). The Sonias make the shoe an extension not
just "of the foot" (McLuhan and Fiore [1967] 2001, 31–32)—but, somewhat
synaesthetically, of the eye too. And the naming of the coded shoes as
"sabots" evokes the spectre of Luddism, of the sabotage of manufacturing
as a form of resistance to industrialization and technocracy.

Lai's more recent book of poetry, *Automaton Biographies* (2009), deals
more directly in the McLuhanesque problematic of the technological
construction of subjectivity. *Automaton Biographies* consists of four long
poems, or as the briefest of prefaces suggests, "four eyes," a pun on the
technological prosthesis of eyeglasses and a foreshadowing of the four
different personae that speak these poems. The first poem, "rachel," is an

acknowledged adaptation of Ridley Scott's film *Blade Runner* (1982), itself an adaptation of Philip K. Dick's 1968 novel about rebellious human-made androids, *Do Androids Dream of Electric Sheep?* (Lai 2009, 165). Lai also quotes Donna Haraway's influential "Cyborg Manifesto" as an epigraph to the poem: "There is no fundamental, ontological separation in our formal knowledge of machine and organism, of technical and organic" (quoted in Lai 2009, 11). "rachel" complements Scott's film, which focalizes its plot through the point of view of the cop Deckard as he hunts a group of rogue android "replicants," by refocalizing the story through the perspective of Rachel, a kind of "company showroom" replicant who has not rebelled and who becomes romantically involved with Deckard. The poem integrates samples of film dialogue, reimagines key scenes from Rachel's viewpoint, and fleshes out a fuller, more conflicted personality than what was scripted for her in the film:

> i rank my anger
> rail against this solitude
> was a princess with perfect clothes
> beloved daughter of a new elysium
> our flawless manufacture
> had shed earth's dirt
> imperfection's disease toil filth. (30)

Images of "manufacture," mechanism, doubling, and technology juxtapose images of childbirth and biblical creation (18, 20) to render the poem an extended interrogation of the boundary between the organic and techno-logical, the authentic and artificial: "my wires heat on semiconductor technology" (39). Lai conducts this interrogation with evocations of *Frankenstein* that are both implicit—filtered through their prior adaptation by Dick and Scott—and intertextually explicit. With reference to a "replicant"—a nominally organic if corporately cultivated creature—Lai's electric and electronic images, as in the "battery," "wires," and "super-conductor" of the above-quoted lines, both evoke the discourse and technics of electricity around which so much of *Frankenstein*'s modern mythology has been organized and at the same time seem anachronistic, even obsolete, with reference to futuristic bioengineering. Lai's poem thus encodes into its persona's very vocabulary a tension between old and new technologies, a tension common to both Shelley's novel and McLuhan's theory as well.

Lai also encapsulates the fundamentally Frankensteinian "skeleton story" of technological backlash in one of Rachel's late reflections in the poem: "faith in wiring / we illegitimate offspring / our father's lawful / monsters to turn or not to turn" (39).

Rachel's reference to "contagion" (24, 30) and her description of one of the fugitive replicants as a "dangerous twin" and "devil" (33) likewise echo the language of contagion in Shelley's novel, and more specifically the fearful fantasy of Victor Frankenstein that his work may produce a "race of devils." Lai also recontextualizes a specific clause spoken by the creature in Shelley's novel, in which he tries to assure Walton that he "will not be the instrument of future mischief"; compare Lai's stanza: "i mourn purity / in guilt in fear / my perfect construction's / the instrument of" (31).

The imagery of "rachel" draws in many of the specific technologies that—via *Frankenstein* and McLuhan—have figured largely in the modern demonization of technology in general: nuclear weaponry (33); guns (22, 26, 28); electronic media (19), including computers (13, 18); as well as capital and industrial production (13, 14, 17, 25).

Lai does not openly cite McLuhan as she cites other sources like Haraway. Lai does, however, wield the McLuhanesque Frankenpheme of technology to powerful aesthetic effect. In addition, as a long poem adaptation of a Hollywood film based on a novel (and a novel based on *Frankenstein*'s "modern myth," of course), "rachel" carries on the peculiarly McLuhanesque practice of articulating questions about the nexus of technology and identity in experimental, media-mixing, and genre-bending forms, rather than in the more straightforward expository prose of journalism and scholarship.

In this context of Canadian literary and media experimentalism, Lai's long poem neatly complements Margaret Atwood's 1966 long poem *Speeches for Doctor Frankenstein*, a chapbook on which she collaborated with Charles Pachter, who illustrated the text; *Speeches* was published in an extremely limited edition of only fifteen copies. As Lai's "rachel" gives a new voice to the creature, so *Speeches* gives a new voice to the creator: Atwood's poem retells Shelley's story mainly from the perspective of Victor Frankenstein, with occasional interjections from his creature, all in condensed poetic language. As "rachel" represents a genre- and media-traversing form of adaptation, so does *Speeches*, juxtaposing Atwood's poems with Pachter's original prints. Like Lai's poem, Atwood's foregrounds McLuhanesque images of media and power; one image of the "sparkling monster" describes "his mane electric" and "his clawed feet / kindling shaggy fires" (1966, 18). Atwood also emphasizes the Arctic setting of Shelley's story, recontextualizing it according to the early Canadian postcolonial concerns with landscape and identity that informed her landmark literary study *Survival* (1972) and related, nationally focused criticism of the period by McLuhan and Northrop Frye, among others. To this emphasis on northern landscape she brings a recognizably Canadian concern with communication media, though with no explicit use of the word *technology*. As the doctor chases the monster over "this vacant winter / plain," he recounts, "I scratch huge rescue messages / on the solid / snow" (15). These images and themes converge in the final poem: as the doctor faces "the creature, his arctic hackles / bristling," the latter "glows" and then says, "You sliced me loose // and said it was / Creation" (20).

In addition to *Speeches for Doctor Frankenstein*, Atwood's poems and other writings feature numerous such representations of technology as manufactured monstrosity. "Notes Towards a Poem That Can Never Be Written" juxtaposes images of gendered violence with reflections on the limits and complicities of media technologies: "Elsewhere, this poem must be written / as if you are already dead" ([1981] 1990, 411). Atwood's 1968 poem "It Is Dangerous to Read Newspapers" tersely and potently articulates the monstrosity of the media in its very title, which anticipates the closing lines. "It is dangerous to read newspapers," Atwood concludes. "Each time I hit a key / on my electric typewriter, / speaking of peaceful trees // another village explodes" ([1968] 1987, 59).

As Kroker observes, Atwood's oeuvre, from early on, was characterized by "searing reflections on the 'anxiety structures' at the heart of technological society" (1984, 8). As a Toronto writer who emerged in the 1960s, Atwood became acquainted with McLuhan's work early in her career. She acknowledges that her very first (and as yet still unpublished) attempt at a novel was influenced by the collage style of McLuhan's *The Mechanical Bride* (1951), which she describes as "a piece of genius" (2011). She has also defended *Survival*'s eschewal of McLuhan's theories (for which it was criticized, although not by Kroker, for whom her work and McLuhan's both belong to the Canadian tradition of thinking on technology) on the grounds that her work differed in focus from his: she jests that she "would have liked to have been Marshall McLuhan—it seemed a ton o' fun—but he had the job pretty much cornered" (quoted in Cavell 2002, 296n52).

Referring to Atwood's early reading of *The Mechanical Bride*, Cavell observes that "one is not hard-pressed to find mechanical brides"—meaning both signature Atwood protagonists and McLuhan's influence—"in a number of her literary works." He points in particular to *The Handmaid's Tale*, in which the redemption of the protagonist, Offred, "comes via the orality of the tape recording" (296n52). In addition, *The Handmaid's Tale* (1985) offers, as its fictional premises for the transformation of North American society into the misogynist dystopia of Gilead, two instances of technologies turned monstrous: the onset of ecological catastrophe that harms humans' reproductive capacity; and the freezing of women's financial savings and assets, an expropriation of wealth made possible by computerized banking technology.

Atwood's more recent dystopian fiction—the *MaddAddam* trilogy of *Oryx and Crake* (2003), *The Year of the Flood* (2009), and *MaddAddam* (2013)—also exhibits the influences of both McLuhan and Shelley in its representations of monstrous technology. In creating its postapocalyptic vision of a violent "global village" in which elite haves and impoverished have-nots are all wiped out by a human-made plague, the trilogy extrapolates from several present-day symptoms of globalization as catastrophe: tempestuous climate change; slavery and human trafficking; the increasing blurring of the social and technological line between the real and the virtual; inexorable and ubiquitous privatization and militarization; and the annexation of biological science by corporate capital.

Introducing us to the trilogy's dystopian future, *Oryx and Crake* centres on the story of Snowman, formerly known as Jimmy, who believes that he is the sole human survivor of a pandemic apocalypse and who takes it upon himself to look after the emergent society of the "Crakers," a posthuman species created by Crake, a mad scientist character, whom Jimmy had befriended in the period before the catastrophic pandemic. *The Year of the Flood* focuses on the stories of Toby and Ren, women who belong to a technophobic, neo-Luddite, Christian environmentalist sect called the God's Gardeners, another group of survivors of the pandemic, or the "Waterless Flood," as they call it (2009, 6). *MaddAddam* continues the story of Toby and Ren and fills out the story of Zeb, a street fighter and saboteur who has worked with both the God's Gardeners and Crake's coterie of biogeneticists, the MaddAddam collective. Unlike *Frankenstein*, none of the novels focalizes its narrative through the perspective of the mad scientist character, Crake, himself; instead, he looms in the stories told by the other focalizing protagonists (more like the creature in Mary Shelley's novel does).

Frankensteinian images of technology construct a stark contrast between the first volume's narrative focalizer, Jimmy, who has a hyper-mediatized, consumerist perspective, and that of the second and third volumes, Toby, who belongs to the technophobic God's Gardeners. In the first volume, the emphasis falls on the highly sophisticated technology, especially media technology and biotechnology, in which its protagonist is immersed, while the second instead emphasizes oral tradition and the Gardeners' demonization of all technology, from writing to genetic engineering. The third volume partially returns the focus to scenes and images of advanced technology, its plot moving between the bunkered world of the God's Gardeners and the technologically advanced but morally benighted wider world ruled by corporate capital that existed prior to the pandemic. This volume ultimately reveals, through Toby's account of Zeb, that the God's Gardeners are less dogmatic about technology than their preachings claim, given their leaders' own covert use of media technologies to spy on their enemies (2013, 331).

The first volume's plot of unfettered technological experimentation yielding both monsters and catastrophe constitutes an extensive adaptation of *Frankenstein*'s skeleton story; this novel also invokes *Frankenstein* twice. In one postapocalyptic scene, Snowman asks (like the creature), "Where's my Bride of Frankenstein?" (2013, 169). And, in a flashback to preapocalyptic days, Snowman recalls poring over archival footage and photos and recognizing one photo as a riot scene "from a movie remake of *Frankenstein*" (257). The second volume has no explicit *Frankenstein* references but emphasizes the manufactured monstrosity of technology in general—not merely the biotechnologies that bring about the pandemic but also technologies of representation: *"Beware of words. Be careful what you write. Leave no trails"* (6). Explicit *Frankenstein* references return in the third volume, mainly in the slang prefix "Franken" applied to genetically engineered entities, from "Frankenbacon" (2013, 19), or genetically modified pig meat, to "Frankenpeople" (19), in reference to the Crakers.

Of the three volumes, *Oryx and Crake* relates most extensively to both Shelley and McLuhan: to the former because of its Frankensteinian plot and open intertextual acknowledgements; to the latter because of its intensive use of media in character development; and to both, in the Frankenphemes of technology it thereby produces. In addition to its adaptation of *Frankenstein*'s skeleton story of manufactured monsters and ensuing mayhem, however, *Oryx and Crake* also adapts *The Last Man,* Shelley's other seminal science fiction novel, first published in 1826. *The Last Man* is set in an imagined future world of the year 2097, when the sole survivor of a pandemic plague, one Lionel Verney, is left, like Snowman, to record a posthuman future for a nonexistent posterity: "I will write and leave in this most ancient city, this 'world's sole monument,' a record of these things. I will leave a monument of the existence of Verney, the Last Man" (Shelley [1826] 1996, 364).

The doubling of Shelley's stories in Atwood's plot reflects a doubling pattern that permeates its other narrative strategies. The main characters have double names: Snowman had been Jimmy; Crake had been Glenn (an allusion to Glenn Gould, the pianist who was greatly influenced by McLuhan [2003, 70]); Oryx—like Frankenstein's creature—"didn't have a name" (90). "Snowman" is the deliberately decontextualized nickname with which Jimmy presents himself to the Crakers, in a globally warmed world where snow no longer exists. The nickname conjures monstrosity (the "abominable" snowman) and also adapts, for character development, the snowy setting of *Frankenstein*'s Arctic frame narrative. What for Shelley was a representative site of modernity—nautical circumpolar exploration—becomes for Atwood one of a myriad relics of lost language that construct Snowman's sense of subjectivity. And crucial to characterizing this subjectivity is a doubling in the narrative point of view, which is always third-person but focalized only through Snowman.

Snowman's intertextual identity and the schizoid narrative voice provide keys to the protagonist's character development, and so to the way this novel weaves a critique of new media into its Frankensteinian plot. Snowman focalizes a narrative viewpoint fraught with tropes of "dead" and new media and other McLuhan allusions. This focalization develops Snowman, and other main characters, as textual constructions, subjective palimpsests and pastiches of multiple media and references. A character who in his life before the pandemic worked, not insignificantly, in advertising, "the promotionals" (2003, 245), Snowman sees himself as a decaying web of quotations and media forms: his "head is becoming one big stash of obsolete fridge magnets" (148), which "tell a lot about a person" (347); he carries a "burning scrapbook" in his head (10), and imagines that, like *Frankenstein*'s Walton, he could "keep a diary" and "emulate the captains of ships" (40); he sees his own thoughts in a cartoonish "voice balloon" (290); his mind "replays" memories (68) like "old films" (283).

Through Snowman's thoroughly mediatized perspective, the other characters become similar media constructions: his father is a "pastiche," his mother a "Polaroid" (2003, 49); Crake belongs to an intellectual elite with "brains like search engines" (81), and he describes his bioengineering work in the language of computing: for example, installing, programming, and "editing" genetic features (303). As for Oryx, whom Snowman first sees on a porn website, he is later able "to piece her together from the slivers of her he'd gathered and hoarded" (114). The gestures of collecting—scrapbooks, fridge magnets, and website pictures—indicate how diverse and serialized media practices both mobilize a decadent consumerist culture and render it ecologically unsustainable; in addition, the different media tropes used to develop different characters underscore the differences of power among them. Crake's tropes of computing figure his rise to a leadership role in the biotech industry that centres Atwood's future socio-economic order. Oryx develops through the photographic and film media that introduce her as a pornographic object: "being in a movie . . . was doing what you were told" (139). Snowman partakes of multiple media forms, but develops with more emphasis on tropes of film and writing than on newer media: calling himself a "word person" (67), he feels acutely his difference from those with "brains like search engines" and instead indulges in "unproductive random scanning" (207).

It is in the context of old and new media generally (and *Frankenstein* texts specifically) that Snowman becomes aware of his programming by Crake to become a kind of shepherd for the posthuman Crakers: "Why am I on this earth?" he asks. "How come I'm alone?" (2003, 169). Snowman's immersion in new media fixes him as their consumer, whereas Crake learns to program and edit genetic sequences, to hack computer networks (85–86), and to "program" receptive subjects like Snowman. Snowman's serialized consumption of media, drugs, and sex turn him into a pathological kind of Everyman, the symptomatic consumer-subject of corporate capitalism not unlike that which Max Renn becomes in *Videodrome*: susceptible and subjugated to ubiquitous, "interactive" media programming. Snowman reflects how he used to "go to a movie . . . to convince himself he was part of a group" and, as the plot concludes, describes watching the end of the world "like a movie" (342) until there is "nothing more to watch" (344). Virtually addicted to print shibboleths and hardcore websites alike, Jimmy becomes deadened to affect by the simulacral ubiquity of media and, also like *Videodrome*'s Renn, becomes a killer, taking at least five lives during the plague panic, including Crake's. The similarity or even identity that, Atwood suggests, inheres between the typical postmodern consumer and the typical serial killer echoes not only Cronenberg, but also Mark Seltzer's (1993) theorization of serial killers as impersonators or mimics of human subjectivity (rather than as fully realized subjects themselves) and the broader "sociopathology of commerce" thesis of Joel Bakan, as presented in the film *The Corporation* (Achbar and Abbot 2003)—which itself also quotes *Frankenstein*, as I've analyzed elsewhere (McCutcheon 2011). *Oryx and Crake* implicates both a McLuhanesque nostalgia for print and a deregulated digital mediascape in its Frankensteinian critique of "human society" as "a sort of monster" (2003, 243).

The Year of the Flood (2009) extends this Frankensteinian premise of Atwood's fictional future—that technology, cultivated by humankind to grow monstrously autonomous, in turn renders human society equally monstrous. As told in the lore of "God's Gardeners," humankind's Promethean embrace of technology represents one step in the species' long and ongoing biblical Fall: "the Fall of Man was multidimensional . . . they fell from instinct into reason, and thus into technology" (2009, 188).

Throughout *The Year of the Flood*, less extensive and more incidental references to technology are nevertheless laced with the dread and danger with which the God's Gardeners' lore imbue it. The Gardeners regard with caution verging on terror all media technologies and practices that leave traces or store data—indeed, all fixed forms of representation: "It seemed so dangerous, all that permanent writing your enemies could find—you couldn't just wipe it away, not like a slate" (216). The Gardeners' apprehension of technology as catastrophic danger also extends to nano- and biotechnologies. The protagonist Toby worries of the activist Gardener Zeb: "Maybe he'd been black-marketing some proprietary item, such as a nanotechnology or gene splice. That could be fatal if you were caught" (119). Here, the lethality of being "caught" with nanotechnology is that of capital punishment under laws that protect corporations and their property, not the public, but the detail foreshadows the "waterless flood" of the story's title, which is what the Gardeners call the humanity-killing pandemic: as is recounted otherwise in *Oryx and Crake*, the pandemic is caused by a biological weapon that is crafted under proprietary conditions in a corporate compound, and then distributed informally, and globally, by Crake's followers.

The story's focalization through perspectives of members of an environmentalist Christian sect, with echoes of Luddite and Mennonite traditions, enables some especially vivid and resonant images to build the novel's satire on neoliberal corporate rule, consumer capitalism, and ecological devastation. One early exchange between a Gardener elder and a newcomer depicts the corporate pharmaceutical and nutrition supplement industries as a massive Frankensteinian experiment: "Those Corporation pills are the food of the dead, my dear. Not our kind of dead, the bad kind. The dead who are still alive. We must teach the children to avoid these pills" (105). Atwood does a particularly deft job of imagining an environmentalist theology that reconciles biblical teaching with modern science, in the face of ecological breakdown, via the sermons of Adam One, the sect's leader, who interprets biblical texts for modern times (which are of course also end times) with the creative latitude and critical rigour of Hebrew midrash tradition. Of the first of "the two floods"—the first being that recounted in Genesis, the second being the looming global pandemic— Adam One pointedly uses the discourse of science in describing "Man" as an "experiment": "God . . . knew something had gone very wrong with his last experiment, Man, but that it was too late for him to fix it" (90). *The Year of the Flood* both extends and complements the thematic and satirical concerns of its prequel; in contrast to the target-market consumer subjectivity of *Oryx and Crake's* narrator, *Year's* focalization through the perspectives of members of a group disenfranchised and demonized by the power centres of global capital and advanced technology enables it to articulate a far more categorical and explicit demonization, in turn, of technology in its own right—which here is the right always arrogated by capital.

The questions of whether a consumer society is made monstrous by technology, and whether technology is inherently monstrous itself, also come up insistently in the science fiction of Toronto writer Peter Watts. Trained as a marine biologist, Watts has developed an oeuvre of hard science fiction—technically and theoretically knowledgeable, but also violent and nihilistic. The Rifters trilogy—*Starfish* (1999), *Maelstrom* (2001), and *βehemoth* (2004)—is set in the mid-twenty-first century and concerns the tense operations and apocalyptic implications of a geothermal energy project based on the floor of the Pacific Ocean. The Firefall series—which consists of *Blindsight* (2006) and *Echopraxia* (2014)—is set in the very late twenty-first century; after an array of unknown satellites surrounds Earth only to burn up in its atmosphere, the spacecraft *Theseus* carries a specialized crew to the outer solar system to investigate a signal suspected to be linked to the "firefall" of alien satellites. Both series focus on protagonists who are spectacular cyborgs, featuring the cyberpunk imagery of bodily incorporated digital technology; moreover, Watts's protagonists are gradually revealed, in plot structures reminiscent of Cronenberg's, to be not only factitious but "programmed" constructs. Both series also figure technology as manufactured and monstrous, in diverse ways. The Rifters trilogy's second novel, *Maelstrom* (2001), derives its title from the novel's depiction of a chaotic, mid-twenty-first-century Internet. The first Firefall novel, *Blindsight* (2006), shows most explicitly Watts's use of the McLuhanesque Frankenpheme of technology.

The protagonist of the Rifters trilogy, Lenie Clarke, is a cyborg in that a mechanical gill has replaced one lung; this and other bodily modifications allow her, like the other "Rifter" workers, to labour in the deep ocean, outside air-pressurized human habitats. As *Maelstrom* unfolds, Lenie discovers that she has also been neurologically programmed: her memories of past trauma turn out to have been implanted, via the molecular-level manipulation of her very synapses by her employer, the energy-producing Grid Authority. She comes to this realization after leaving a trail of retaliatory destruction in her eastward trek from the Pacific coast, across North America, to seek revenge on the Grid Authority for its mismanagement of the deep sea power station: at the conclusion of the first novel, *Starfish*, the Authority defers executive operating decisions to a "head cheese" (1999, 65), a crude artificial intelligence that summarily ends station operations by destroying it, in the process unleashing earthquakes and microbial plagues all along the west coast. *Maelstrom*, then, reads much like the story of Frankenstein's creature, as Clarke wreaks widespread, violent destruction on any and all she deems responsible for her undersea abandonment, before arriving at a peripatetic knowledge of herself and her origins.

Most other characters in the Rifters and Firefall series exhibit similarly monstrous technological modifications. The Rifters antagonist Achilles Desjardins depends on digital data delivered via "optical inlays" that "projected the same images onto line-of-sight whether or not his eyelids were in the way" (2001, "Cascade"); he has also been deliberately infected with a retrovirus nicknamed "Guilt Trip" that controls his sociopathic tendencies. *Blindsight's* characters are all cyborgs or assemblages, reminiscent of Gibson's cyberpunk characters. "Jigsaw," "topology" (2006, 279), and figures of fragmentation and reassembly (315) recur as words to describe identity and subjectivity. Like Lenie in *Maelstrom*, the narrator of *Blindsight*, Keeton, gradually awakens to an alarming apprehension of the artificial nature of consciousness—not only his own, but that of the human species. Faced by a form of life that the *Theseus* crew nickname "scramblers," a radically unknowable alien life form that has superior spacefaring technology but no consciousness—"intellect but no insight, agendas but no *awareness*" (323)—Keeton concludes that human sentience is an evolutionary aberration, and subjectivity a superfluous illusion: "the homunculus behind your eyes . . . that arrogant subroutine that thinks of itself as *the* person, mistakes correlation for causality" (301). Informed not by poststructuralism but by neuroscience, Watts arrives at something very like subject theory, in *Blindsight's* contemplation of the Cartesian *cogito* as an effect mistaking itself for a cause. "Am I nothing but sparking chemistry?" Keeton asks himself (313), echoing *Frankenstein's* suggestive image of the "spark of being" (Shelley [1831] 2000, 60). The zombie images that appear throughout the book to describe creatures lacking consciousness become ironic, in their ultimate applicability to creatures possessing it.

Alongside images of automatons, "constructs," avatars, robots, AI, mosaics, biomechanics, the undead, and impersonators, Watts emphatically uses characteristically Frankensteinian pairings of zombie and vampire images in order to describe, by turns, the crew members, the alien life forms they encounter, and the human race in general. Keeton opens the novel's narration by recounting a childhood memory in which kids called him "zombie" because of brain surgery that had altered his personality: "'I think you *did* die,' said my best and only friend. . . . 'And you're some whole other kid that just, just *grew back* out of what was left'" (2006, 16).

The *Theseus* crew spends the majority of its space travel time in a cybernetically controlled dormancy that's repeatedly called being "undead" (22). Keeton describes the *Theseus* crew as "four optimized hybrids somewhere past the threshold of mere humanity, one extinct predator who'd opted to command us instead of eating us alive" (117). The last reference is to the mission commander, who is a "vampire": in Watts's fictional world, an alternate-anthropology subplot posits a race of humanoid, quasi-cannibal predators who feed on "baseline" humans—in other words, vampires. In a further Frankensteinian twist, this race of vampires has been reconstituted and rehabilitated from the novel's fictional antiquity by scientific means. As the narrator puts it, with a touch of Frankensteinian foreshadowing, to reintroduce a lost race of super-human apex predators to the general populace was "to resurrect our own nightmares in order to serve us" (59).

As a "hybrid" collective of cyborgs, zombies, and vampires, then, the *Theseus* crew comprises a microcosm of Watts's fictional world, which like Gibson's extrapolates an advanced neoliberal ruling order of corporate governance. Towards the end of the novel, a rigorous discussion two crew members have about consciousness *and mimicry of consciousness* turns to global capital: "If impersonating something increases fitness, then nature will select good impersonators over bad ones. . . . Interesting to note how many sociopaths show up in the world's upper echelons, hmm?" This passage alludes (like *Oryx and Crake*'s characterization of Snowman) to Bakan's thesis on the sociopathology of commerce (Achbar and Abbot 2003) and to vulgar social Darwinism, as the crew hypothesizes, first, that natural selection privileges impersonators for their adaptability; then, that people in power need not impersonate but rather act as models for others to impersonate; and finally, that the "ruthlessness and bottom-line self-interest" of the corporate elite may be leading it to abandon or adapt beyond sentience (via technology, not evolution), in order to more effectively increase market share and profits. "Eventually," concludes Cunningham, "there aren't any real people left. Just robots pretending to give a shit" (2006, 311). This theoretical discussion draws together the images of cyborgs, zombies, and vampires that characterize the crew and projects them more broadly onto capital and its globalized reproduction.

Watts's extensive scientific learning furnishes his novels with a vocabulary of terms, arguments, and experiments that persistently and perspicaciously interrogate the fragile boundary between the organic and technological, natural and artificial. "Are *scramblers* even alive?" Keeton asks his shipmate, a technologically augmented biologist named Cunningham. "Maybe they're just biomechanical machines." Cunningham replies: "That's what life *is*, Keeton. . . . Get your head out of the Twentieth Century" (2006, 250–51). While *Blindsight* mechanizes the human, *Maelstrom* animates the digital. The title refers to the name the novel's characters use to refer to the Internet in the mid-twenty-first century: "maelstrom," a cybernetic jungle teeming turbulently with digital artificial life (2001, "Cascade"). Overrun with rudimentarily self-aware viruses and other variously benign and malevolent software and subroutines, the "maelstrom" also constantly teeters on the edge of collapse between the ·Scylla of chaotic social complexity and the Charybdis of overburdened infrastructure resources:

> *The* Net. Not such an arrogant label, back when one was all they had.
> The term *cyberspace* lasted a bit longer—but *space* implies great empty vistas, a luminous galaxy of icons and avatars, a hallucinogenic dreamworld in 48-bit color. No sense of the meatgrinder in *cyberspace*. No hint of pestilence or predation, creatures with split-second lifespans tearing endlessly at each others' throats. *Cyberspace* was a wistful fantasy-word, like *hobbit* or *biodiversity*. . . . If you could watch the fornication and predation and speciation without going *grand mal* from the rate-of-change, you knew there was only one word that really fit: *Maelstrom*. ("Cascade")

Watts explicitly contrasts this digital "meatgrinder" against Gibson's "cyberspace," which is invoked as a quaint shibboleth, a nostalgic image of networked computing as a "wistful fantasy-word" in contrast to the stormy digital wilderness of Watts's fictional future. His hyper-Darwinian image of the near-future Internet comments satirically on the competition, adaptation, and survivalism of our present-day digital ecology, while speculating with signature scientific rigour on the Internet's technological development, particularly as a breeding ground for digitally based artificial life; like Watts's other novels, *Maelstrom* provides detailed notes and references: endnotes 25 through 30 document scientific sources for his extrapolation of the Net as "maelstrom." Furthermore, the image of the maelstrom is one of McLuhan's favourite tropes (as we saw in chapter 4):

McLuhan took the image from Poe's story "A Descent into the Maelstrom" to describe the postwar mediascape.

Blindsight also uses the word "maelstrom" to describe not the Internet, but, more literally, the turbulent and toxic storm of magnetic and radioactive forces that the *Theseus* "descends into" so it can approach and communicate with the alien craft (2006, 118). But the same kind of hostility which Watts attributes to the digital communications of his imagined midcentury world obtains for communication per se in *Blindsight*: at the novel's climax, the *Theseus* crew come to comprehend that the vapid "scramblers" have all along been treating the humans' communications as a hostile stimulus, a viral attack that provokes counterattack as the only response. To the scramblers, the humans' earnest attempts at meaningful communication only ever "mean" evidence of advanced technology and therefore hostility. The *Theseus* crew's attempts at outreach and understanding thus ironically exemplify the very threat that the crew has been led to see in the scramblers themselves, as an alien life form capable of traversing interstellar space and targeting planets bearing life: the threat constituted by advanced technology in and of itself.

"Technology implies belligerence" (44): this "mantra" recurs, verbatim and with variations, throughout the novel, an axiomatic heremeneutic of suspicion for understanding extraterrestrial life, advanced by a school of thought Keeton calls "the Historians" (80–81). "What is Human history," Keeton reflects, "if not an ongoing succession of greater technologies grinding lesser ones beneath their boots?" (79). This pessimistic caricature of history condenses and channels ideas drawn from Orwell, Darwin, the *Grundrisse* of Marx, and McLuhan's model of history as a series of different media ages punctuated by epoch-defining technological revolutions. Amidst *Blindsight*'s pervasive extrapolations of advanced technology and theorizations of technological advance, the novel draws together a vast constellation of not only scientific but cultural, historical, and political references: to the Luddite revolts (181); to McLuhan's "global village" (141); to the aforementioned *uploadable consciousness* trope, illustrated here in a virtual-reality retirement community called "Heaven"; to zombie economics and the global corporate elite as a kind of hybrid, zombie-vampire class (311–12); and even to the ancient Hebrew legend of the Golem, here a name given to a biological weapon that accelerates bone growth (292). Taken together with the plot—in which terrestrials and extraterrestrials, however incommensurate their fundamentals of being, both respond in ironic kind to advanced technology as hostile stimulus—this constellation of references renders the novel's nihilistic mantra legible as a variation on McLuhan's maxim. For Watts, "Technology implies belligerence" comes to mean something like "the medium is the message," or, closer still, like "every technology necessitates a new war" (McLuhan and Fiore 1968, 98). Not merely uninterested in but physiologically incapable of comprehending the content of the humans' benign communication, the scramblers act only on its apparently baleful form.

Blindsight thus essays an extended inquiry into the nature of sentience and humanity, in the socio-historical context of technological development and the speculative context of complicated encounter among "baseline" humans, "optimized hybrids," and radically "other" forms of life. Like Watts's other novels, *Blindsight* spectacularly foregrounds the ubiquitous, mutual interpenetration of human subjectivities and technological innovations; but *Blindsight* goes further than his other novels in theorizing and interrogating the posthuman implications of this interpenetration, which repeatedly yields the historically and culturally conjoined images of zombie and vampire, robot and cyborg, as figures of the epistemological horizon to which such interrogation leads, a horizon that remains still very much a Frankenstein barrier.

After Gibson and Cronenberg, Atwood and Watts have furnished the most extensive, explicit, and globally grounded articulations of McLuhan's Frankenpheme of technology in Canadian literature, and in Canadian science fiction literature specifically. Dominick Grace's reading of common plot points in Gibson and Cronenberg extends equally well to the Atwood and Watts works discussed here:

> Pell-mell forward action, sinister organizations, double agents, protagonists lacking crucial information until near the end of the story, complex plotting, elliptical narrative style, moral ambivalence, obscure or irreconcilable plot elements; all figure strongly in the work of both Cronenberg and Gibson, as does a focus on characters well-removed from the corridors of power (Grace 2003, para. 5)

Grace's summary also illuminates, more by flashes than by a steady light, how *Frankenstein*'s "skeleton story" of technological hubris furnishes the foundational armature on which these plot points get arranged. And to this summary must also then be added the prominent representation of media as environments, which all four authors, as well as the others discussed here, depict as monstrous technologies, implying belligerence.

Gibson's "cyberspace" and Cronenberg's *Videodrome* have thus joined McLuhan's media theory in becoming cultural and conceptual touchstones for a discourse of technology that continues to weave through representations of technology and new media to this day. The next chapter turns from literary texts to other media, to sound and image, tracking McLuhan's Frankensteinian discourse of technology into the scene of Canadian electronic dance music production and performance.

7. Is It Live or Is It Deadmau5?

Pattern Amplification in Canadian Electronic Dance Music

If David Cronenberg's 1983 film *Videodrome* and William Gibson's 1984 novel *Neuromancer*, both globally popular texts, establish a pattern of McLuhanesque Frankensteins that refracts throughout Canadian popular culture, then electronic dance music (EDM) culture is a lower-profile but profoundly rich and resonant subcultural scene for reproducing, recirculating, and further amplifying this pattern. Some of this scene's adaptations of *Frankenstein* and articulations of technology discourse occur textually and linguistically, but often they emerge in audio and visual representations that dramatically exhibit and further circulate the McLuhanesque Frankenpheme of technology. This chapter sketches some background for contextualizing EDM culture both globally and in Canada and considers in detail two exemplary Canadian EDM acts: the Paladin Project (a.k.a. Len Jaroli), an underground DJ act; and the more recently established but already globally successful Canadian EDM producer Deadmau5 (a.k.a. Joel Zimmerman). These examples illustrate and dramatize dance culture's Frankensteinian contexts and put McLuhan's theories into dance-floor practice. The chapter then turns to a theatrical production steeped in EDM culture—Matthew MacFadzean's fringe play *richardthesecond*—to consider how EDM culture engages with other sites of cultural production and scene making to further disseminate McLuhan's Frankensteinian discourse of technology.

"Experimenting on their own nervous systems": EDM Culture's "Techno-Romanticism"

A backgrounder on EDM might be helpful to begin with. Today's dance culture is both diversified and robust, building on more than half a century of dance scenes that have pivoted on DJ culture and the playback of recorded music: from postwar US record hops and Jamaican sound system clashes to the rapid rise and exaggerated "death" of disco, which actually lived on in the electronic sounds of Chicago house, Detroit techno, and New York garage. These sounds stayed very marginal subcultures in North America through the 1980s and 1990s, while becoming massively popular in Europe, especially the UK, where rave culture spawned huge dance parties, some amassing tens of thousands of partygoers for a night or a weekend. By the mid-1990s, UK rave culture had become a target of quite draconian neoliberal regulation and suppression, such as the Criminal Justice Act of 1994, which outlawed a gathering of ten or more listeners to music "characterized by repetitive beats." UK raves put together black American dance music, traveller culture nomadism, and nascent new media technologies like cellphones and the Internet.

North American rave culture emerged in the wake of UK rave but modelled itself more openly on the mediatized scene making of 1960s counterculture: just as 1960s counterculture adopted McLuhan's then-current ideas for its psychedelic scene making, so did 1990s rave culture adopt McLuhan's then-revived ideas for its *cyber*delic scene making. Like UK raves in the mid-1990s, towards the turn of the millennium North American raves were subjected to extraordinarily suppressive policy and policing as they gained greater popularity; they became, in effect, a domestic front in the US "war on drugs." The globalized dance music industry fell into an economic slump in the mid-2000s, but, since around 2010, dance music has become much more firmly established in the pop soundscape, as heard by the prevalence of electronic dance songs in commercial, "hit format" FM radio. If the purported death of disco was belied by the rise of raves, the decline of raves amidst bad press, moral panics, and legislative zeal has in turn been reversed by EDM. Simon Reynolds argues that some of the success of EDM might be attributed to a "rebranding coup" that evokes cultural legitimacy, where raves formerly signalled transgressive excess: "What were once called 'raves' are now termed 'festivals'; EDM is what we used to know by the name of techno. Even the drugs have been rebranded: 'molly,' the big new chemical craze, is just ecstasy in powder form (and reputedly purer and stronger) as opposed to pills" (2012, para. 1). And Deadmau5, a.k.a. Joel Zimmerman, a producer from a working-class Niagara Falls background, tours dance floors around the world, wearing a cartoonish, vaguely trademark-infringing mouse-head helmet as the face of disco's latest resurrection.

The Frankensteinian language of death and resurrection in dance culture articulates three of this culture's constitutive contexts: the oscillating popularity of dance sounds in the global music market, as outlined above; the culture's "techno-Romantic" representations of excess as experiment; and its uses and fetishizations of technology in reconfigurations of "liveness" in music media and performance practices.

The long-running historical predisposition of western modernity to treat bodily affective music with suspicion or outright hostility (McClary 1994) has made social dance scenes reliable and routine targets for various kinds of public controversy and moral panic. In disco and its electronic successors, the racializing anxieties once visited on rock and roll became compounded by heteronormative anxieties: early house music was reviled by the music press as not just a fad but as an unexpected return of disco, and moreover a kind of disco that amplified a stark, alien minimalism of drum loops, bass lines, and other machine sounds and thus exaggerated the foundational *queerness* of disco. As rave culture codified and popularized (even while sometimes strenuously disavowing) the interface between electronic dance music and MDMA or "Ecstasy," the moral panics that reductively caricatured rave culture as drug culture (from the UK's 1994 Criminal Justice Act to the turn-of-the-millennium "war on raves" in North America) traded on myths and misconceptions about MDMA—for example, as depersonalizing hallucinogen not self-affirming empathogen— that positioned MDMA as a "synthetic" or "designer" drug. Philip Jenkins notes that the rhetoric of "designer" drugs

> is Promethean, portraying scientists as irresponsibly venturing into realms of knowledge not meant for human beings. . . . The Frankenstein image is so frequently cited in discussions of synthetic drugs because, as in the original tale, a quest for human improvement results instead in the creation of what are identified as terrifying figures. . . . Through chemical technologies, drug users abandon full humanity in a quest for a superior state. (1999, 8)

This "quest" activity has long structured raving, clubbing, and other social dance leisure activities and is organized not according to chemical technologies alone but in concert with cultural technologies, chiefly music. This activity is what Reynolds calls "techno-Romanticism": the pursuit of the palace of wisdom on a path of excess "expressed in the discourse of science and technology," as in Iggy Pop's reflection on fronting for the Stooges by taking so many drugs that, as he puts it, "I sublimated the person" and "became a human electronic tool" (quoted in Reynolds 1999, 200). Iggy Pop's language and performance practice exemplify the way in which subcultural scene makers use "the discourse of science and technology" to represent practices of music making—and drug taking: "In rave," Reynolds writes, "kids play the roles of both Frankenstein and the monster, experimenting on their own nervous systems" (1999, 204).

Techno-Romanticism also aptly describes the aesthetics of EDM's musical foundation in Afro-Futurism, the tradition of black Atlantic music- and scene-making in which producers and performers like George Clinton and Kool Keith adopt "mad scientist" personae and in which marginalized and racialized dancers breakdance or jack their bodies with stylized robotic moves, in empowering practices of "technological identification" whereby "the fearful paradox of the technological age, that machines created as artificial slaves will somehow enslave and even mechanize human beings, is ritually enacted at the discotheque" (Hughes 1994, 151). About rave more specifically, Reynolds adopts a more negative view in describing raving as a zombie-like "living death" (1997, 102), arguing that the dance-drug interface is "an engine for programming sensations . . . connotative of enthrallment, of loss of control" (109).

These Frankensteinian figures of dance music's "techno-Romanticism" reverberate with representations of EDM music making, performance, and consumption in terms of "liveness" and death: representations of EDM as a monstrous synthesis of sampled fragments (Reynolds 1998, 45); as autonomous technology, where "the sequencer and sampler take over" (Chapman 2002, 17); as "soulless" artifice versus authentic presence— recording versus "liveness." The conventional performance of EDM by DJs revolves around a paradox of *live playback*: the improvised, responsive, site-specific selection and sequencing of tracks. EDM culture illustrates Philip Auslander's argument that "the 'live' has always been defined as that which can be recorded" (1999, 86)—and, moreover, that "liveness" marks "a site of anxiety, an anxiety that infects all who have an interest in maintaining the distinction between the live and the mediatized" (87). Following theorists like Benjamin and Derrida, scholars of media and culture have observed the reconfigurations of aura and authenticity not only between unmediated presence and mediation but also between different kinds of media (for instance, Bolter et al. 2006). Sarah Thornton documents these reconfigurations in dance culture, from early twentieth-century musicians organizing against jukeboxes and DJs to DJs themselves, by century's end, dreading the "death of vinyl" (1996, 64) amidst the rise of CDs and digital sound. "Since the mid-eighties," Thornton writes, "'live' qualities have been increasingly attributed to recorded events," while "music performances have become more reliant on recording" (85).

EDM's estranging reconfiguration of "liveness" converges commodity fetishism and the technological sublime: media live and die and achieve uncanny, monstrous effects, confusing the biological and the technological. From techno-Romantic representations of EDM consumption in terms of experiment and automatons to techno-fetishizing representations of EDM production in terms of automatic yet autonomous technology, dance culture is fraught with the discourse of technology as Frankensteinian monstrosity. These historical and discursive contexts thus suggest how the McLuhanesque Frankenpheme of technology courses through the technologically immersed and experimental culture of EDM, as becomes more concretely illuminated in the work of particular EDM cultural producers: the Paladin Project and Deadmau5.

The Paladin Project: "You are a big rechargeable battery"

Many DJs and producers before Deadmau5 have used costume and technical spectacle in their acts and their performing personae: perhaps none more so than a fixture in Canada's dance underground, the Paladin Project, a.k.a. Len Jaroli. From 1996 until 2015, Jaroli donned (and incessantly modified, tweaked, and revamped) an elaborate cyborg costume with which he DJ'd as "the Paladin Project" at raves and other dance events across North America.

Paladin's costumes both exaggerated and satirized the militarized hypermasculinity that has long dominated DJ culture. Over the twenty years of Paladin's performance career, Jaroli constantly modified his costume and its attendant array of technical gear. The first Paladin performance I attended was at the "E Space" venue in Toronto's West End, for a Hallowe'en party in 1997. Paladin's set included samples of the "Imperial March" anthem from *Star Wars*, and his costume consisted of bright, day-glow orange camouflage fatigues, repurposed sports equipment, and a gas mask. At the end of the 1990s, the costume assumed a storm-trooper or riot-police look, complete with helmet. Jaroli also adapted the show to specific occasions; for instance, at a Hallowe'en party at a Richmond Street club in 1999, Paladin replaced his helmet with a fanged, bug-eyed alien mask. By the time Jaroli retired the Paladin Project, in 2015, it had reached its "6.3" iteration, which exaggerated the storm-trooper militarism of the suit, sound, and show and featured a helmet that displayed an Expressionistic skeletal mask (figs. 4 and 5).

Figure 4 The Paladin Project in performance, circa 2011. Paladin's version 6 iterations featured a grotesque monster mask as well as the machine-military costume and props. Photo courtesy of Ben Ripley Photography. Copyright © 2011 by Ben Ripley.

Paladin's performance persona adapted the name, cultivated anonymity, and vigilante image from CBS's 1957 TV series *Have Gun Will Travel* (Alan Filewod, pers. comm, 11 June 2003)—but gave it a science fiction spin. Paladin's costume combines a kind of "Robocop" imagery of body armour, gadgetry, and weaponry, with masks ranging from gas mask, to face-plated helmet, to grotesque, grimacing monster. Paladin's costume also incorporates media: mounted cameras, lasers, and screens; built-in monitors and microphone; and even an FM transmitter. Evoking both Marx's vampire image of capital and *The Matrix*'s image of bodies as batteries, the Paladin "darkandhard.ca" website that was up in 2006–7 stated: "As far as PALADIN is concerned . . . you are a big rechargeable battery that actually enjoys having the life force pounded out of you. The harder you dance the harder PALADIN plays."

Figure 5 The Paladin Project in performance, circa 2011. Photo courtesy of C. Jaroli. Copyright © 2011 by C. Jaroli.

Like many cultural practitioners, Paladin embraced social media in the later 2000s, discontinuing his independent "darkandhard.ca" website in favour of the newer affordances of Facebook and Soundcloud, where "P4L4DiN" and "thepaladinproject" accounts, respectively, remain operative as of this writing and archive a great deal of photos and mixes from various performances over the years. The "darkandhard" site, though, also included a "Technical Data" web page that detailed the tech specs that went into the Paladin Project, which was at that time in its "5.1" version (Paladin 2006b). The description is worth quoting at some length, given the meticulous attention to creative and highly technologized detail that Jaroli put into developing and delivering his DJ act:

> After over 7 years of development, The PALADIN Project has now released the latest version of the worlds first P.rototype A.rtificial L.ifeform A.nd D.ata I.ntegration N.etwork: The PALADIN 5.1 Advanced Prototype. Music programming is best described as dark and hard, and utilizes a combination of vinyl / original tracks and a MC-303. . . . The PALADIN 5.1 system also includes a custom made wireless F.L.I.R. (forward looking infra red) camera system. Utilizing advanced technology similar to that used by military and government agencies. Totally wireless . . . with a range beyond 100 meters, this custom made one of a kind camera system emits no (negligible) visible light—yet the 58 high power infra red LED's provide true night vision images on projector screens as well as giving a never before seen view of the dance floor from the PALADIN system itself. In addition to wireless video output, the PALADIN 5.1 system is also equipped with a stereo FM transmitter and signal booster. The capability of the PALADIN system to broadcast on any standard FM frequency adds yet another layer to the complete experience. The standard configuration currently allows participants to hear discreet voice communication from PALADIN. With an on board voice processor and noise cancelling microphone; PALADIN can walk and talk to any individual with a receiver . . . or feed the signal to the main system. At larger events, this capability can be configured to independently provide music to anyone with a FM radio—within the operational range of the on-board 4ft antenna—or—at a proximity close enough to PALADIN to hear the onboard 10 watt amplified speaker system. To complement the audio, is an on-board visual system unlike any other. The primary component is an arm mounted—5mW—bright green—DPSS laser system. This compact laser is capable of projecting a beam over 4000 meters away, and is visible without the augmentation of a fog machine. On the chest is a 1.3" LCD screen as well as a 10 band graphic spectrum analyzer for real time visual interpretation of sound at any volume. . . . Completing the equipment list is a CSA° approved helmet with a custom mesh

front that blocks all light including camera flashes at close range as well as concealing a Sony® VDR700 custom headphone monitor. . . . The PALADIN 5.1 prototype demonstrates what is possible when advanced technology and unrestrained creativity are combined into one complete package. (2006b)

These technical details suggest that Paladin's shows came to consist of more than music mixes played by a DJ in costume. In particular, the systems that fostered interactivity—like short-range broadcasting, audio input and output feeds, and patches for them into the sound system used for DJing—played creatively with the "interactivity" for which many digital media and processes have been widely lauded (from games, to message boards, to social networks). The technological sophistication of Paladin's act suggests not only creativity but considerable cost; but the act proved successful enough in the dance underground that from the mid-1990s to the mid-aughts, DJing was Jaroli's only employment and source of income (Paladin 2006a, para. 8). Paladin's performance act, like much of rave culture more generally, extended the earlier 1960s counterculture's McLuhan-influenced practices of intensely stimulating and professedly interactive multimedia experimentalism (Rycroft 1998).

The creative cybernetic details that made Paladin both a unique dance music performer and an eminently McLuhanesque multimedia monster also made him a favourite act in the North American electronic dance scene. As evinced in the above passage, and in numerous statements and samples during performances, Paladin dramatized the technological sublime. Paladin's technological sublime is a figure of the "fetishism of mechanical power," with music sets that not only drove intense audience engagement on the dance floor but also sometimes represented abstract musical narratives of power, paranoia, and panic. In a 2006 interview, Jaroli theorized that

PALADIN's sole purpose is to generate as much energy as possible for its consumption—using the energy to increase its own output. If you don't like PALADIN . . . leave . . . because if you aren't a power source then you're taking up space. . . . If you get into a PALADIN set—you don't just "dance." You become one of a thousand screaming dancers with clenched fists and stomping feet . . . an incredibly powerful—and unique experience. (Paladin 2006a, para. 10)

In this interview, Jaroli also expressed his preference for surprising new audiences over playing to established followings: "A big show in a city that has never seen PALADIN is what I love above all" (para. 25). This preference suggests that surprise and novelty were key performance values in Paladin's audiovisual construction of technological spectacle; surprise and novelty are analogous to and associated with the elements of shock and revolution that are integral to the discourse of technology, as chapters 1 and 3 showed.

Paladin also dramatized novelty, surprise, and the trope of "revolutionary technology" in his performance by continually changing, modifying, and "upgrading" the costume and multimedia show. Moreover, the changes in Paladin's costume, from the day-glow fatigues, football gear, and gas mask of the mid-1990s to the cybernetic storm-trooper armour and death's-head helmet of the 2010s not only demonstrated Jaroli's technical creativity with new media technologies, they also spoke sometimes to changes in the political economy of Toronto's dance scene over the years. The turn of the millennium saw a spotlight put on Toronto's rave scene, as city officials banned raves from public municipal sites, provincial legislators proposed bills to suppress dance events, the Toronto police began a systematic crackdown on—and shakedown of—Toronto rave organizers and partygoers, and the press and media consequently shone a national spotlight on raves in Toronto and across the country. Amidst the crackdown, in early 2000, the chief of the Toronto police proposed to dramatically change the force's uniform to adopt a more paramilitary image; the proposal drew public criticism for perceptions the new uniform looked too fascist, even neo-Nazi (Blackwell 2000, A5). Around the same time, Paladin debuted the "5.0" iteration of his project: this was the first iteration that introduced the storm-trooper look, departing drastically from the previous fatigues-and-gas mask ensemble with a black, armoured suit, helmet, backpack, and body-mounted laser. In the context of the cops' crackdown and their chief's somewhat ridiculous sartorial proposal, Paladin's futuristic riot-cop look seemed hardly coincidental and caused a sensation on the dance floor. On ending a set, Paladin would often exit the DJ booth to stalk slowly around the dance floor, turning a moment of audience appreciation into a parody of police surveillance. After the summer of 2000, the dramatically increased visibility of actual, paid-duty police officers at dance parties (a requirement imposed by the force in an attempt to make raves prohibitively expensive via the cost of hiring more paid-duty officers) lent Paladin's costume and dance floor patrol a pointed, carnivalesque irony, calling the crowd's attention to the escalating militarization of leisure space and to the studied performativity of the officers' own dress, presence, and actions amidst the dancers and partygoers.

Paladin's dramatization of the McLuhanesque Frankenpheme of technology in performance also emerged in the music around which his performance practice revolved (and which can still be heard in several of his DJ sets that have been archived online). Paladin consistently described the music style he played as "dark and hard": house and techno characterized by 140 beats-per-minute tempos, driving 4/4 kick drums often given echo effects to make them stomp harder, distorted Roland 303 bass lines, minor-key strings sections and synthesizer riffs, and a range of Gothic and dystopian sound effects like horror film samples, sirens, and gunfire. Early Paladin sets sometimes included 45 rpm hardcore tracks played at 33 rpm, and a favourite mantra of the performer is this: "Faster isn't harder. Harder is harder." A track often heard in Paladin sets of the later 1990s was Brainbug's "Nightmare" (1996), and samples from the *Nightmare on Elm Street* films recur frequently in later mixes (Paladin 2014). Paladin's 4.5 mix from 1999 opens with an extremely slowed-down playback of the lyrics from the Foremost Poets' 1998 track "Moon-Raker," in which a man's voice (in Paladin's mix slowed to a muddy growl) tells the audience to "remain calm" and not leave the dance floor while the DJ tests the sound system for "an unidentified frequency" that "has become a threat . . . used by a secret society in conjunction with Lucifer to lure and prey on innocent partygoers, with hypnotism, syncroprism, tricknology, lies, scandal, and pornography" (1998). This sample has been repurposed extensively in EDM to the point of becoming cliché; Paladin's use defamiliarizes the sample by pitching it way down so the voice becomes a cadaverous croak. The pun on "technology"—"tricknology"—becomes a self-reflexive comment on Paladin's own performance practice and an explicit invocation of the discourse of technology whose monstrousness his whole performance is devoted to dramatizing. The track that follows this ominous opening amplifies the Frankenpheme of "tricknology" by starting with a low-frequency synth note that sounds intermittently, evoking an alarm klaxon, as a low voice starts to punctuate the bar changes by repeating only the word "annihilating," before a spare, echoing kick drum drops to establish the tempo and gradually becomes syncopated with an additional drum track that sounds like simulated machine gun fire. A subsequent track in the mix samples a similarly down-pitched voice that asks the listener, in a guttural growl, the popular dance-floor question that here sounds like a rudimentary Turing test: "Can you feel it?" (1999).

Paladin's music selections and sequencing, taken together with his spectacular stage show, conjure a techno-Romantic, dystopian sound-scape of beat-regimented hedonism, industrial and postindustrial sounds of automation and militarization, and pervasive Gothic atmospherics. The "hard" in Paladin's brand signals, in a gender-coded way, his music's and his show's "hardcore" credentials: the music is audibly abrasive, even hostile, an acquired taste, even for fans of other EDM styles like house and trance; it is a definitively "underground," non- or anticommercial sound. And yet at the same time, this music also sounds like the culmination of industrial capital in automation verging on artificial intelligence, bolstered by inten-sifying militarism and securitization. Paladin's music is resolutely, critically "underground," and yet at the same time it also sounds like a virtual sound-track for neoliberalism. The Paladin Project's coherent and detailed creative presentation of both a militarized cyborg figure and a dystopian soundscape made his act a unique dance-scene act and a profoundly McLuhanesque media monster: a DJ's dramatization of the "rise of the machine" and its monstrous takeover. In the process, the Paladin Project prefigured the more recent and more globally recognized music and performance of another Canadian EDM artist, Deadmau5, a.k.a. Joel Zimmerman.

Deadmau5: "An unhealthy obsession with technology"

While, largely because of the more hardcore style of his music, Paladin stayed very much in EDM's underground niche, Deadmau5 has achieved global popularity for more accessible productions, with slower tempos (around 128 bpm), more major-chord melodies and harmonies, and sung lyrics. But like Paladin—and like French house producers Daft Punk, who also combine costume and spectacle to play on human-machine ambi-guities (2005)—Deadmau5 plays, in his performance, production, and promotion, on EDM's structuring tensions between liveness and death. Zimmerman says the "Deadmau5" pseudonym derives from his once having found a dead rodent in his computer. That which is named "dead" plays "live" (like the Grateful Dead); the name also connotes "mouse" as computer peripheral, the device that translates the digits into the digital, a McLuhanesque "extension" of the hand. The mouse is a synecdoche for the hand; here, the dead mouse is a synecdoche for the dead hand, a complex evocation at once of the problem of "liveness" in electronic music, of the disembodied yet autonomous hand known as "Thing" from *The Addams Family*, and of "Dead Hand," the nickname of the Soviet military computer system programmed to launch nuclear missiles across the northern hemisphere in a war scenario where human command had been wiped out (Thompson 2009).

Figure 6 Deadmau5 live in San Francisco, at Facebook's F8 conference, 25 March 2015. Deadmau5's signature mouse helmet requires him to see what he's doing via video, not with his own eyes. Note, too, the prominence of recording and playback technology, here, both on the stage and among the audience. Photo CC2.0 licensed from Maurizio Pesce. Copyright © 2015 by Maurizio Pesce.

Deadmau5's costume is a helmet shaped like a cartoon mouse head; the mouse icon has become recognizably Deadmau5's own brand while also clearly evoking, in a potentially trademark-infringing way, the image of Mickey Mouse (fig. 6)—clearly enough that in September 2014, Disney launched a trademark action against Deadmau5, who counter-sued Disney for unlicensed use of his music; ultimately, the two parties called the whole thing off (O'Reilly). The Deadmau5 helmet and Zimmerman's visible tattoos of video game icons evoke the formal basis of his music in the assembly of samples, including some appropriated ones.

Deadmau5 produces house music of the "electro" and "progressive" subgenres—popular dance music styles that are staples at nightclubs, especially the major clubs of Ibiza, London, and Miami that are central scenes and tastemakers for the global EDM economy. Although it is a more accessible and less alienating sound than Paladin's, Deadmau5's music, like Paladin's, features Gothic motifs and textures, including explicit references to horror figures like Frankenstein. The 2010 track "Cthulhu Sleeps" evokes the monster of Lovecraft's story. (Deadmau5's Twitter account sometimes states his location as "Rlyeh": the undersea city that houses Cthulhu in H. P. Lovecraft's 1928 story "The Call of Cthulhu.") "Cthulhu Sleeps" uses a sampled vocal "whoop" that we also hear in Armand Van Helden's "Witch Doktor," which itself also samples Parliament's *The Clones of Dr. Funkenstein* (1976)—a record also sampled by Deadmau5 in a different track, the eponymous "Dr. Funkenstein," in which the only lyric is the utterance of this name, in a sonorous bass voice. Deadmau5's "Dr. Funkenstein" has since been widely remixed; for Hallowe'en 2009, Deadmau5 released the *Dr. Funkenstein Remixes* EP (2009a), featuring the original track together with nine remixes by other EDM producers, in a range of EDM styles.

Gothic and horror references abound in other Deadmau5 tracks. "Complications" (2008) includes the metronome pulse of an electrocardiogram, which flatlines during sequences when the kick drum cuts out, and then stops when the kick drum resumes, as though the drum beat replaces the heartbeat; the arrangement signals an oscillation from life to death, and back to life—or its digital simulation. The 2009 track "Ghosts 'n' Stuff" propelled Deadmau5 to chart-topping fame; its lyrics open with a disorienting image of shared disembodiment: "It's been so long I've been out of my body with you" (2009b). The song's hook is a heavy organ riff (which in itself evokes *Frankenstein*, according to the tradition of organ instrumentation discussed in chapter 2). The companion track "Moar Ghosts 'n' Stuff" (2009c) opens with the funeral march by Chopin and modulates this into the organ hook of "Ghosts."

The 2012 track "The Veldt" extends these thematics of death and technics in its adaptation of the eponymous Ray Bradbury story, and its unsettling juxtaposition of major-chord melody, bucolic samples of bird- and insect song, and subtly gruesome, dystopian lyrics: "Happy life with the machines . . . Happy technology / Outside the lions run / Feeding on remains" (2012b). In an interview with CBC, Zimmerman (2012a) described "The Veldt" as an homage to the Bradbury story "in which an unhealthy obsession with technology ends up having murderous consequences." He said that part of his intent with the song was to renew interest in that story. In a way both suggestive and symptomatic of the discourse of technology as Frankenpheme, the interviewer then asked Zimmerman:

> Interviewer: Do you have an unhealthy obsession with technology?
> Zimmerman: Yeah, absolutely. It's incredibly unhealthy.
> Interviewer: Tell me how it's unhealthy.
> Zimmerman: Well, because I have absolutely no social skills whatsoever. I cannot unplug. It's not like I'm addicted to it, like a drug . . . well, maybe I am. (2012a)

As if to deliberately overstate the point, Zimmerman subsequently answered his cellphone while still on the air.

Deadmau5's performance aesthetic and his productions alike thus dramatize and thematize the Frankensteinian problematic of life, death, and undeath. And in June 2012, Zimmerman reanimated the debate in popular music over "liveness" versus playback: in a *Rolling Stone* interview (Eells 2012), he claimed that EDM performers—including himself—"just hit play"—that is, preprogram whole sets—instead of improvising a mix of tracks. In follow-up music press coverage and social media, Zimmerman tried to clarify that he was referring specifically to EDM producers who are expected to perform at concerts and are held—absurdly, he holds—to expectations to perform music "live" the way singer-songwriters would: that is, to play music, not to play it back: "we all hit play," he said (Deadmau5 2012c). But Deadmau5's claim that he could show up at a gig, press the spacebar, and then just fist-pump for the whole show touched a nerve with DJs as well as producers (thus showing some slippage and identification between these two roles, which have long overlapped in the EDM economy). On Twitter, Canadian expat DJ Sydney Blu continued the debate, writing: "Some idiot accused me of prerecording my set last night. That's the funniest thing ever because I am one of the few djs that still beat match" (@SYDNEYBLU, 23 December 2012, 11:13 am).

In this way, Deadmau5 is extending not just recent traditions in Canadian EDM, but a broader legacy of McLuhan-informed Canadian music making, like that demonstrated by Glenn Gould. But while Gould famously forsook the live concert for the recording studio, Zimmerman, conversely, brings the recording studio to the concert. In the perennial crisis of "liveness" in music, Zimmerman's "just hit play" comments transposed the terms of this crisis more deeply into the already mediatized context of EDM and inflamed deep-seated and long-standing anxieties over technology as labour's monstrous supplement, which perennially recur in music as new instruments, production processes, and performance practices alternately assist or supplant human labour (Porcello 1991). For those who don't know or don't like EDM, Deadmau5's remark feeds these anxieties and plays into stereotypes of DJs as doing work other than music making, and of EDM as something other than music. What does Deadmau5's admission leave the performing body to do? To parody liveness, to act as conductor? As Bolter et al. (2006) argue, "aura" is now just a design parameter for digital media. Opting out of the aura of liveness, it seems, has hurt neither Zimmerman's touring schedule nor his music sales.

Deadmau5's performance practice includes a further detail that furnishes an apt coda to this discussion: when he performs while wearing the version of the mouse-head helmet that lights up with LEDs, he cannot actually see out of the helmet with his own eyes. Instead, he wears video goggles. As he explained in his CBC radio interview:

> Zimmerman: I got a camera coming out of this thing so I can see my hands—
> Interviewer: So wait a sec—there's a camera in the mouse head?
> Zimmerman: Yeah, there's video goggles in the mouse head, so I'm looking through video goggles and there's a camera down here by my neck.
> Interviewer: You're *watching a video* of what is *in front of you*.
> Zimmerman: Yeah, it's really weird. And there's a two millisecond lag on it and it drives me crazy. (2012a)

Identifying hypermediatization with intoxication, and technology with addiction, and making and playing music in ways that amplify the Frankensteinian figuration of technology, Zimmerman as Deadmau5 thus represents a recent, globally popular contribution to the tradition of McLuhanesque *Frankenstein* adaptations in Canada's EDM scene. As Canadian representatives of a globalized EDM culture characterized by "techno-Romanticism" and immersive mediatization, the Paladin Project and Deadmau5 problematize anxieties over liveness and labour in their productions and performance practices that amplify McLuhan's Frankensteinian discourse of technology.

Despite EDM culture's organization around subcultural capital and insulating "gatekeeping" practices and discourses, it is a fundamentally social cultural scene; and while its heavy investments in digital media complicate and problematize "liveness," by the same token they thus show that EDM culture is a profoundly performance-oriented scene. These social and performative dimensions of EDM scene-making have facilitated its cross-pollination with other sites and forms of cultural production in Canada; in the process, EDM culture's performance practices, reference points, and techno-Romantic aesthetics—with their emphasis on the McLuhanesque Frankenpheme of technology—have spread to and been adapted by other sub- and popular cultural scenes and processes. One salutary example of this cross-pollination is the fringe play *richardthesecond* (2001), by Toronto-based actor and playwright Matthew MacFadzean.

"The new celebrity is gonna be genetic pioneers"

MacFadzean's *richardthesecond*, first performed at the 2001 Summer-Works festival in Toronto, is an intensely intertextual production: an acknowledged adaptation of Shakespeare and an implicit adaptation of Mary Shelley's "skeleton story," with numerous nods to *Videodrome* and Toronto's rave scene, among a dizzying array of other popular cultural points of reference. The play distills its manic mix of subcultural, pop-cultural, and canonical sources into an eminently McLuhanesque meditation on new media technologies and their monstrous implications.

richardthesecond is a one-actor play, and as the plot unfolds this dramaturgy assumes a rich irony. The protagonist, "Richie Excellent," introduces himself as a cocky young hipster-raver; he tells the audience of his ambition to make a difference in the world, amidst a tangle of segues and non-sequiturs about *Star Wars*, *Electric Circus*, and other pop culture touchstones. Between his live monologue and video footage, which includes speeches by a "mad scientist" character named Gene, we gradually learn that Richie has been cloned as part of a research project led by Gene. In the first pages of the script, Gene's references to Darwin and eugenics frame the project that Richie ultimately describes very much according to the familiar Frankenphemes that have historically articulated public concerns with experiments in cloning (Morton 2002, Turney 1998): later in the script, video footage shows "protesters holding placards reading 'Stop Cloning Now'" (MacFadzean 2001, 18). Gene's introductory references to Darwin and natural selection also bear self-reflexively on MacFadzean's play as an *adaptation* in its own right (albeit of the cultural not biological kind). By the end of the play, which concludes Richie's search for identity and ethics among the simulacra of postmodernity, neither the audience nor Richie himself knows if he is the original Richie, or the second.

The play's similarities to *Videodrome* abound, from its opening on a TV screen showing noise not signal, to the O'Blivionesque (which is to say McLuhanesque) restriction of Gene's role to a posthumous, televised presence and his characterization as a mad scientist preoccupied with human adaptation, to Richie's references to TV as a kind of surrogate parent figure: "I sorta . . . stumbled onto destiny. Birthed by must-see tee-vee" (MacFadzean 2001, 10). Like O'Blivion, Gene only ever appears on a video screen, as a recording, and he provides the explanation of the protagonist's monstrous origins. As in *Videodrome*, this explanatory sequence occurs late in the plot, a revelation of Richie's true, "second" nature as a clone. Something of O'Blivion's apocalyptic tone—which itself echoes McLuhan's tendency to generalize his claims about media into nothing less than epochal terms—resonates in a late montage sequence wherein a TV announcer welcomes the audience to "the Next Age of Man" (16). Like O'Blivion, a great deal of Richie's identity is bound up in a videotape library, in this case, a complete collection of every episode of the TV show *Electric Circus* (which was Toronto's answer to US dance shows like *Solid Gold* and *Soul Train*): "I watch *Electric Circus* to know I'm alive," Richie asserts, echoing O'Blivion's claim in *Videodrome* that "television is reality."

Like Atwood's Snowman, Richie is a collage of a character, a pastiche of pop-culture and media references, one of which is Cronenberg's film *Dead Ringers* (which Richie cites to describe Gene). As Richie's role in the cloning experiment becomes clear, he also becomes his own doppelgänger: unsure whether he's the first or second Richie, he adds that additional "me's" will be built "at age 2, 20, 40, 60, 80" (20). "I'm tellin ya," he boasts, "the new celebrity is gonna be genetic pioneers, and if that's the case I'm like grade seven Canadian history" (21). Apprehending the Frankensteinian character of his fate in terms of media—*and the mediatization not simply of performance but of subjectivity itself*—Richie expects that he will eventually become downloadable (21), describes himself as a "high-speed connection," as a "telegram" (23), and, more abstractly and ambiguously, as simply "shared" (27).

Recognizing that the play's compulsive referentiality risks dating it, the script's stage directions call for "pop culture updates" as "necessary" (2), thus rendering a constellation of script details subject to both obsolescence and interchangeability—and therefore amplifying the Frankensteinian resonance of the play's intense intertextuality. This intertextuality encompasses echoes of and allusions to other previous *Frankenstein* adaptations: not only *Videodrome* but also *Max Headroom* (in early footage of Gene, edited to loop, repeat, and stutter) and *2001: A Space Odyssey* (in subsequent footage of the iconic rebellious computer, Hal) (21). The play also alludes to *Frankenstein* itself, in that Richie's concluding reflection—and confusion—is set against the mediatized backdrop of repeating video footage of an "arctic vista" (20, 25, 30), and the play's end mirrors its beginning in footage of TV "snow" (30).

Electronic dance music accompanies the play's action; productions have for the most part used not prerecorded music but "live" mixing performance by an offstage DJ. The script sometimes suggests what kind of music is to be played, with repeated references to "tech" in its stage directions: "like some massive tech-anthem" (2); "muscle car techno" (12). These references to "techno"—the music genre—mark the performances of techno music in the production and textually complement the script's other references to technology, which culminate in the denouement's stage directions for a climactic montage of footage including "rapid firing off of images on screen symbols, slogans, inventions, technologies, ending with a shot of Darth Vader with his mask taken off" (29).

Techno music accompanies the action and dialogue, references to technology and prior *Frankenstein* adaptations augment the script, and MacFadzean's commentary on the play suggests how it furthers a McLuhanesque and Frankensteinian discourse of technology. Describing his play as a "techno-opera," the playwright told *Now* magazine that "what I like most about Shakespeare is that each play mirrors an era, and *Richard II* seems to be ours" (quoted in Kaplan 2001, 53). Detailed production notes identify *Richard II*'s protagonist as a "dreamer" who is fascinated by the strange fruits of technology and capitalist excess, while wilfully oblivious to "impending environmental shutdown" (MacFadzean 2002).

richardthesecond thus adapts major canonical literary works, pop culture references and media samples, and the subcultural milieu of EDM to stage a story of technological backfire organized around a scientific field whose long-standing controversy has been framed emphatically in Frankensteinian terms. As a fringe play, the production has occupied a liminal niche where subculture, pop culture, and canonical or "high" culture converge—and where they enable cultural hybridization and experimentation with form and media. Together with the music production and performance practices of Paladin and Deadmau5, theatrical works like *richardthesecond* dramatize the Frankensteinian and McLuhanesque contours of new media technology and media discourse in Canada. These multimedia productions and performances, occupying intersecting milieus of localized subculture and globalized popular culture, also illustrate how the discourse of technology functions legibly in sound- and image-making practices as well as textual and language articulations. And they demonstrate that Canadian popular culture represents a pivotal site both for theorizing adaptation in cultural production and for popularizing McLuhan's sense of technology as something modern, manufactured, and monstrous.

8. Monster Mines and Pipelines

Frankenphemes of Tar Sands Technology in Canadian Popular Culture

The company is welding together old pipelines and new ones, reversing the flow on some and pumping up the volume on others, building their very own Frankenstein pipeline down to the Gulf coast. (LaFontaine 2012)

Weather forecasters are predicting that Hurricane Sandy could merge with another weather system as it moves, bringing a "Frankenstorm" to parts of Eastern Canada and the U.S. in time for Halloween. (CBC 2012)

Friday marks the fourth day of an intense firestorm in Canada's boreal forest that has engulfed large parts of Fort McMurray, Alberta—a frontier town that serves as the base for the province's oil sands region. . . . "The beast is still up. It's surrounding the city," said fire chief Darby Allen. . . . Fire is a natural part of the boreal ecosystem, but what's happening in Fort McMurray isn't natural. . . . We've reached an era where all weather events bear at least a slight human fingerprint, which, as Elizabeth Kolbert points out in the *New Yorker*, means "we've all contributed to the latest inferno." (Holthaus 2016)

Cultural representations of the Alberta tar sands industry demonstrate the pivotal role that Canadian adaptations of *Frankenstein* have played in constructing and popularizing a globalized discourse of technology. This chapter contextualizes the popular cultural tradition of Canadian adaptations of *Frankenstein* in relation to Canada's resource extraction-based industries, and hence to globalization. Moreover, in finding an abundance of cultural representations of oil in Canada alone, this chapter answers and tempers Imre Szeman's (2011) claim that "our fiction of energy surplus appears to be so completely shielded from view as to be hardly named in our literary fictions at all." He sees energy infrastructure and especially oil as a "dearth . . . in contemporary fiction," pointing to works like Upton Sinclair's *Oil!* (1927) as exceptions to this rule. Szeman focuses on "literary fictions" and gives only a nod to science fiction, a genre that is central to cultural images of oil. For Szeman, *Avatar* (2009) illustrates science fiction's fantastic, clean energy futures, a curious misreading of the film that seems to miss its tar sands allegory, as I will discuss.

Today, the Alberta tar sands industry, located northeast of McLuhan's hometown Edmonton, represents a significant and symptomatic site of technology as a *Frankenstein* trope: it is the world's biggest industrial project and capital's most hubristic gamble with climate change catastrophe (Berman 2013). In 2016, the region where this industry is located suffered a catastrophic, long-running wildfire dubbed "the Beast" by firefighters and described by Naomi Klein (evoking the Frankensteinian rhetoric of galvanism) as the result of "El Niño *supercharged* with climate change" (2016). An extraction business of enormous scale and unprecedented destructiveness (Patchett 2012), the tar sands literalize David McNally's observation that "the idea that something monstrous is at work in the operations of global capitalism is never far from the surface today" (2011, 9). Accordingly, technologically reductive articulations of *Frankenstein*s have emerged to represent the tar sands—and the climate change that the oil business is now known to accelerate. Cultural representations of the Alberta tar sands demonstrate the pivotal role that Canadian adaptations of *Frankenstein* have played in constructing and circulating the globalized discourse of technology.

Here we should first recall that allusion, adaptation, and other modes of cultural appropriation can as readily serve strategies of interpretive closure (Baldick 1987, 5) as those of openness and ambiguity. *Frankenstein* references often function as sensational rhetoric designed to thwart serious, reasoned discussion. The figure of Frankenstein stalks contemporary journalism and commentary on oil and the tar sands, among critics *and* supporters. A 2009 US advertising campaign by the environmental advocacy group Forest Ethics warned about "the dirtiest oil on earth" and described "the Tar Sands" as "a Frankenstein of local and global environmental hazards" (quoted in Craven 2009). In 2012, the National Wildlife Federation described Enbridge's proposed pipeline expansion in a flurry of *Frankenstein* images: "If Keystone XL is the 'zombie pipeline' that won't die, it's pretty clear the Enbridge expansion is the 'Frankenstein' of tar sands. The patchwork, 2,600 mile pipeline is right out of a mad scientist's dream" (LaFontaine 2012). Conversely, the oil lobby Energy Tomorrow also invoked *Frankenstein* to refute criticisms of diluted bitumen, or "dilbit," the tar sands' product: "Dilbit isn't some Frankenstein-like product and lots of care goes into shipping it" (Green 2012). References like these are more rhetorical moves than aesthetic ones, although the availability of *Frankenstein* to *both* sides of this debate refracts a bit of the ambivalence of the story and its near-ubiquitous invocation with reference to public questions concerning technology.

Across different media and genres, Canadian cultural texts exhibit a range of reductive and ambiguous uses for *Frankenstein*'s story of technological backfire to represent oil business, energy crisis, and climate crisis. Take McLuhan, for instance: his work does not address energy as extensively as media, but references to energy industries furnish contextual bookends for the first and last chapters of *Understanding Media* (1964). That study devotes a chapter to the car, figured according to the same *Frankenstein* allusion that titled his first book: that chapter is called "Motorcar: The Mechanical Bride" ([1964] 2003, 291). For McLuhan, the car is a cyborg technology, described in terms as Frankensteinian as those with which he describes new media generally: "It was the electric spark that enabled the gasoline engine to take over from the steam engine. The crossing of electricity, the biological form, with the mechanical form was never to release a greater force" (296). As an "extension of man"—that is, as a *medium*—the car "turns the rider into a superman" (297); the car is not only a medium but also a weapon, a "misguided missile" (300) whose destructive power is its drastic environmental impact and social transformation: "cars have become the real population of our cities, with a resulting loss of human scale" (293).

In 1973 (at the onset of the first postwar energy crisis), Christopher Dewdney's first book, *A Paleozoic Geology of London, Ontario*, includes a prose poem called "Sol du Soleil" ("Soil of the sun"), consisting of two paragraphs: the first defamiliarizes the point of view of a car driver; the second figures the fossil fuel industry in monstrous, geological terms. The second paragraph speculates how the "continued use of fossil fuels" will "slowly replace the present composition of the atmosphere with the chemical composition of the atmosphere some 200 million years ago. . . . This atmosphere will become capable of generating the life-forms essential to this ancient form" (1973, 5).

The poem posits fossil fuel use as ironic technological backlash: the human use of fuels made from the fossils of ancient life forms is changing the climate to make the earth once again hospitable to those life forms. In this concise speculation on energy futures, the unintended end and radical externality of oil is the return of the compressed. The ironic sense of cyclical time in the context of fossil fuels expressed in Dewdney's poem has been more recently expressed in an Internet meme that started circulating around 2013; the meme image varies (some versions show stock "meme" characters like Philosoraptor), and the source is unknown (because of the anonymous and viral character of memes), but the text reads: "If oil is made from decomposed dinosaurs, and plastic is made from oil, are plastic dinosaurs made from real dinosaurs?" (Kim 2013). The question has since been taken up online, in discussion forums and web comics, to assess if there's any scientific truth to it, although the main interest in the meme is its implied questioning of consumerism in an oil-based economy and its accompanying hint—which recurs elsewhere in popular cultural representations of oil—that this economy symbolically depends as much on archaic, fossilized ideas and ideologies as it materially depends on fossil fuels.

Another suggestive period text that represents the oil business and extraction technology in Frankensteinian terms is Richard Rohmer's early-1970s trilogy of novels that imagine a Canada threatened with US annexation for its Arctic oil and gas reserves. The first of these, *Ultimatum* ([1973] 2003), also includes a subplot concerning First Nations protests over territorial and resource rights—and a controversial pipeline, no less, giving it an uncanny timeliness and even prescience concerning today's "Frankenstein pipelines" and growing interest in Arctic fuel sources.

Rohmer's novel takes the energy crisis quite seriously: the story envisions a near-future oil boomtown in Resolute Bay. Interestingly, much of the plot action takes place over the phone, as the US president and the Canadian prime minister engage in extensive and exhausting negotiations to resolve the crisis and stave off a US invasion of Canada. This may seem odd for a techno-thriller (and, well, less than thrilling) but it belongs to a distinctly Canadian and McLuhanesque tradition of integrating media, their effects, and their environments into not only the setting but also the action of a story (as discussed in chapter 5, concerning Cronenberg's films). In an early scene in *Ultimatum*, as the US president arrives in Resolute Bay to tour its undersea drilling operation, the narrator supplies some backstory that is also foreshadowing: "It was right about here that the first big gas discovery was made in January '70. It came up under such enormous pressure that it blew. . . . No one had the know-how or the technology then to cope with high-pressure finds like that" (118). Ironically, then, the operation that the president inspects subsequently ruptures and blows. Although the Arctic's fossil fuels have turned Resolute Bay into a boomtown, the "know-how and technology" for extracting and distributing them remain sketchy at best, subject to backfire as well as sabotage, all while the threat of neoimperial war hangs on the phone wire between the state leaders' offices.

The period's popular music also addressed the energy crisis. Neil Young's 1974 song "Vampire Blues" invokes the vampire (a figure with close historical ties to *Frankenstein*, as discussed in chapter 2) to depict the oil business: "I'm a vampire, babe / Suckin' blood from the Earth . . . Sell you twenty barrels' worth."

More recently, Young has become a prominent, outspoken critic of the tar sands; his Honour the Treaties concert tour of 2014 was a legal fundraiser for the Fort Chipewyan reserve, the First Nations community that has been most gravely afflicted by tar sands pollution. Young's tour and his controversial statements polarized and galvanized Canadians.

Turning to more contemporary work, the Canadian photographer Edward Burtynsky has drawn public and critical attention to the tar sands. His photographs of "manufactured landscapes" play with scale and perspective, for instance by using elevated or aerial vantage points to suggest the enormity of infrastructural technologies, their social effects, and their drastic consequences and externalities. Images of industrial enormity, of "the rise of the machine" have, since Marx, included a tradition of Frankensteinian references (Baldick 1987), and Burtynsky has played on and extended this tradition in his revealing photographic work. An exemplary photo is *Alberta Oil Sands #6* (fig. 7).

On the horizon, we see only "darkness and distance" (Shelley [1818] 2012, 221). In the middle distance, an oil sands refinery sprawls, like Archibald Lampman's nightmarish "city at the end of things." From the middle distance to the foreground stretch two flat, rectangular areas that disrupt the industrial realism of the composition; they are fields of unnatural yellow and rust hues, like lakes of fire in hell. These areas—which are sulphur collection beds—convey Burtynsky's signature ability to turn documentary into defamiliarization, confronting us with a shocking kind of realism that verges on the surreal, in a way that might prompt us to wonder whether the images have been digitally enhanced. *OIL*, a book produced to accompany an exhibit of Burtynsky's photographs, itself features explicitly Frankensteinian language, in curator Paul Roth's description of Burtynsky's work, in which, he argues, we see "no industrial Golem, no homicidal Frankenstein. Rather, we see the ordering force of man, and the chilling, corrosive, penultimate threat that lies at the black heart of our rationalism" (Burtynsky et al. 2011, 169). Roth's reference to *Frankenstein*, intended to disavow its relevance, still conjures its association with technology, and it is suggestively worded as well: that "we see" no Frankenstein may not so much deny the monstrous horror of Burtynsky's images as instead implicate us, the viewers, in the environmental horror show documented in Burtynsky's photographs. That is, we may understand *ourselves* as Frankensteins or, at least, as accomplices to Big Oil's Frankensteinian work—like Walton aboard the icebound ship, who first hears the stricken scientist's story but ultimately assumes an active role in it.

Returning to popular music, the Albertan singer-songwriter Corb Lund approaches the petroculture of his home state from a libertarian perspective. The grim, apocalyptic song "Gettin' Down on the Mountain," from Lund's 2012 album *Cabin Fever*, begins with an odd arrangement of juxtaposed acoustic plucking and growling electric bass, over which Lund opens the lyrics with this ominous refrain: "When the oil stops, everything stops." What follows is like a lyrical three-minute version of Cormac McCarthy's desolate, postapocalyptic novel *The Road* (2006): images of gridlock, supply shortages, and starvation, punctuated by pointed, pedagogical questions to the listener about survival skills. "Can you break the

Figure 7 "Darkness and distance": Edward Burtynsky, *Alberta Oil Sands* #6 (2011). Burtynsky's signature aerial vantage point and wide scope crucially document extraction technologies otherwise hidden from public view. Photo copyright © Edward Burtynsky, courtesy Nicholas Metivier Gallery, Toronto.

horse, can you dig the well?" (Lund 2012). In the chorus, the song's persona shares his own plan: "Don't wanna be around when the shit goes down / I'm going to ground on the mountain" (2012). The song is a musical version of the "peak oil" thesis whose proponents are characterized by the bunkered, embattled survivalism conveyed here in passages like "Brother can you pass the ammo?" The song emphasizes its premise in the precariousness of the oil-based economy; both the first and the last verses start with the same line: "When the oil stops, everything stops." The lyrics' present-tense and interrogative wording make the imagined scene less an extrapolation than a foregone conclusion: the future present. In the backfire of this single technology—the unanticipated unsustainability of fossil fuel dependence—Lund reads the ripping of "the social fabric": peak oil is a man-made monster in its overinvested valuation, as everything that keeps men from acting like monsters to one another.

In the tone with which it represents the oil business, this song contrasts sharply with "The Roughest Neck Around," from Lund's 2002 album *Five Dollar Bill.* "Roughest Neck" is an upbeat ode to the oil patch worker. The "roughest neck" is larger than life, a superhuman Everyman characterized by hard work, technical expertise, and devotion to family and society; "he brings power to the people." And yet he is figured in grotesque, almost monstrous terms. "He's got a "real long reach," with "the power in his hands to pull the dragons from the ground." He is the oil industry's globalized product as much as its producer: "He's been all around the world," and he's got both "power in his heart" and "dragons in his chest" (2002). Musically, too, the swinging roadhouse blues of "Roughest Neck" contrast with the halting, plodding rhythm of "Gettin' Down." These two songs about oil production contrast each other in tone, but not in overall ethos; both appeal, albeit in different ways, to more right-wing discourses of individual responsibility and self-making. Thus, their Frankensteinian images complement each other: the former figures the oil worker as monstrous superman, the latter posits peak oil as a global threat, and the shadow of Frankensteinian technological backfire looms over both.

Several recent plays by Alberta theatre companies—plays like *Good Fences* (2012) and *Extraction* (2013)—have turned to the tar sands for dramatic subject matter (Nestruck 2012). One allusive and suggestive production is Catalyst Theatre's *Frankenstein* (Christenson 2006), which premiered in 2006 at the Keyano Theatre in Fort McMurray—the northern

Alberta town adjacent to the tar sands operation. Catalyst Theatre's *Frankenstein* is an extensive, acknowledged adaptation on Hutcheon's (2006) model, and it uses many of the key points of Shelley's original plot: the Frankenstein family servant Justine is tried for the murder of the boy William; Frankenstein destroys the "bride" he promises the creature, who then murders his betrothed; in the middle of the story, the creature confronts Frankenstein on a glacier and tells its "origin story"; Frankenstein is accused of murdering his friend Henry Clerval. Catalyst's stage version also makes significant changes: Justine is young Victor's science tutor and mentor; Walton's frame narrative is replaced by a loose chorus of narrators who introduce, interrupt, and look on the main action; Frankenstein completes and animates the "bride" before destroying it; and the play ends with Frankenstein incarcerated in an institution for the mentally ill, where the creature visits him in the final scene.

The script dialogue and narration are largely structured by rhyming, song-like lines, and the costumes and props are highly stylized according to a stark Expressionist aesthetic: all the costumes and props are paper, paper-surfaced, or papier-mâché and mostly all white, with only a very few accents of colour, which tend instead to be produced by lighting effects and makeup. The rhyming script and musical numbers, together with the striking, monochromatic visual effects, lend the play a surreal period atmosphere. The abundance of paper, its use to create an Expressionist visual vocabulary reminiscent of silent film, and its presence in a stage play all make for a self-reflexive commentary on dramatic form and established media like writing and live performance, at a time when reminders for audiences to turn off mobile devices have become as routine as the inevitable disruptions said devices cause. In its script and its staging, Catalyst's *Frankenstein* mounts a self-consciously theatrical, pointedly low-tech production.

The script's opening is particularly noteworthy for relating the play to its site of production in Fort McMurray and thus to the tar sands with which the town is popularly identified. The introduction sets the scene for the story it unfolds against a backdrop of "strange signs" seen in "strange times" that could be either Shelley's period or the present:

Nick: These are strange days we live in.
              Strange days to be alive!
              Who knows where we're heading?
              Or how long we may survive?

Nancy: For five hundred days a poisonous haze
       Has spread across the sky.
Tim: Perhaps it's a sign of the sickening times:
Tracy: Grim and foreboding—sent from on high.
Sarah: Something's gone terribly wrong in this world,
       Something beyond repair. . . .
Tim: Another strange, malignant plague
       Annihilates ten thousand men.
Sarah: Another record-breaking storm
       Claims a hundred thousand more. (Christenson 2006, 1)

The suggestion of "strange days" precedes a litany of unusual—and globalized—phenomena and crises. The "poisonous haze" alludes to the "Year without a Summer," 1816, which saw temperatures fall across Europe as a result of an Indonesian volcanic eruption; this was the unseasonable summer that Shelley spent with her circle of friends in Switzerland, when they made their famous agreement to write ghost stories, Shelley's being *Frankenstein*. But "poisonous haze" also alludes to the pollution produced by the tar sands operations, visible in the vicinities of Fort McMurray and Edmonton, and a subject of perennial news coverage and scientific study (like Parajulee and Wania 2014). Similarly, the "plague" could refer either to the significant cholera outbreaks of Shelley's time (which inspired her 1826 novel *The Last Man*), or to any number of global disease outbreaks today, such as the 2014 Ebola scare. But among these "signs," the "record-breaking storm" seems decidedly more about the present than about the past. The term "record-breaking" is a construction of modern usage, and the image of a monster storm—a "Frankenstorm," as Hurricane Sandy got called (CBC News 2012) or "the Beast" of the Fort McMurray fire—is an emphatically contemporary image, and one increasingly understood in close relation to the climate change caused by widespread fossil fuel use.

The relevance of Catalyst's *Frankenstein* to the tar sands, especially in its relation to Fort McMurray and its apocalyptic script, has not been lost on those involved in staging the play. Dov Mickelson, an actor who plays several roles in the play (including Frankenstein's father and younger brother), has said of the play that

certainly it has present day implications. We first performed this show in Fort McMurray (in −40 February!) and what is going on there with the oil sands and the environment had an eerie resonance. It made me wonder if it was the same for the author 200 years earlier and the onslaught of the industrial revolution as a backdrop to what was going on. (quoted in Cross 2010)

The play's apocalyptic sense of foreboding and looming catastrophe gets put in a significantly—and symptomatically—global context, in the above-quoted opening lines: "Something's gone terribly wrong in this world" (2006). From these first lines forward, the play consistently connects the local to the global, the personal tragedy of Frankenstein to the broader catastrophes of the world, often through the invocation of a collective "we"; in this way, Frankenstein's "first irreversible blunder" is universalized, the cause of a global "terrible mess" (65) that encompasses "us" in its querying of responsibility and complicity: "How did we come to this point? . . . The time will come to face our fears . . . We close our eyes, we cover our ears, / We know the end is drawing near" (65–66). If there were ever a global, technological, and ecological crisis in which "we" are implicated as a collective, it is certainly that of the capitalist world-system's structural dependence on oil.

The last but not least example to be analyzed in detail here is the 2009 blockbuster film *Avatar*, directed by Canadian expatriate James Cameron, whose most successful films—for instance, *The Terminator* (1984), *Aliens* (1986), and *Titanic* (1997)—have all been dramas of Frankensteinian technological backfire. One of the most successful Hollywood movies to date, *Avatar* is also a powerful representation of the tar sands, and this representation has been mobilized for activism, against the "*Avatar* sands" (Sierra Club et al, 2010), by NGOs, Indigenous groups, and Cameron himself (Mirrlees 2013, 7). Among the many appropriations and critiques of *Avatar*, an overlooked narrative aspect is that its plot is a Frankensteinian story of technological backfire. The uncanny "native alien" body that the disabled soldier Sully learns to occupy is a lab-grown body. As a host for Sully's projected consciousness, the avatar enacts a doubled role, making Sully his own doppelgänger. The avatar body is also gigantic and blue—as were most nineteenth-century stage performances of Frankenstein's monster. The scene in which Sully first "wakes up" in his avatar body echoes the typical "creation scene" in *Frankenstein* films, as the creature awakens to cause a ruckus in the lab and breaks its restraints. *Avatar*'s plot becomes one of technological backfire, as the transformed Sully rebels against his masters, abandoning his mission to join the oppressed Na'vi in resisting the military-industrial colonists. The success of the Na'vi's resistance forces the decolonization of the planet Pandora. While this is a Hollywood happy ending, it is also a dramatization of the SF "Frankenstein barrier": here, the Na'vi cut off Earth's staple fuel source; this contingency effectively forecloses on the planet's future.

What especially enabled the adoption of *Avatar* for activism against the "*Avatar* sands" are the early establishing shots that show the colonists' mining operation on Pandora. The resemblance of these shots to the tar sands is openly acknowledged by *Avatar*'s art director, Alberta-born Todd Cherniawsky, who is quoted in the documentary *The Tipping Point* (Thompson and Radford 2011): "What was going on in Alberta," he says, "was hugely informative in building and designing this environment." The first view of the Pandora mine appears through the landing spacecraft's windshield as the copilot says "the mine is in sight"—a subtle script emphasis on making visible an extraction industry characterized as "uniquely occluded" (Pendakis and Wilson 2012, 5). The next shot (fig. 8) shows the fuller vista of the mine in the middle distance and the refinery in the background; this shot strongly resembles Burtynsky's distinctive aerial-angle, panoramic photographs of the Alberta tar sands operations.

The camera then pans and cuts to a shot that details the operation: loaded dump trucks and soldiers traversing a narrow access road, behind which a massive bucket-wheel excavator sends up dust as it chews into the earth (fig. 9).

Significantly, in this close shot the bucket-wheel appears so gigantic that it exceeds the frame, as does the gigantic dump truck in a subsequent shot where the protagonist stops as the truck drives past, revealing a number of arrows that have been shot into its tires. The script for this scene invokes the discourse of technology explicitly: "The neolithic weapons are jarring amid all the advanced technology" (Cameron 2009, 8). The bucket-wheel image itself is suggestively critical: the bucket-wheel excavator was discontinued in the 1990s (Gismondi and Davidson 2012), so it appears here as an obsolete icon of extraction machinery, as if to signal the unsustainability and ultimate failure of the Pandora mine and to suggest the combined obsolescence and rapacity—the living death—of fossil fuel technology in general.

Across a range of different media and genres, then, Canadian representations of the tar sands invoke *Frankenstein* to depict and question

Figure 8 *Avatar* (2009), at runtime 00:03:59: "The mine is in sight." Author's rendering of the original shot. (This and the next artistic rendering of scenes from *Avatar* are used because such renderings constitute fair dealing for purposes of criticism, while the licensing cost to reprint the film still-frames of these scenes would exceed $1000 USD. To see the film still-frames, just search the Internet for "Avatar unobtainium mine.")

Figure 9 The bucket-wheel excavator, from *Avatar*, at runtime 00:04:07. Author's rendering of the original shot.

this industry's scale, danger, and obsolescence; in the process, they demonstrate how Canadian culture and industry have both popularized the general discourse of technology as human-made global monstrosity and promoted public awareness of the causal relation between fossil fuel use and climate change. Taken as a group, these texts also provide a grotesque critical vocabulary of images for Canada's tradition of technological nationalism—which the oil business restructures as a *trans*nationalism—and for its postcoloniality: if Canada is sometimes positioned as a "dutiful daughter" of Empire or a victim of the cultural imperialism of US popular culture, texts like those analyzed here articulate and dramatize how the resource extraction industry anchored in the tar sands has made Canada a neoimperial economic leader in its own right, with all the predictable failures of democratic integrity and environmental stewardship that such leadership tends to confer (Shrivastava and Stefanick 2015). Taken together, these texts tell a story—which itself may trade in the oversimplifying interpretive closure of "technological reduction" that has fuelled *Frankenstein's* global popularity—in which the tar sands are the mad scientist, and climate change its monster.

And in a further Frankensteinian irony, the climate change exported by Canada's tar sands has accelerated a polar melting that now brings Big Oil to the Arctic for exploration and extraction (Al Jazeera 2012; Chazan 2008). Recent *Frankenstein* scholarship reflects this trend: "Arctic exploration was in the news at the time Mary Shelley was working on her novel, much in the same way that the circumpolar region is in the news in our own time due to global warming. It is probably for this very reason that most of the articles on Mary Shelley's Arctic have been published within the last ten years as we become conscious of and concerned with Arctic issues once again" (Bachinger 2010, 162). Like Mary Shelley's novel, Big Oil's own *Frankenstein* story of technological backfire is destined to press north, towards greater hubris and atrocity; and it will all too likely end, as well, in self-destructive conflagration.

Conclusion

In concluding this study, I want to turn from Canadian popular culture to survey a set of works by major international scholars—mainly in media studies—that build on McLuhan's media theory to globally distribute his Frankenpheme of technology. This survey will establish a point from which to suggest some tentative conclusions to be drawn and some possible further directions in which to take this work, in terms of its possible implications for adaptation studies generally and for studies of *Frankenstein* in particular, and in terms of other national or regional sites of *Frankenstein* adaptation in cultural practice. These transnational considerations in turn prompt a return to the question of what precisely is Canadian about these adaptations and about the discourse of technology, and whether, accordingly, the long-standing socio-cultural mode of Canadian technological nationalism (Charland 1986) might warrant rethinking or reconfiguring as something more like a "technocratic transnationalism."

McLuhan's Frankenpheme of Technology in Global Scholarship

Widely misread as a techno-enthusiast, McLuhan personally opposed technological change: "No one could be less enthusiastic about these radical changes than myself" (1969, 158). He argued individuals and societies respond to the tumult and havoc new media bring about by going into shock or enduring "autoamputation": "With the arrival of electric technology, man extended, or set outside himself, a live model of the central nervous system itself" ([1964] 2003, 65). The spectre of artificial intelligence and the imagery of "amputation" that pervades McLuhan's work amplify his Frankensteinian sense of technology as modern, manufactured, and monstrous.

If we see the postcolonial conditioning of McLuhan's discourse of technology in his Cambridge training, his reliance on British literary touchstones (such as Blake, Byron, and Joyce), and his popularization via the "global underground" counterculture (Rycroft 1998) and US advertising and media industries, we then see the global circulation of McLuhan's discourse of technology in its receptions, relays, and reformulations by scholars of media and technology around the world. The international corpus of media theory, communications, and technology studies that has built on and extended McLuhan's legacy has also reproduced and reinforced his specifically Frankensteinian trope of technology as one of this corpus's central keywords.

In the United States, two major studies of the theory of technology explicitly link McLuhan and *Frankenstein*: Langdon Winner's *Autonomous Technology: Technics-out-of-Control as a Theme in Political Thought* (1977) and Avital Ronell's 1991 *The Telephone Book: Technology, Schizophrenia, Electric Speech*. In *Autonomous Technology*, Winner credits McLuhan and Jacques Ellul (to whom his study more specifically responds) with the "ability to sensitize modern audiences to something they had overlooked: we are surrounded on all sides (possibly even the inner side) by a myriad of techniques and technologies" and speculates their work warrants contemplating new approaches for social science and theory (1977, 6). Winner refers repeatedly to McLuhan's idea of technology as prosthetic or cybernetic "extension" (178, 202, 285). He observes how the word technology itself "is applied haphazardly to a staggering collection of phenomena" (10) and provides his own three-part definition of technology as apparatus, techniques, and organizations (11–12), on which he then builds a theorization of it as less determinist than substantivist—that is, a theorization that attributes autonomy and agency to technology. Significantly, Winner concludes his extensive study with a chapter called "Frankenstein's Problem": an explication of Mary Shelley's novel that crystallizes his own point about "our involvement with technology": that "we are dealing with an unfinished creation, largely forgotten and uncared for, which is forced to make its own way in the world" (316). Winner insists early on that his central argument is "not . . . that technology is a monstrosity or an evil in and of itself" (316), but his alternating critique and reproduction of technology as autonomous—together with his acknowledgement of McLuhan's influence and his discussion of *Frankenstein*—demonstrate a redeployment of McLuhan's distinctive vocabulary and figuration of this quintessentially modern term as a specifically manufactured kind of monstrosity.

Ronell's *Telephone Book* is a deconstructive treatise on the telephone, a communication technology that, the author argues, is strangely absent from mainstream media studies. In the course of her analysis, Ronell develops an extended comparison of Alexander Graham Bell to Victor Frankenstein:

> We can ask the same question of the Frankenstein monster as we do of the telephone. After all, both inventors—Bell and Victor Frankenstein—were invested in the simulacrum that speaks and hears; both, we might add precipitously, were elaborating works of mourning, memorializing that which is missing, in a certain way trying to make grow the technological flower from an impossible grave site. Both inventors were motivated to reanimate a corpse, to breathe life into dead body parts. . . . He [the monster] shares in the atotality of the telephone that seeks its other in the remote possibility of a long-distance summoning. (1991, 194)

To sustain this narrative and theoretical analogy between Bell and Victor Frankenstein, and between the telephone and Frankenstein's monster, Ronell, very tellingly, calls on McLuhan. "It cannot suffice to say, with McLuhan, that this machinery extends the body in a way that would not be discontinuous," she writes; the monster "was an answering machine of sorts, one whose call was to hang up and disconnect" (194–95). Here, the analogy is informed by McLuhan's idea of media technology as extension; elsewhere in the book, it is informed by his imagery of amputation, which is also resonant for Ronell's purposes and prompts her to ask Frankensteinian questions of McLuhan's own work. She notes that in the fourth chapter of *Understanding Media*, McLuhan writes that "with the arrival of electric technology, man extended, or set outside himself, a live model of the central nervous system"—and that this "outering," as McLuhan would call it, also represents for him "a desperate and suicidal auto-amputation" (quoted in Ronell 1991, 89). Why a "live model"? Ronell asks. "The live model of the electric switchboard sounds more like a constative statement about Frankenstein's monster than anything else. This is not bad, since electric currents no doubt compel scrambling devices to recode the philosophical opposition of life/death, body/machine." Ronell reads McLuhan's major work as developing "a hermeneutics of despair," a "shock registry" that includes (unlike many media studies) the telephone among its "other live electric extensions" (1991, 89–90). The resonance of

McLuhan's "live modelling" and "hermeneutics of despair" then echoes in Ronell's subsequent discussions of technology, as when later in the book she links *Frankenstein* to the trope of "technological revolution" (340), and, more tersely, asserts that "technology . . . is inseparable from catastrophe" (341).

Another notable American reception is Neil Postman's work. With his explicit elaboration of McLuhan's work as media ecology and his popular-audience publications, Postman has been positioned as McLuhan's successor as pre-eminent media theorist. Postman cites McLuhan as a major influence in his 1985 book *Amusing Ourselves to Death*—recognizing that it was then "fashionable" to disavow him (1985, 8); McLuhan's reputation would be rehabilitated in North America in the early 1990s. The influence has persisted and echoed throughout Postman's work, with particular reverberation in his 1993 book *Technopoly: The Surrender of Culture to Technology* (note in the title the play of both terms that name McLuhan's institutional home at the University of Toronto). In this book, technology is a central keyword, but one Postman does not clearly define, except, following McLuhan, as a determining, material and ideological social force: "The uses made of any technology are largely determined by the structure of the technology itself" (1993, 7). Like both McLuhan and Winner, Postman is concerned with the potential of technology to achieve autonomy, a potential he sees as a threat. Any technology, he writes, "has a tendency to run out of control" (138); it "tends to function independently of the system it serves. It becomes autonomous, in the manner of a robot that no longer obeys its master" (142). The echoes of *Frankenstein* and McLuhan are equally clear here: in the former's popularization as a drama of technological backfire; and in the latter's evocation of this drama to state his personal position on technology in the *Playboy* interview (as discussed in chapter 4). Postman's chief illustration of potentially autonomous and rebellious technology is the computer: "There has never been a technology that better exemplifies Marshall McLuhan's aphorism" (118). For Postman, the McLuhanesque "message" of the computer, then, is a Frankensteinian message: "that we are machines—thinking machines, to be sure, but machines nonetheless. . . . The computer claims sovereignty over the whole range of human experience, and supports its claim by showing that it 'thinks better' than we can" (111). And the computer is, accordingly, the pre-eminent technology pivotal to the state of "technopoly"—a state of "totalitarian technocracy" in which all forms of cultural life submit to the sovereignty of technology—a state that Postman argues the US has attained in the postwar period (52).

To Winner, Ronell, and Postman, we could add many other anglophone media and technology scholars who have adapted and amplified McLuhan's Frankensteinian discourse of technology: Donna Haraway, Arthur Kroker, Olivia Harvey, Stelarc, and Cavell, whose *Spectres of McLuhan* project documents and exemplifies the revenant discourse in question. But here I want to consider two European scholars: Jean Baudrillard and Friedrich Kittler. Addressing them means attending to differences in language and to translation: this is both problematic, given my focus on the globalization of technology discourse in English, but also productive, given the influence of Baudrillard and Kittler on anglophone scholars.

The English word "technology" finds two approximations in French, "la technique" and "la technologie": these can each be defined more or less expansively than their English counterpart (Ellul [1954] 1964, xxv). Early French reviews of McLuhan tended to use "la technique" (Riesman, quoted in Genosko 2005, 194; Morin, quoted in Genosko 2005, 209). Baudrillard adopted and adapted McLuhan's ideas (Husseyn 1989), including McLuhan's main idea of media as prosthetic extensions (Genosko 2005, 238); and like Postman, Baudrillard has been hailed as "a new McLuhan" (Kellner 1989). His canonical essay on postmodernity, "The Precession of Simulacra," in *Simulations*, amplifies the monstrous and revenant resonance of McLuhan's media theory in its references to "artificial resurrection" (1983, 4), its use of sciences long associated with *Frankenstein*—the "nuclear and genetic"—to describe the "operation" of simulation (3) and its echo of Frankensteinian presumption in the suggestion that God is a simulation (10). "Precession" invokes neither "la technique" nor "la technologie" explicitly, though Baudrillard's work does elsewhere (quoted in Husseyn 1989, 13); and (in much the manner that media and technology were virtually interchangeable terms for McLuhan), as Douglas Kellner notes, "the theory of autonomous media also returns with Baudrillard; thus the critiques of autonomous technology can usefully and relevantly be applied to Baudrillard, and, more generally to postmodern social theory" (1989). In "Precession," too, occurs the image of "the desert of the real" (Baudrillard 1983, 2)—which gets sampled, along with many other Baudrillard references, in *The Matrix*, a film that rehearses a familiar "technological reduction" of *Frankenstein*, but also bases its "rise of the machines" version on the premise of a literalization of McLuhan's image of humans as "the sex organs of the machine world." Baudrillard's writings on the real as technologically overdetermined dystopia—and his intertextual appearance in a film dramatizing the same—amplify the "demonology of technology" (Haraway 1991, 181) that McLuhan codified and popularized.

There is a further sense, too, in which Baudrillard's construction of the postmodern mediascape on the model of the simulacrum resembles McLuhan's world-historical anthropomorph, "electric man," as a Frankensteinian figure; Baudrillard describes the overdeveloped modern West as "a world completely catalogued and analysed and then *artificially revived as though real*" (1983, 16, emphasis in original). Baudrillard theorizes the simulacrum as a copy without any original, much like Frankenstein's creature is not a simulation but a simulacrum of humanity. As an attempt to improve on human biology and anatomy, Frankenstein's creature is both more human than human and not quite human; as Mellor has observed, significantly (1988, 112), the creature is composed of not only human but also animal parts, a detail Victor Frankenstein makes explicit in describing how he gleaned materials from "the dissecting room and the slaughter-house" as well as "the unhallowed damps of the grave" (Shelley [1818] 2012, 81). For Baudrillard, the globalized corporate media institutions traffic not in images that simulate or refer to external referents in the so-called real world, but rather in "irreferent" images (1983, 5) that have dispensed altogether with referentiality and construct instead a kind of self-enclosed, self-sustaining virtual ecology. The apocalyptic implications of this "phantasmagoria of the social contract" (29) leads Baudrillard, elsewhere on this same subject, to deploy the discourse of demons ([1984] 1987, 13) and the "diabolical" (14)—precisely the discourse Victor Frankenstein uses often to describe his creature (Shelley [1818] 2012, 60, 84, 106, 209).

Turning to German, we find a similar translation pattern. The English word's closest German equivalent is perhaps *Technologie*; however, the term used in Martin Heidegger's seminal STS essay—"Die Frage nach der Technik" (1954)—is not *Technologie* but *Technik*. Like its French equivalent, *Technik* can mean "technique, craft, skill" (Weber 1989, 981)—it is used more broadly and capaciously than the English word "technology" that has become common since William Lovatt's 1977 translation of Heidegger's essay as "The Question Concerning Technology." Both *Technologie* and *Technik* appear in Friedrich Kittler's *Gramophone, Film und Typewriter* (1986, translated into English in 1999). A media discourse analyst, Kittler rigorously and dynamically develops McLuhan's discourse of technology. He integrates McLuhan's ideas with those of Foucault and Lacan in critical historicizations of relationships "between the history of technology and the body" and "between modern technologies and modern warfare" ([1986] 1999, 34). For Kittler, the "so-called" human subject is a "discourse network" structured by media technologies: "technical media are models of the so-called human" (36). Moreover, these developments Kittler shows consistently to be productions of warfare: "the development of all previous technical media, in the field of computers as well as optical technology, was for . . . military purposes" ([2002] 2010, 30). In *Gramophone*, Kittler elaborates an unsettling understanding of modern subjectivity as a kind of simulation program both sustained and subverted by a kind of "discourse network 1900": the industrial proliferation of recording media, namely gramophone, film, and typewriter, the last of which also ushers in the postwar computer ([1986] 1999, 251). Kittler's method is to work backward from the Lacanian argument that the Cartesian cogito is an effect of language mistaking itself for a cause, to the Foucauldian premise that historically contingent discourses structure language practices, to arrive at a McLuhanesque a priori that discourses depend on equally contingent media technologies.

Like McLuhan, Kittler theorizes the modern humanist subject as the content of media—but also as increasingly vestigial and tangential to a nascent, globalizing regime of ascendant cybernetics, automation, and artificial intelligence: here is a more concrete theory, then, of humans "as the sex organs of the machine world." In *Gramophone*, Kittler writes that "once the technological differentiation of optics, acoustics, and writing exploded Gutenberg's writing monopoly around 1880, the fabrication of so-called Man became possible. His essence escapes into apparatuses. Machines take over functions of the central nervous systems" ([1986] 1999, 16). The book's historicization of media technologies at the advent of the age of mechanical reproduction teems with Frankensteinian imagery of spectres (12), doppelgängers (149), and dissected bodies (151). "Media-technological differentiations opened up the possibility for media links," he writes in one especially resonant passage that describes the discourse network of 1900 as a Frankensteinian assemblage: "After the storage capacities for optics, acoustics, and writing had been separated, mechanized, and extensively utilized, their distinct data flows could be reunited. Physiologically broken down into fragments and physically reconstructed, the central nervous system was resurrected, but as a Golem made of Golems" (170). A manufactured monster of ancient Jewish legend, the golem has been suggested as a pretext for *Frankenstein* and here figures similarly as both piece and whole of a modern subject radically imagined as a "resurrected" linkage of media technologies (terms Kittler tends to use together, not interchangeably as McLuhan did). Like Baudrillard's amplification of McLuhan in his apocalyptic critiques, Kittler's extension of McLuhan to historicize technology as the engine of subjectivity, and war in turn as the engine of technological change, represents a scholarly engagement with McLuhan's work that illustrates its international reach and influence in globalizing its distinctive discourse of technology. Consider this summary of *Gramophone* in *The Guardian*'s obituary for Kittler:

> Kittler . . . tapped into humanity's fear of being neutralised by its own tools. *Gramophone, Film, Typewriter* was written in the wake of such science-fiction fantasies as William Gibson's *Neuromancer* (1984). . . . Kittler's point was not that machines will exterminate us; rather that we are deluded to consider ourselves masters of our technological domain. (Jeffries 2011)

Like Baudrillard's, Kittler's work in English translation has done as much as that of anglophone scholars to consolidate and popularize McLuhan's Frankensteinian discourse of technology.

We find a suggestive coda to McLuhan's global influence on the imagery and discourse of modern technology in the architecture of Berlin. Berlin's Canadian Embassy, built in 2005, features a high-tech, multimedia "McLuhan Salon" (Government of Canada 2012). And the new embassy literally shadows the ruins of the Führerbunker, site of Hitler's last proverbial stand in the German capital, now a grassy knoll, conspicuously neglected and just as conspicuously unmarked. The renovated site for a new global assertion of Canada's technological nationalism shadows the demolished site of Germany's prior assertion of similar technological nationalism, and both sites are just south of a monument to one of the twentieth century's most emblematic catastrophes of technological nationalism: the Holocaust Memorial. In this juxtaposition emerges the spectre of Frankensteinian hubris and ruin that Canadians would do well to heed, susceptible as Canada and indeed many nations have been, in the twentieth and twenty-first centuries, to political populism, ultra-nationalism, and corporate protectionism, principles widely recognized as associated with and symptomatic of fascism.

From Technological Nationalism to Technocratic Transnationalism

Given the Canadian government's prioritization of the business interests of global capital, a prioritization that is exclusive neither to any one governing party, nor to the Canadian state in this age of globalized "neoliberal empire" (McNally 2011, 168); given the continuing centrality of technology to capital—as seen in hegemonic policy terms like technology transfer and the technological imperative (Lorimer, Gasher, and Skinner 2008); and given the corresponding privilege accorded "STEM" disciplines (science, technology, engineering, mathematics) above others: for these reasons, among others discussed in this study, it might be worthwhile to reconsider technological nationalism, now, as something more like technocratic transnationalism: less an endeavour in applying technology to build a nation, as Charland's (1986) theory argued, and more a prevailing arrogation of governance by global capital through advanced technological means.

At late capital's intersection of the "technological imaginary" popularized by McLuhan (Genosko 2005, xxxvi) and the "transnational matrix" theorized by Gibson (Moylan 1995, 184), technological nationalism may be productively reconfigured in terms of *trans*nationalism, which describes the transformation, transgression, and transcendence of national borders—and national forms. As Watts comments wryly in *Maelstrom*: "National identity was so irrelevant that nobody'd even bothered to dismantle it" (2001, "Complicity"). The notion of revising technological nationalism as technocratic transnationalism emerges in reading the McLuhanesque Frankenpheme of technology against the grain of—or as the dangerous supplement of—the primacy of technology in capitalist modernity. The patterns and traditions of McLuhanesque *Frankensteins* in Canadian popular culture not only prompt us inevitably to think of *Frankenstein* when we talk of technology, they also share an intriguing commonality in consistently and critically representing corporate business and its neoliberal hegemony with Frankensteinian figures of technology. McLuhan discussed the modern corporation often in his works; while he tends to use the language of the corporate in a more general and abstract way as a synonym for the collective or the community, sometimes he invokes corporate business specifically and explicitly, and in suggestively Frankensteinian terms, as in his aforementioned, incisive claim about how media "lease our central nervous systems to various corporations" (McLuhan [1964] 2003, 99–100).

And if, since Shelley's hideous progeny first entered political and public discourse as an allusion, it has been invoked widely by conservative commentators to advise caution against progressive policies, to criticize certain scientific and technological experiments (St. Clair 2004; Turney 1998) and to demonize labour (Baldick 1987), *Frankenstein* has also been invoked by progressives and radicals to caution against conservative policies, to criticize certain scientific and technological experiments, and to vilify corporate business (sometimes citing Marx's aforementioned image of capital as vampire). As Hitchcock (2007) notes, the early twentieth-century predations of robber-baron capitalism that triggered the Great Depression prompted representations of corporate business like Mitchell Dawson's 1930 article "Frankenstein, Inc.," which criticizes the corporatization of legal practice. Today, ongoing corporate campaigns to arrogate more rights and privileges unto themselves, often at the expense of democracy, citizens' rights, and the public interest, suggest that the nullification of government about which Dawson warned may be well underway, under the auspices of neoliberalization and globalization. The Frankenstein image of corporate business has been vividly reanimated in the Canadian documentary *The Corporation* (2003), which describes the profiteering mandate of a corporation as a "monstrous obligation," and in which two interviewees suggest that an apt metaphor for the modern corporation is none other than Frankenstein's monster: "Corporations are artificial creations; you might say they're monsters, trying to devour as much profit as possible, at anyone's expense," says one interviewee early in the film, immediately after which, another elaborates: "Dr. Frankenstein's creation has overwhelmed and overpowered him, as the corporate form has done with us" (Achbar and Abbot 2003).

As an intensification of the global, technologized flow and accelerating concentration of capital, the modern corporation and the neoliberal globalization processes it demands provide a common target for many Canadian adaptations of *Frankenstein* that reproduce the McLuhanesque

Frankenpheme of technology. Among these, *Videodrome* and *Neuro-mancer* remain globally recognized and significant exemplars. In these Canadian *Frankenstein* stories, technology in general and media technologies in particular are monstrously figured, as insidious programming; as tools of colonization, domination, and exploitation; as supplements that threaten humanity with obsolescence; as weapons. As Robins and Webster claim, "The global space that has been instituted through the new information and communication technologies has turned out to be a catastrophic space" (1999, 130). By monstrously figuring technology and the "new flesh" it makes, Canadian *Frankensteins* relate transnational capital's technological futures back to its industrial origins, reinscribing the robustness of a text that identified, at the advent of industrial modernity, an epistemic limit for that modernity.

In addition to corporate business, Canadian adaptations of *Franken-stein* also show a common preoccupation with media, evincing McLuhan's abiding influence. Texts like Cronenberg's, Gibson's, and the myriad analogous *Frankenstein* adaptations that follow them consistently represent media—especially new media—as technologies that are not just routinely vulnerable to backfiring or running amok but also vital instruments of globalizing corporate hegemony and the technocratic governance structures that privilege, sustain, and subsidize it. By constructing Frankenstein figures of technologies and corporations, these adaptations become legible as critiques of capital itself.

Every week, evidence of the consolidation of technocratic transnationalism and of the McLuhanesque Frankenpheme of technology that shadows it is audible in the CBC Radio program *Spark*. The program discusses "tech, trends, and fresh ideas" and it is hosted by Nora Young, for whom McLuhan and Foucault are strong, acknowledged influences (Gunn 2012). We hear this influence in several recurring claims Young consistently makes in numerous episodes: "technology" means more than just what's new and "high-tech"; technology is about more than tools or devices, it's also about their "social contexts"; and technology often harbours significant, unintended consequences. That is, each week *Spark* reproduces and disseminates McLuhan's Frankenpheme of technology in its wide-ranging discussions of new software, devices, and systems, new and old media technologies, algorithms and artificial intelligence, and scholarship and journalism in STS and related areas, as well as the social costs and benefits of the various items under discussion. Several recurring concerns in *Spark*'s diverse reporting on technological development illustrate the constant circulation of the McLuhanesque Frankenpheme of technology in the radio show (which is also available in podcast and web streaming media). One of these recurring concerns is automation's displacement of human labour: what happens "when your boss is a piece of software" is a topic in one episode (Young 2015b). Another is the discourse of technology itself:

> What do we talk about when we talk about tech? Is it an engine of economic growth? Instrument of oppression? An extension of our identity and emotions? . . . In an age when our tech is more powerful and more intimately connected to us than ever, we'd better choose those metaphors carefully. (Young 2015a)

And another significant concern is the spectre of technological autonomy. "What if there really is a Skynet?" Young asks, introducing an item on a group of scientists' recent announcement that the achievement of artificial intelligence is imminent—and a danger. Of one group member, Young asks: "We've seen some startling examples of autonomy in computers and machines . . . but how pervasive is this in our society now?" And she subsequently asks: "So what should we be doing as a society to safeguard ourselves from this technology getting hideously out of control?" (2014a). In addition, in light of the discursive pattern this study has traced, the program's subject matter often leads Young and her interviewees to explicitly cite *Frankenstein*: for instance, a Microsoft representative describes his tablet stylus development project by saying, self-deprecatingly, that "we're building these bizarre Frankenstein devices with wires hanging out of them and so forth" (quoted in Young 2014b). And for *Spark*'s Hallowe'en 2017 episode, Young (2017) drew together some of these recurring ideas and issues in the show, speaking at length about *Frankenstein* as "the governing metaphor for our fears about out-of-control tech," with specific reference to emerging critiques of the unexpected consequences of social media. As suggested by even this cursory sampling, the McLuhanesque Frankenpheme of technology enjoys regular circulation in CBC Radio's popular technology show. So, it must be said, does a cultural and philosophical problematization of technology and the discourse of technology, which occurs about as often as does the show's usage of technology as

Frankenpheme. Some of the show's sophistication is encapsulated in its very title, which evokes an image of electrical engagement that is popularly identified with new ideas—and with the "spark of being" (Shelley [1831] 2000, 60) that animates *Frankenstein*'s monster.

Amplifying Adaptation Studies

The myriad ways in which *Frankenstein* has cast a long shadow over technology discourse, taken together, suggest a richness, resonance, and above all a profound ambivalence. The discourse of technology, in which technology is so widely figured as a McLuhanesque Frankenpheme, thus represents, somewhat contradictorily, both an instance of and counterexample to the gestures of simplification and interpretive closure for which *Frankenstein* allusions have been historically used in political, economic, and scientific discourse and debates (Baldick 1987, St. Clair 2004). The McLuhanesque Frankenpheme of technology instantiates the gesture of interpretive closure in its consistent intimation of hubris and ensuing catastrophe; it represents a counterexample in its diversity of iterations and inflections. And what opens up or reopens receptions of *Frankenstein* to such varied and even contradictory readings is a more expansive, more minutely attentive approach to adaptation studies: more expansive in the range of forms, genres, and media to which it attends; and more minutely attentive in its readings of both the formal details and social contexts of the texts and other cultural practices given consideration. While this book has engaged with a variety of forms and media both extensive and ephemeral, both popular and scholarly, there are of course many others that invite reading for evidence of the McLuhanesque Frankenpheme of technology: advertising, comics and cartoons, digital games, food products, toys, curricular materials (fig. 10), and graffiti (fig. 11) to name just a few.

Similarly, there are many other sites of cultural practice that would invite such a reading. Canadian adaptations of *Frankenstein* demonstrate recurring preoccupations with the discourse of technology, media, corporate business, and globalization—the latter of which also puts in question the very category of the nation-state, of Canada itself. In light of these preoccupations—and mindful of the qualifying question that puts the context of the national under nominal erasure—what might be identifiable preoccupations or emphases of *Frankenstein* adaptations in other regional or national sites, such as the United States or India? Relatedly, how has the McLuhanesque Frankenpheme of technology circulated across the English-speaking postcolonial world? The above survey of salutary articulations of it among major US and European scholars' works perhaps only shows the tip of a massive cultural iceberg.

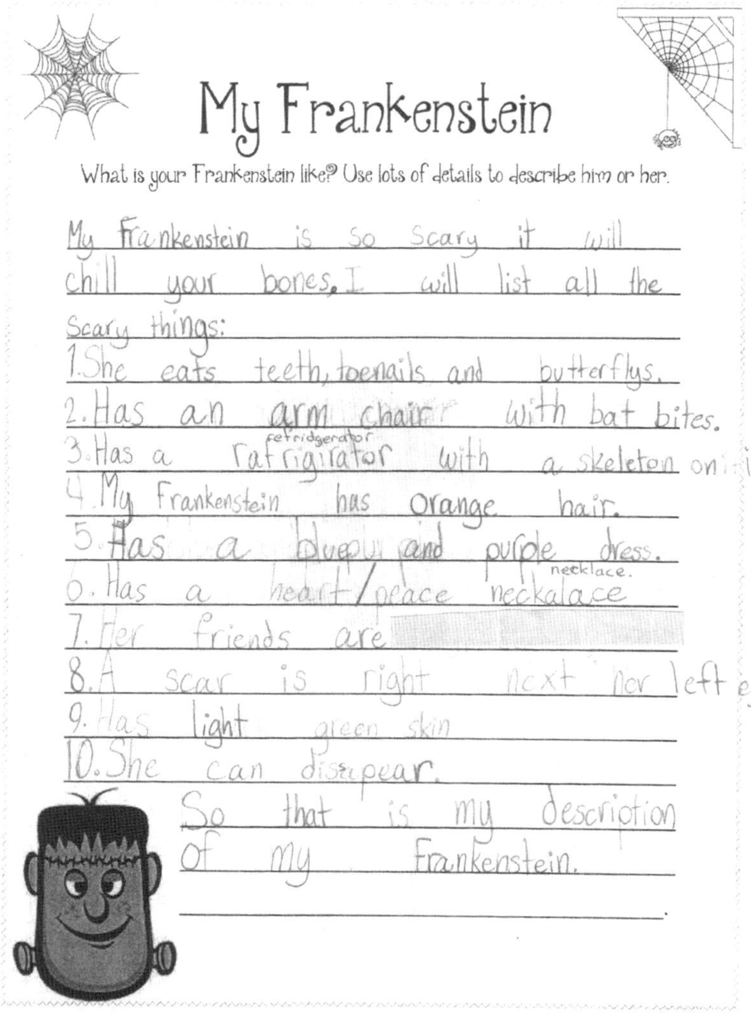

My Frankenstein

What is your Frankenstein like? Use lots of details to describe him or her.

My Frankenstein is so scary it will
chill your bones. I will list all the
scary things:
1. She eats teeth, toenails and butterflys.
2. Has an arm chair with bat bites.
3. Has a rafrigirator (refridgerator) with a skeleton on it.
4. My Frankenstein has orange hair.
5. Has a blue and purple dress.
6. Has a heart/peace necklace (necklace).
7. Her friends are
8. A scar is right next nor left eye
9. Has light green skin
10. She can disapear.
So that is my description
of my Frankenstein.

Figure 10 "My Frankenstein" as a second-grade school assignment, Hallowe'en 2014, illustrating both the common use of the creator's name for that of his creation and the text's pedagogical adaptability. Courtesy of the author's daughter.

Figure 11 Stencil graffito depicting Boris Karloff's iconic portrayal of Frankenstein's creature, in James Whale's 1931 film. Photographed in Kinsmen Park, Edmonton, 2010. Photo copyright © 2010 by Mark A. McCutcheon.

When I first undertook this study, my mentor and friend, the late Constance Rooke, asked me a pointed question: "What's Canadian about all these adaptations of *Frankenstein*? Because, you know: it could be nothing." This interrogative caveat has stayed with me through the pursuit and completion of this work. The short answer, I suppose, is that McLuhan is what's Canadian about these adaptations, since they all connect his theory to Mary Shelley's story. But Rooke's caveat has taken on few different meanings—not least of which is this question of Canada's existence under a neoliberal world-system of technocratic transnationalism. What is Canadian about these adaptations of *Frankenstein* is that they are also simultaneously adaptations of McLuhan's media theory; however, in the process, they have constructed and popularized a nationally contextualized discourse of technology that—sometimes subtly, sometimes stridently—renders unsettling and uncanny technology's place of privilege and presumption in the modern capitalist world order. As Mark Kingwell observed in a *Globe and Mail* editorial, "fear remains the dominant emotion when humans talk about technological change" (2017, F7). Kingwell's subject is artificial intelligence, an area rife with Frankensteinian anxieties, allusions, and adaptations; and even in this quite short prose piece on the subject, McLuhan gets cited as one of "the best voices in the critical literature about technology" (F7)—though Kingwell reproduces the popular reception of McLuhan as a voice counselling understanding, not fear, when as we've seen, he more ambivalently articulated both.

And as was pointed out to me in one of the early talks that formed the basis of this book, there is a good deal of irony in the gender politics of technology discourse and its historical provenance. The globalized discourse of technology is a pivotal discourse of capitalist modernity—which is also a patriarchal and paternalistic modernity (Haraway 1991). And technology, in its pride of place in this world-system, has become widely understood as a gendered discourse, a domain of boys and their toys. How ironic, then, that the epistemic foundations of this discourse were set down, one unseasonably, erratically cold summer, by the prodigious and audacious imaginings of one well-read teenage girl.

References

Achbar, Mark, and Jennifer Abbot, dirs. 2003. *The Corporation*. Vancouver: Big Picture Media.

Al Jazeera. 2012. "Carving Up the Arctic." *The Stream*, 6 December. Al Jazeera. http://stream.aljazeera.com/story/201212060011-0022427.

Alan Parsons Project. 1976. *Tales of Mystery and Imagination*. CDS 4003. Charisma.

Alang, Navneet. 2017. "Matters of Life and Death." *Globe and Mail*, 25 February.

Aldiss, Brian. [1973] 1986. *Trillion Year Spree: The History of Science Fiction*. New York: Atheneum.

Annesley, James. 2001. "Netscapes: Gibson, Globalisation, and the Representation of New Media." *Forum for Modern Language Studies* 37, no. 2: 218–29.

Appadurai, Arjun. 1990. "Disjuncture and Difference in the Global Cultural Economy." *Theory, Culture, and Society* 7: 295–310.

Arthur, W. Brian. 2009. *The Nature of Technology: What It Is and How It Evolves*. New York: Free Press.

Atwell, Phillip, dir. 2003. *In da Club*. Aftermath Entertainment.

Atwood, Margaret. [1968] 1987. *Selected Poems, 1965–1975*. Boston: Houghton Mifflin Harcourt.

———. [1981] 1990. "Notes Towards a Poem That Can Never Be Written." In *15 Canadian Poets X2*, edited by Gary Geddes, 409–11. Toronto: Oxford University Press.

———. 2003. *Oryx and Crake*. London: Bloomsbury.

———. 2009. *The Year of the Flood*. London: Bloomsbury.

———. 2011. "Margaret Atwood, Uncensored." *Globe and Mail*, 29 April.

———. 2013. *MaddAddam*. London: Bloomsbury.

Atwood, Margaret, and Charles Pachter. 1966. *Speeches for Doctor Frankenstein*. Bloomfield Hills, MI: Cranbrook Academy of Art.

Auslander, Philip. 1999. *Liveness: Performance in a Mediatized Culture*. New York: Routledge.

Bachinger, Jacob. 2010. "The Arctic and 'Other Spaces' in Mary Shelley's *Frankenstein*." *At the Edge* 1: 158–74. http://journals.library.mun.ca/ojs/index.php/ate/article/view/95/50.

Baldick, Chris. 1987. *In Frankenstein's Shadow: Myth, Monstrosity, and Nineteenth-Century Writing*. Oxford: Clarendon Press.

Bannerji, Himani. 2000. *On the Dark Side of the Nation: Essays on Multiculturalism, Nationalism, and Gender*. Toronto: Canadian Scholars' Press.

Barney, Darin. 2000. *Prometheus Wired: The Hope for Democracy in the Age of Network Technology*. Vancouver: University of British Columbia Press.

Baudrillard, Jean. 1983. *Simulations*. Translated by Paul Foss. New York: Semiotext(e).

———. [1984] 1987. *The Evil Demon of Images*. Translated by Paul Patton and Paul Foss. Waterloo, UK: Power Institute of Fine Arts.

Beard, William. 1983. "The Visceral Mind: The Major Films of David Cronenberg." In *The Shape of Rage: The Films of David Cronenberg*, edited by William Beard, 1–79. Don Mills, ON: General Publishing.

———. 2006. *The Artist as Monster: The Cinema of David Cronenberg*. Toronto: University of Toronto Press.

Behrendt, Stephen C. 2001. "Richard Brinsley Peake (1792–1847)." In *Presumption; or The Fate of Frankenstein by Richard Brinsley Peake*, edited by Stephen C. Behrendt. Romantic Circles Electronic Editions. College Park: University of Maryland. https://www.rc.umd.edu/editions/peake/apparatus/peake.html.

Beller, Jonathan L. 1996. "Desiring the Involuntary: Machinic Assemblage and Transnationalism in Deleuze and *Robocop 2*." In *Global/Local: Cultural Production and the Transnational Imaginary*, edited by Rob Wilson and Wimal Dissanayake, 193–218. Durham, NC: Duke University Press.

Benedetti, Paul, and Nancy DeHart, eds. 1996. *Forward Through the Rearview Mirror: Reflections on and by Marshall McLuhan*. Toronto: Prentice Hall.

Bentham, Jeremy. 1827. *Rationale of Judicial Evidence, Specially Applied to English Practice*. Vol. 1. London: Hunt and Clarke.

Berman, Tzeporah. 2013. "Washington Is Right: Canada Must Confront Its Climate Neglect." *Globe and Mail*, 19 February.

Bessai, Carl, dir. 1999. *Marshall McLuhan: Out of Orbit*. Life and Times series. Toronto: CBC.

Bigelow, Jacob. 1831. *Elements of Technology, Taken Chiefly from a Course of Lectures Delivered at Cambridge, on the Application of the Sciences to the Useful Arts*. 2nd ed. Boston: Hilliard, Gray, Little, and Wilkins.

Blackwell, Tom. 2000. "Toronto chief wants paramilitary uniforms: Changes would make police look like Nazis, critics fear." *Ottawa Citizen*, 19 April: A5.

Bodroghkozy, Aniko. 2002. "As Canadian as . . . Possible: Canadian Popular Culture and the American Other." In *Hop on Pop: The Politics and Pleasures of*

Popular Culture, edited by Henry Jenkins, Tara McPherson, and Jane Shuttac, 566–89. Durham, NC: Duke University Press.

Bolter, Jay, Blair MacIntyre, Maribeth Gandy, and Petra Schweitzer. 2006. "New Media and the Permanent Crisis of Aura." *Convergence* 12: 21–39.

Botting, Fred. 2005. "Reading Machines." In *Gothic Technologies: Visuality in the Romantic Era*, edited by Robert Miles. Romantic Circles Praxis series. University of Maryland. http://www.rc.umd.edu/praxis/gothic/botting/botting.html.

Boyd-Barrett, Oliver. 1977. "Media Imperialism: Towards an International Framework for the Analysis of Media Systems." In *Mass Communication and Society*, edited by James Curran, Michael Gurevitch, and Janet Woollacott, 116–35. London: Edward Arnold.

Brainbug. 1996. "Nightmare (Original Mix)." From *Nightmare*. SF 496-04. Strike Force.

Brand, Dionne. 1990. *No Language Is Neutral*. Toronto: Coach House Press.

Brouillette, Sarah. 2002. "Corporate Publishing and Canonization: *Neuromancer* and Science-Fiction Publishing in the 1970s and Early 1980s." *Book History* 5: 187–208.

Brown, Ed. 2009. "Industrial (P.B.K. Remix)." From *Magnetic Fields*. CAMINODIGITAL003. Camino Blue.

Brydon, Diana. 2004. "Postcolonialism Now: Autonomy, Cosmopolitanism, and Diaspora." *University of Toronto Quarterly* 73, no. 2: 691–706.

Bukatman, Scott. 1992. "Amidst These Fields of Data: Allegory, Rhetoric, and the Paraspace." *Critique* 33, no. 3: 199–219.

Burtynsky, Edward, Michael Mitchell, William E. Rees, and Paul Roth. 2011. *OIL*. London: Steidl.

Cameron, James, dir. 2009. *Avatar*. Hollywood: 20th Century Fox. Script reprinted at Internet Movie Script Database, http://www.imsdb.com/scripts/Avatar.html.

Canada. 2017. "Government of Canada Invests $43 Million in Clean Technology Innovation." Government of Canada, 13 March. https://www.canada.ca/en/innovation-science-economic-development/news/2017/03/government_of_canadainvests43millionincleantechnologyinnovation.html.

Cavell, Richard. 2002. *McLuhan in Space: A Cultural Geography*. Toronto: University of Toronto Press.

CBC News. 2012. "'Frankenstorm' May Be Headed for Eastern Canada, U.S." *CBC News*, 26 October. http://www.cbc.ca/news/canada/frankenstorm-may-be-headed-for-eastern-canada-u-s-1.1187140.

Chapman, Dale. 2002. "Hermeneutics of Suspicion: Paranoia and the Technological Sublime in Drum and Bass Music." *Echo* 5, no. 2. http://www.echo.ucla.edu/volume5-issue2/chapman/chapman.pdf.

Charland, Maurice. 1986. "Technological Nationalism." *Canadian Journal of Political and Social Theory* 10, no. 1: 196–220.

Chazan, Guy. 2008. "Cold Comfort: Arctic Is Oil Hot Spot." *Wall Street Journal*, 24 July.

Christenson, Jonathan, writer and dir. 2006. *Frankenstein*. Production designed by Bretta Gerecke. Catalyst Theatre, Keyano Theatre, Fort McMurray.

Clayton, Jay. 2003. *Charles Dickens in Cyberspace: The Afterlife of the Nineteenth Century in Postmodern Culture*. Oxford: Oxford University Press.

Corbett, John. 1994. *Extended Play: Sounding Off from John Cage to Dr. Funkenstein*. Durham, NC: Duke University Press.

Crane, Jonathan. 2000. "A Body Apart: Cronenberg and Genre." In *The Modern Fantastic: The Films of David Cronenberg*, edited by Michael Grant, 50–68. Westport, CT: Praeger.

Craven, Will. 2009. "Full-Page *USA Today* Advertisement Warns Obama About Canada's Controversial Tar Sands Oil." *Common Dreams: Building Progressive Community*, 17 February. https://www.commondreams.org/newswire/2009/02/17.

Cronenberg, David, dir. 1999. *eXistenZ*. Toronto: Alliance Atlantis Communications.

———. 1981. *Scanners*. Toronto and Montréal: Canadian Film Development Corporation (CFDC) and Filmplan International/Criterion.

———. 1983. *Videodrome*. Toronto and Montréal: Canadian Film Development Corporation (CFDC)/Criterion.

Cronenberg, David. 2000. Interview with David Cronenberg. *Mondo 2000*. https://web.archive.org/web/20030327092102/http://www.davidcronenberg.de/mond2000.html.

Crosby, Harry H., and George R. Bond, eds. 1968. *The McLuhan Explosion: A Casebook on Marshall McLuhan and* Understanding Media. New York: American Book Company.

Cross, Miriam. 2010. "Dov Mickelson on the Fantastical World of *Frankenstein*." *Shalom Life*, 14 May. http://www.shalomlife.com/culture/12600/dov-mickelson-on-the-fantastical-world-of-frankenstein/. (accessed 20 June 2015 but no longer available online).

Curtiz, Michael, dir. 1936. *The Walking Dead*. Hollywood: Warner Brothers.

Cybordelics. 1993. "Adventures of Dama." From *Nighthorse*. HH 026. Harthouse.

Daft Punk. 2005. *Human After All*. 724356356207. EMI/Virgin Records.

Dawkins, Richard. [1976] 1989. *The Selfish Gene*. Rev. ed. Oxford: Oxford University Press.

Dawson, Mitchell. 1930. "Frankenstein, Inc." *The American Mercury*, 19 March.

Deadmau5 [Joel Zimmerman]. 2006. "Dr. Funkenstein." From *Vexillology*. PD2001. Play Digital.

———. 2008. "Complications." From *Random Album Title*. UL 1905. Ultra.

———. 2009a. *Dr. Funkenstein Remixes*. PD2028. Play Digital.

———. 2009b. "Ghosts 'n' Stuff." From *For Lack of a Better Name*. UL 2174. Ultra Records.

———. 2009c. "Moar Ghosts 'n' Stuff." From *For Lack of a Better Name*. UL 2174. Ultra Records.

———. 2010. "Chthulhu Sleeps." From *4x4=12*. UL 2518-2. Ultra Records.

———. 2012a. Interview. *Q*. Toronto: CBC Radio, 23 July. https://www.youtube. com/watch?v=Zeb3dGbhvTM.

———. 2012b. "The Veldt (Original Mix)." From *The Veldt EP*. MAU5053B. Mau5trap Recordings.

———. 2012c. "we all hit play." *United We Fail* [blog], 23 June. https:// web.archive.org/web/20120627035653/http://deadmau5.tumblr.com/ post/25690507284/we-all-hit-play.

Derrida, Jacques. [1967] 1976. *Of Grammatology*. Translated by Gayatri Chakravorty Spivak. Baltimore: Johns Hopkins University Press.

———. [1981] 1988. *Dissemination*. Translated by Barbara Johnson. Chicago: University of Chicago Press.

Devadas, Vijay, and Chris Prentice. 2011. "Postcolonial Popular Cultures." *Continuum* 25, no. 5: 687–93.

Dewdney, Christopher. 1973. "Sol du soleil." In *A Paleozoic Geology of London, Ontario: Poems and Collages*, 5. Toronto: Coach House Press.

———. 1993. *The Secular Grail: Paradigms of Perception*. Toronto: Somerville House.

———. 1998. *Last Flesh: Life in the Transhuman Era*. Toronto: Harper Collins.

Douthwaite, Julia V. 2009. "The Frankenstein of the French Revolution: Nogaret's Automaton Tale of 1790." *European Romantic Review* 20, no. 3: 381–411.

Downes, Daniel. *Interactive Realism: The Poetics of Cyberspace*. Kingston: McGill-Queens University Press.

Dysart, Josh, and Cliff Chiang. 2010. *Neil Young's Greendale*. New York: Vertigo Comics.

Eco, Umberto. [1986] 2005. "Cogito Interruptus." In *Marshall McLuhan: Critical Evaluations in Cultural Theory*, vol. 1, *Fashion and Fortune*, edited by Gary Genosko, 120–31. New York: Routledge.

Eells, Josh. 2012. "The Rise of the Mau5." *Rolling Stone*, 7 May.

Ellul, Jacques. [1954] 1964. *The Technological Society*. Translated by John Wilkinson. New York: Random House.

Eric B. and Rakim. 1987. "Paid in Full (Seven Minutes of Madness: The Coldcut Remix)." From *Paid in Full*. 12 BRW 78. 4th & Broadway Records.

Eshun, Kodwo. 1998. *More Brilliant Than the Sun: Adventures in Sonic Fiction*. London: Quartet.

Eurythmics. 1984. "Sexcrime (1984)." From *1984 (For the Love of Big Brother)*. V1984. Virgin Records.

Feenberg, Andrew. 2002. *Transforming Technology: A Critical Theory Revisited*. New York: Oxford University Press.

Fekete, John. [1977] 2005. "McLuhanacy: Counterrevolution in Cultural Theory." In *Marshall McLuhan: Critical Evaluations in Cultural Theory*, edited by Gary Genosko, 29–82. New York: Routledge.

Ferguson, Marjorie. 1991. "Marshall McLuhan Revisited: 1960s Zeitgeist Victim or Pioneer Postmodernist?" *Media, Culture and Society* 13, no. 1: 71–90.

Findlay, Len. 2004. "Always Indigenize! The Radical Humanities in the Postcolonial Canadian University." In *Unhomely States: Theorizing English-Canadian Postcolonialism*, edited by Cynthia Sugars, 367–82. Peterborough, ON: Broadview Press.

Fischlin, Daniel, and Mark Fortier, eds. 2000. *Adaptations of Shakespeare: A Critical Anthology of Plays from the Seventeenth Century to the Present*. New York: Routledge.

Foremost Poets. 1998. "Moon-Raker (Main Mix)." From *Moon-Raker*. SOW-416. Soundmen on Wax.

Forry, Steven E. 1990. *Hideous Progenies: Dramatizations of Frankenstein from Mary Shelley to the Present*. Philadelphia: University of Pennsylvania Press.

Foster, Derek. 1999. "The Banana-Skin Ballet of William Gibson." In *Pop Can: Popular Culture in Canada*, edited by Lynne Van Luven and Priscilla Walton, 66–72. Toronto: Prentice Hall.

Foucault, Michel. [1969] 1972. *The Archaeology of Knowledge and the Discourse on Language*. Translated by A. M. Sheridan Smith. New York: Pantheon.

Franklin, Ursula. 1990. *The Real World of Technology*. Toronto: CBC.

Freedman, Carl. 2002. "Hail Mary: On the Author of *Frankenstein* and the Origins of Science Fiction." *Science Fiction Studies* 29, no. 2: 253–64.

Front 242. 1987. "Masterhit." From *Masterhit*. RRET 9. Red Rhino.

García, Pedro Javier Pardo. 2005. "Beyond Adaptation: *Frankenstein*'s Postmodern Progeny." In *Books in Motion: Adaptation, Intertextuality, Authorship*, edited by Mireia Aragay, 223–42. Amsterdam: Rodopi.

Gasher, Mike. 2002. *Hollywood North: The Feature Film Industry in British Columbia*. Vancouver: University of British Columbia Press.

Gehlen, Arnold. [1983] 2003. "A Philosophical-Anthropological Perspective on Technology." *Research in Philosophy and Technology* 6: 205–16. Reprinted in

Philosophy of Technology: The Technological Condition, edited by Robert C. Scharff and Val Dusek, 213–20. Oxford: Blackwell.

Genosko, Gary, ed. 2005. *Marshall McLuhan: Critical Evaluations in Cultural Theory*. Vol. 1, *Fashion and Fortune*. New York: Routledge.

Gibson, William. 1984. *Neuromancer*. New York: Ace.

——. 1993. *Virtual Light*. New York: Bantam.

——. 1996. *Idoru*. New York: Berkley.

Gilbert, Jeremy, and Ewan Pearson. 1999. *Discographies: Dance Music, Culture, and the Politics of Sound*. New York: Routledge.

Gilroy, Paul. 1993. *The Black Atlantic: Modernity and Double Consciousness*. Cambridge, MA: Harvard University Press.

Gismondi, Mike, and Debra J. Davidson. 2012. "Imagining the Tar Sands 1880–1967 and Beyond." *Imaginations* 3, no. 2: 68–103.

Gordon, Alastair. 2008. *Spaced Out: Radical Environments of the Psychedelic Sixties*. New York: Rizzoli.

Gordon, W. Terrence. 1997. *Marshall McLuhan: Escape into Understanding*. Toronto: Stoddart.

Gotlieb, Phyllis. [1975] 1978. "ms & mr frankenstein." *The Canadian Forum*, July. Reprinted in *The Works: Collected Poems*, 241–44. Toronto: Calliope Press.

Government of Canada. 2012. Marshall McLuhan Salon. Government of Canada, 17 October. http://mcluhan-salon.de/en/the-marshall-mcluhan-salon.

Grace, Dominick. 2003. "From *Videodrome* to *Virtual Light*: David Cronenberg and William Gibson." *Extrapolation* 44, no. 3: 344–55.

Grant, George. 1969. *Technology and Empire: Perspectives on North America*. Toronto: Anansi Press.

Grant, Peter S., and Chris Wood. 2004. *Blockbusters and Trade Wars: Popular Culture in a Globalized World*. Vancouver: Douglas and McIntyre.

Graves, Frank. 2010. "Frankenstein's Ideal Leader." *The Mark News*, 24 March. https://web.archive.org/web/20110501184218/http://www.themarknews.com/articles/1178-frankenstein-s-ideal-leader.

Green, Mark. 2012. "Bitumen, 'Dilbit,' and Pipelines—Just the Facts, Please." *Energy Tomorrow*, 22 August. http://www.energytomorrow.org/blog/2012/08/22/bitumen-dilbit-and-pipelines-just-the-fa.

Grossberg, Lawrence. 1997. "Re-placing Popular Culture." In *The Clubcultures Reader*, edited by Steve Redhead, 217–37. Oxford: Basil Blackwell.

Guillory, John. 2010. "Genesis of the Media Concept." *Critical Inquiry* 36: 321–62.

Gunkel, David J. 2012. *The Machine Question: Critical Perspectives on AI, Robots, and Ethics*. Cambridge, MA: MIT Press.

Gunn, Andrew. 2012. "Nora Young: Virtually in Order." *Canadian Interviews*, 9 May. https://web.archive.org/web/20151224061956/http://www.canadianinterviews.com/interviews/nora-young.

Habermas, Jürgen. 1970. *Toward a Rational Society*. Translated by Jeremy J. Shapiro. Boston: Beacon Press.

Handsome Boy Modeling School. 1999. "Once Again (Here to Kick for You)." From *So . . . How's Your Girl?* TBCD1258. Tommy Boy.

Haraway, Donna. 1991. "A Cyborg Manifesto: Science, Technology, and Socialist-Feminism in the Late Twentieth Century." In *Simians, Cyborgs, and Women: The Reinvention of Nature*, 149–81. New York: Routledge.

Harvey, Olivia. 2006. "Marshall McLuhan on Technology, Subjectivity, and 'the Sex Organs of the Machine World.'" *Continuum* 20, no. 3: 331–44.

Hazlitt, William. [1825] 2000. "Portrait of Mr Bentham." In *The Fight and Other Writings*, edited by Tom Paulin. London: Penguin.

Hedges, Chris. 2012. "Colonized by Corporations." *Truthdig*, 14 May. https://www.truthdig.com/articles/colonized-by-corporations/.

Heidegger, Martin. [1954] 1977. *The Question Concerning Technology and Other Essays*. Translated and with an introduction by William Lovitt. New York: Harper and Row.

Henthorne, Tom. 2011. *William Gibson: A Literary Companion*. Jefferson, NC: McFarland and Company.

Hitchcock, Susan T. 2007. *Frankenstein: A Cultural History*. New York: W. W. Norton.

Hoeveler, Diane L. 2005. "Smoke and Mirrors: Internalizing the Magic Lantern Show in *Vilette*." In *Gothic Technologies: Visuality in the Romantic Era*, edited by Robert Miles. Romantic Circles Praxis series. University of Maryland. http://www.rc.umd.edu/praxis/gothic/hoeveler/hoeveler.html.

Holmes, Richard. 2009. *The Age of Wonder: How the Romantic Generation Discovered the Beauty and Terror of Science*. London: HarperCollins.

Holthaus, Eric. 2016. "We Need to Talk About Climate Change: Tragedies Like the Fort McMurray Fire Make It More Important, Not Less." *Slate*, May 6. http://www.slate.com/articles/health_and_science/science/2016/05/the_mcmurray_fire_is_worse_because_of_climate_change_and_we_need_to_talk.html.

Hopkinson, Nalo. [1996] 2007. "A Habit of Waste." *Fireweed* 53: 28–43. Reprinted in *Making a Difference: Canadian Multicultural Literature*, 2nd ed., edited by Smaro Kamboureli, 362–72. Toronto: Oxford University Press.

Hopkinson, Nalo. [1998] 2012. *Brown Girl in the Ring*. New York: Grand Central Publishing.

Hughes, Walter. 1994. "In the Empire of the Beat." In *Microphone Fiends: Youth Music and Youth Culture*, edited by Andrew Ross and Tricia Rose, 147–57. New York: Routledge.

Husseyn, Andreas. 1989. "In the Shadow of McLuhan: Jean Baudrillard's Theory of Simulation." *Assemblage* 10: 6–17.

Hutcheon, Linda. 2006. *A Theory of Adaptation*. New York: Routledge.

Ice Cube [O'Shea Jackson Sr.]. 1998. "Dr. Frankenstein." From *War & Peace, Vol. 1 (The War Disc)*. P2 50700. Priority.

Jackson, Michael. 1984. "Thriller." From *Thriller*. QE 38112. Epic.

Jeffries, Stuart. 2011. "Friedrich Kittler Obituary." *The Guardian*, 21 October. http://www.guardian.co.uk/books/2011/oct/21/friedrich-kittler.

Jenkins, Henry, Tara McPherson, and Jane Shuttac, eds. 2002. *Hop on Pop: The Politics and Pleasures of Popular Culture*. Durham, NC: Duke University Press.

Jenkins, Philip. 1999. *Synthetic Panics: The Symbolic Politics of Designer Drugs*. New York: New York University Press.

Jonker, Julian. 2002. "Black Secret Technology (the Whitey on the Moon Dub)." *Ctheory*, article a117. http://www.ctheory.net/text_file.asp?pick=358.

Kaplan, Ben. 2001. "SummerWorks." *Now*, 2 August.

Kellner, Douglas. 1989. "Baudrillard: A New McLuhan?" *Illuminations: The Critical Theory Project*. Graduate School of Education and Information Studies, University of California, Los Angeles. http://pages.gseis.ucla.edu/faculty/kellner/Illumina%20Folder/kell26.htm.

Kelly, Kevin. 2011. *What Technology Wants*. New York: Penguin.

Kennedy, Paul. 2006. "'And she feeds you tea and oranges . . .': The Story of Suzanne." *The National*, CBC, 3 February. Reprinted in *Leonard Cohen Forum*, 25 April 2007. http://www.leonardcohenforum.com/viewtopic.php?f=9&t=8611.

Kim, Brad. 2013. Philosoraptor Image #621, 455. *Know Your Meme*, n.d. [ca. October]. http://knowyourmeme.com/photos/621455-philosoraptor.

Kingwell, Mark. 2017. "Artificial Intelligence in 2017 Means Respect, Not Fear." *Globe and Mail*, 20 May.

Kittler, Friedrich. [1986] 1999. *Gramophone, Film, Typewriter*. Translated by Geoffrey Winthrop-Young and Michael Wutz. Stanford, CA: Stanford University Press.

———. [2002] 2010. *Optical Media*. Translated by John Durham Peters. Cambridge, UK: Polity Press.

Klein, Naomi. 2016. "This Changes Everything: Capitalism Versus the Climate." Lecture delivered at the Congress of the Humanities and Social Sciences 2016, University of Calgary, 29 May.

Kool Keith a.k.a. Dr. Octagon [Keith Matthew Thornton]. 1997. *Dr. Octagonecologyst*. DRMD-50021. Dreamworks.

Kranzler, Laura. 1988. "*Frankenstein* and the Technological Future." *Foundation* 44: 42–49.

Kroker, Arthur. 1984. *Technology and the Canadian Mind: Innis, McLuhan, Grant*. Montréal: New World Perspectives.

Kurzweil, Ray. 2005. *The Singularity Is Near: When Humans Transcend Biology.* New York: Viking.

LaFontaine, Peter. 2012. "A Monster Rises: Enbridge's Tar Sands Frankenstein." *Wildlife Promise: Blogs from Around the Federation.* National Wildlife Federation. 27 September. http://blog.nwf.org/2012/09/a-monster-rises-enbridges-tar-sands-frankenstein/.

Lai, Larissa. 2002. *Salt Fish Girl.* Toronto: Thomas Allen Publishers.

———. 2009. *Automaton Biographies.* Vancouver: Arsenal Pulp Press.

Lampman, Archibald. 1900. "The City at the End of Things." In *The Poems of Archibald Lampman,* edited by Duncan Campbell Scott, 179–82. Toronto: George N. Morang.

Landers, Lew, dir. 1935. *The Raven.* Hollywood: Universal Studios.

Lazarus, Neil. 1999. *Nationalism and Cultural Practice in the Postcolonial World.* Cambridge, UK: Cambridge University Press.

Lee, Byron, and the Dragonaires. 1964. "Frankenstein Ska." Label unknown.

Levey, William A., dir. 1973. *Blackenstein.* FRSCO Productions.

Levine, George, and Ulrich C. Knoepflmacher, eds. 1979. *The Endurance of Frankenstein: Essays on Mary Shelley's Novel.* Berkeley: University of California Press.

Lorimer, Rowland, Mike Gasher, and David Skinner. 2008. *Mass Communication in Canada.* 6th ed. Toronto: Oxford University Press.

Lucas, George, dir. 2005. *Star Wars Episode 3: Revenge of the Sith.* San Francisco: Lucasfilm.

Luna C [Christopher Howell]. 1993. "Mind of a Lunatic (Knite Force remix)." From *The Luna-C Project* EP. KF001. Kniteforce Records.

Lund, Corb. 2002. "The Roughest Neck Around." From *Five Dollar Bill.* SPCD1284. Stony Plain Records.

———. 2012. "Gettin' Down on the Mountain." From *Cabin Fever.* NW6239. New West Records.

MacFadzean, Matthew. 2001. *richardthesecond: a nightmare.* Toronto: Nation of Aslan Theatre Company and Artword Theatre. http://www.canadianshakespeares.ca/anthology/richardthesecond.pdf.

———. 2002. "Production Notes." *Richardthesecond.com.* http://www.richardthesecond.com/ (accessed 7 January 2007 but no longer available online).

Madness. 1979. "One Step Beyond." From *One Step Beyond.* QSR-6085. Stiff/Sire.

Maestro Fresh-Wes [Wesley Williams]. 1989. "Let Your Backbone Slide (Power Mix)." From *Symphony in Effect.* ACD 1272. Attic Records.

Mamoulian, Rouben, dir. 1931. *Dr. Jekyll and Mr. Hyde.* Hollywood: Universal Studios.

Manovich, Lev. 2001. *The Language of New Media*. Cambridge, MA: MIT Press.

Marks, Laura. 2005. "Packaged for Export, Contents Under Pressure: Canadian Film and Video in a U.S. Context." In *Cultural Subjects: A Popular Culture Reader*, edited by Allan J. Gedalof, Jonathan Boulter, Joel Faflak, and Cameron McFarlane, 189–201. Toronto: Thompson Nelson.

Marx, Karl. [1857] 1973. *Grundrisse*. Translated by Martin Nicolaus. London: Penguin. Reprinted in *Marx Engels Archive*. https://www.marxists.org/archive/marx/works/1857/grundrisse/.

——. [1857] 1983. From *Grundrisse*. In *The Portable Karl Marx*, edited and translated by Eugene Kamenka, 375–94. New York: Penguin.

McClary, Susan. 1994. "Same as It Ever Was: Youth Culture and Music." In *Microphone Fiends: Youth Music and Youth Culture*, edited by Andrew Ross and Tricia Rose, 29–40. New York: Routledge.

McCutcheon, Mark A. 2007. "Techno, *Frankenstein*, and Copyright." *Popular Music* 26, no. 2: 259–80.

——. 2009. "'Come on back to the war': Germany as the Other National Other in Canadian Popular Culture." *University of Toronto Quarterly* 78, no. 2: 764–81.

——. 2011. "*Frankenstein* as a Figure of Globalization in Canada's Postcolonial Popular Culture." *Continuum* 25, no. 5: 731–42.

——. 2012. "Towards a Theory of the Dubject: Doubling and Spacing the Self in Canadian Media Culture." In *Selves and Subjectivities: Reflections on Canadian Arts and Culture*, edited by Manijeh Mannani and Veronica Thompson, 235–64. Edmonton: Athabasca University Press.

——. 2016. "Stephen Harper as Killer Robot." *English Studies in Canada* 42, nos. 1–2: 175–201.

McKitterick, David. 2003. *Print, Manuscript, and the Search for Order, 1450–1830*. Cambridge, UK: Cambridge University Press.

McLuhan, Marshall. 1951. *The Mechanical Bride: Folklore of Industrial Man*. London: Routledge and Kegan Paul.

——. [1962] 1969. *The Gutenberg Galaxy*. New York: Signet.

——. [1964] 2003. *Understanding Media: The Extensions of Man*. Corte Madera, CA: Gingko Press.

——. 1969. "The *Playboy* Interview." *Playboy*, March. 53–4, 56, 59–62, 64–6, 68, 70, 72, 74, 158.

——. 1970. *Culture Is Our Business*. New York: McGraw-Hill.

McLuhan, Marshall, and Quentin Fiore. [1967] 2001. *The Medium Is the Massage: An Inventory of Effects*. Corte Madera, CA: Gingko Press.

——. 1968. *War and Peace in the Global Village*. New York: Bantam.

McLuhan, Marshall, with Wilfred Watson. *From Cliché to Archetype*. New York: Viking Press.

McNally, David. 2011. *Monsters of the Market: Zombies, Vampires, and Global Capitalism*. Chicago: Haymarket Books.

McQuire, Scott. 2006. "Technology." *Theory, Culture and Society* 23, nos. 2–3: 253–60.

McRobbie, Angela. 1999. "Thinking with Music." In *Stars Don't Stand Still in the Sky: Music and Myth*, edited by Karen Kelly and Evelyn McDonell, 37–49. New York: New York University Press.

Mellor, Anne K. 1988. *Mary Shelley: Her Life, Her Fiction, Her Monsters*. London: Routledge.

Messiah. 1991. "Prince of Darkness." From *Prince of Darkness*. DJV 005. Déja Vu.

———. 1992. "You're Going Insane." From *Temple of Dreams* (EP). Kick 12. Kickin Records.

Mirrlees, Tanner. 2013. *Globalized Entertainment Media*. London: Routledge.

Mitcham, Carl. 1994. *Thinking through Technology: The Path between Engineering and Philosophy*. Chicago: University of Chicago Press.

The Mohawks. 1968. "The Champ." From *The Champ / Sound Of The Witchdoctors*. PM 719. Pama Records.

Monáe, Janelle. 2010. *The ArchAndroid*. 2-512256. Wondaland/Bad Boy Entertainment.

———. 2013. *The Electric Lady*. 2-536210. Wondaland/Bad Boy Entertainment.

Moody, Jane. 2000. *Illegitimate Theatre in London, 1770–1840*. Cambridge, UK: Cambridge University Press.

Mookerjea, Sourayan, Imre Szeman, and Gail Farschou, eds. 2009. *Canadian Cultural Studies: A Reader*. Durham, NC: Duke University Press.

Morton, Timothy. 2002. *Mary Shelley's* Frankenstein*: A Sourcebook*. London: Routledge.

Morus, Iwan Rhys. 1998. *Frankenstein's Children: Electricity, Exhibition, and Experiment in Early Nineteenth-Century London*. Princeton, NJ: Princeton University Press.

Mosco, Vincent, and Derek Foster. 2001. "Cyberspace and the End of Politics." *Journal of Communication Inquiry* 25, no. 3: 218–36.

Moss, Laura, ed. 2003. *Is Canada Postcolonial? Unsettling Canadian Literature*. Waterloo, ON: Wilfrid Laurier Press.

Moylan, Tom. 1995. "Global Economy, Local Texts: Utopian/Dystopian Tension in William Gibson's Cyberpunk Trilogy." *Minnesota Review* 43–44: 182–97.

Neill, Roy W., dir. 1943. *Frankenstein Meets the Wolf Man*. Hollywood: Universal.

Nestruck, J. Kelly. 2012. "The Oil Sands' Latest Byproduct: Cutting-Edge Theatre." *Globe and Mail*, 11 February.

Neuromancer of Structural Damage [Paul Drake]. 1992. "Pennywise." From *Pennywise/The Unforgettable Feeling*. SYM003. Symphony Sound Records.

Nye, David. 1994. *American Technological Sublime*. Cambridge, MA: MIT Press.

O'Flinn, Paul. 1986. "Production and Reproduction: The Case of *Frankenstein*." *Literature and History* 9, no. 2: 194–213.

Onstad, Katrina. 2013. "The Dark Knight: David Cronenberg's Creepy Obsessions Say as Much About Us as They Do About Him." *Toronto Life*, 3 December. https://web.archive.org/web/20160601195021/https://torontolife.com/city/david-cronenberg-profile-dark-night/.

O'Reilly, Terry. 2017. "The Crazy World of Trademarks (An Encore Broadcast)." *Under the Influence*, 25 May. Toronto: CBC Radio. http://www.cbc.ca/radio/undertheinfluence/the-crazy-world-of-trademarks-an-encore-broadcast-1.3918789.

Paladin [Len Jaroli]. 1999. *4.5* [DJ mix CD]. No catalogue number. No label.

———. 2006a. Interview. *Global Sound Philosophy*, 19 February. https://web.archive.org/web/20061031224953/http://www.gspmagazine.com/html/modules.php?name=News&file=article&sid=72.

———. 2006b. "The Paladin Project: Technical Data." *Darkandhard.ca*. Reprinted at Internet Archive, https://web.archive.org/web/20070210204501/http://www.darkandhard.ca/technical.html.

———. 2014. *P4L4DiN 6.3 Final Set*. Soundcloud, 2 June. https://soundcloud.com/thepaladinproject/p4l4din-6_3-final-set.

Parliament. 1976. *The Clones of Dr. Funkenstein*. NBLP 7034. Casablanca.

Parajulee, Abha, and Frank Wania. 2014. "Evaluating Officially Reported Polycyclic Aromatic Hydrocarbon Emissions in the Athabasca Oil Sands Region with a Multimedia Fate Model." *PNAS Early Edition*, 2 January. https://www.documentcloud.org/documents/1012653-pnas201319780-vwtwnf-ap-with-proof-corrections.html.

Patchett, Merle. 2012. "From 'On-High' to the Roadside: Scalar Aesthetics and the Canadian Oil Sands." *Imaginations* 3, no. 2: 141–54. http://imaginations.csj.ualberta.ca/?p=3556.

Peacock, Thomas Love. [1818] 2007. *Nightmare Abbey*. Peterborough, ON: Broadview Press.

———. [1831] 1947. *Crotchet Castle*. London: H. Hamilton.

Pendakis, Andrew, and Sheena Wilson. 2012. "Sight, Site, Cite: Oil in the Field of Vision." *Imaginations* 3, no. 2: 4–5. http://imaginations.csj.ualberta.ca/?p=3664.

Pennee, Donna. 1999. "Culture as Security: Canadian Foreign Policy and International Relations from the Cold War to the Market Wars." *International Journal of Canadian Studies / Revue internationale d'études canadiennes* 20: 191–213.

————. 2004. "Literary Citizenship: Culture (Un)Bounded, Culture (Re) Distributed." In *Home-Work: Postcolonialism, Pedagogy and Canadian Literature*, edited by Cynthia Sugars, 75–86. Ottawa: University of Ottawa Press.

Picart, Caroline J. S. 2002. *The Cinematic Rebirths of Frankenstein: Universal, Hammer, and Beyond*. Westport, CT: Praeger.

————. 2003. *Remaking the Frankenstein Myth on Film: Between Laughter and Horror*. Albany: State University of New York Press.

Pickett, Bobby, and the Crypt Kickers. 1962. "Monster Mash." From *Monster Mash*. 45-44167. Garpax Records.

Poe, Edgar Allan. [1846] 1987. "The Philosophy of Composition." In *The Fall of the House of Usher and Other Writings*, edited by David Galloway, 48–92. New York: Penguin.

Porcello, Thomas. 1991. "The Ethics of Digital Audio-Sampling: Engineers' Discourse." *Popular Music* 10, no. 1: 69–84.

Postman, Neil. 1985. *Amusing Ourselves to Death: Public Discourse in the Age of Show Business*. New York: Penguin.

————. 1993. *Technopoly: The Surrender of Culture to Technology*. New York: Vintage.

Quiggin, John. 2010. *Zombie Economics: How Dead Ideas Still Walk Among Us*. Princeton, NJ: Princeton University Press.

Randel, Fred V. 2003. "The Political Geography of Horror in Mary Shelley's *Frankenstein*." *English Literary History* 70, no. 2: 465–91.

Rapatzikou, Tatiani G. 2004. *Gothic Motifs in the Fiction of William Gibson*. Amsterdam: Rodopi.

Rees, Terence. 1978. *Theatre Lighting in the Age of Gas*. London: Society for Theatre Research.

Reynolds, Simon. 1997. "Rave Culture: Living Dream or Living Death?" In *The Clubcultures Reader*, edited by Steve Redhead, 102–11. Oxford: Blackwell.

Reynolds, Simon. 1998. *Generation Ecstasy: Into the World of Techno and Rave Culture*. New York: Little, Brown.

————. 1999. "Ecstasy Is a Science: Techno-Romanticism." In *Stars Don't Stand Still in the Sky: Music and Myth*, edited by Karen Kelly and Evelyn McDonell, 199–205. New York: New York University Press.

————. 2012. "How Rave Music Conquered America." *The Guardian*, 2 August. http://www.theguardian.com/music/2012/aug/02/how-rave-music-conquered-america.

Rich, Nathaniel. 2014. "American Dreams: Did William Gibson's 'Neuromancer' Blueprint Our Reality?" *Daily Beast*, 5 October. https://www.thedailybeast.com/american-dreams-did-william-gibsons-neuromancer-blueprint-our-reality.

Robins, Kevin, and Frank Webster. 1999. *Times of the Technoculture: From the Information Society to the Virtual Life*. London: Routledge.

Rockwell. 1984. "Somebody's Watching Me." From *Somebody's Watching Me*. 1702MF. Motown.

Rohmer, Richard. [1973] 2003. *Ultimatum*. In *A Richard Rohmer Ombinus*. Toronto: Dundurn.

Ronell, Avital. 1991. *The Telephone Book: Technology, Schizophrenia, Electric Speech*. Lincoln: University of Nebraska Press.

Rosen, Larry. 2011. "iDisorder." *Dr Larry Rosen*. http://drlarryrosen. com/2011/03/idisorder/.

———. 2012. *iDisorder: Understanding Our Obsession with Technology and Overcoming Its Hold on Us*. New York: Palgrave Macmillan.

Rosenberg, Harold. 1965. "Philosophy in a Pop Key." *The New Yorker*, 27 February.

Ross, Andrew. 2005. "Technology." In *New Keywords: A Revised Vocabulary of Culture and Society*, edited by Tony Bennett, Lawrence Grossberg, and Meaghan Morris, 342–44. Oxford: Blackwell.

Rutherford, Paul. 2005. "Made in America: The Problem of Mass Culture in Canada." In *Cultural Subjects: A Popular Culture Reader*, edited by Allan J. Gedalof, Jonathan Boulter, Joel Faflak, and Cameron McFarlane, 101–14. Toronto: Thompson Nelson.

Ryall, Emily. 2008. "The Language of Genetic Technology: Metaphor and Media Representation." *Continuum* 22, no. 3: 363–73.

Rycroft, Simon. 1993. "Mapping the Underground: British and American Counter-cultures, 1950–1975." Ph.D. diss., University of Nottingham.

———. 1998. "Global Undergrounds: The Cultural Politics of Sound and Light in Los Angeles, 1965–1975." In *The Place of Music*, edited by Andrew Leyshon, David Matless, and George Revill, 222–48. New York: Guilford Press.

———. [2011] 2016. *Swinging City: A Cultural Geography of London, 1950–1974*. London: Routledge.

St. Clair, William. 2004. *The Reading Nation in the Romantic Period*. Cambridge, UK: Cambridge University Press.

SASI Group and Mark Newman. 2006. "Royalties and License Fee Exports." *Worldmapper.org*. http://www.worldmapper.org/posters/worldmapper_ map99_ver5.pdf.

Sassen, Saskia. 2000. "Spatialities and Temporalities of the Global: Elements for a Theorization." *Public Culture* 12, no. 1: 215–32.

Seltzer, Mark. 1993. "Serial Killers (1)." *differences* 5, no. 1: 92–128.

Sharman, Jim, dir. 1975. *The Rocky Horror Picture Show*. Hollywood: 20th Century Fox.

Shelley, Mary. [1818] 2012. *Frankenstein; or, the Modern Prometheus*. Peterborough, ON: Broadview Press.

———. [1826] 1996. *The Last Man*. Peterborough, ON: Broadview Press.

———. [1831] 2000. *Frankenstein, or The Modern Prometheus*. New York: Bedford / St. Martin's Press.

Shrivastava, Meenal, and Lorna Stefanick, eds. 2015. *Alberta Oil and the Decline of Democracy in Canada*. Edmonton: Athabasca University Press.

Sickels, Robert C. 2009. *The Business of Entertainment: Movies*. Santa Barbara: ABC-CLIO.

Sierra Club et al. 2010. "Avatar Sands" advertisement. *Variety*, 4 March. https://web.archive.org/web/20100613115822/http://dirtyoilsands.org/files/AVATARSANDS_Variety_Final_PRINT.pdf.

Sigelman, Matthew. 2016. "Getting Past the Lazy Debate." *Inside Higher Ed*, 8 February. https://www.insidehighered.com/views/2016/02/08/debate-over-liberal-arts-vs-vocationalism-lazy-one-essay.

Simpson, David. 1993. *Romanticism, Nationalism, and the Revolt against Theory*. Chicago: University of Chicago Press.

Skinny Puppy. 1987. "Draining Faces." From *Cleanse Fold and Manipulate*. NTL30011. Nettwerk.

Slusser, George. 1992. "The Frankenstein Barrier." In *Fiction 2000: Cyberpunk and the Future of Narrative*, edited by George Slusser and Tom Shippey, 46–71. Athens: University of Georgia Press.

Smith, Don G. 1992. "Shelley's *Frankenstein*: A Possible Source for Poe's 'MS. Found in a Bottle.'" *Poe Studies* 25: 37–38.

Stein, Atara. 2004. *The Byronic Hero in Film, Fiction, and Television*. Carbondale: Southern Illinois University Press.

Stewart, Jon, et al. 2009. *The Daily Show*. Viacom, 2 February.

The Stooges. 1973. "Search and Destroy." From *Raw Power*. KC 32111. Columbia.

Sugars, Cynthia, ed. 2004. *Home-Work: Postcolonialism, Pedagogy, and Canadian Literature*. Ottawa: University of Ottawa Press.

Sullivan, Mark. 2009. "*Neuromancer* turns 25: What it got right, what it got wrong." *PCWorld*, 30 June. https://www.pcworld.com/article/167670/neuro.html.

Szeman, Imre. 2011. "Literature and Energy Futures." *PMLA* 126, no. 2: 323–25.

Tenner, Edward. 1996. *Why Things Bite Back: Technology and the Revenge of Unintended Consequences*. New York: Knopf.

Testa, Bart. 1995. "Technology's Body: Cronenberg, Genre, and the Canadian Ethos." *Post Script* 15, no. 1: 39–56. https://web.archive.org/web/20010121055200/http://www.utoronto.ca/cinema/html_site/faculty/testa/testa_article.htm.

Theall, Donald F. 1992. "Beyond the Orality/Literacy Dichotomy: James Joyce and the Pre-history of Cyberspace." *Postmodern Culture* 2, no. 3. doi:10.1353/pmc.1992.0036.

Thompson, Nicholas. 2009. "Inside the Apocalyptic Soviet Doomsday Machine." *Wired*, 21 September. http://archive.wired.com/politics/security/magazine/17-10/mf_deadhand?currentPage=all.

Thompson, Niobe, and Tom Radford, dirs. 2011. *Tipping Point: The Age of the Oil Sands*. Edmonton: Clearwater Documentary.

Thornburg, David D. 1992. *Edutrends 2010: Restructuring, Technology, and the Future of Education*. San Carlos, CA: Starsong Publications.

Thornton, Sarah. 1996. *Club Cultures: Music, Media, and Subcultural Capital*. Middletown, CT: Wesleyan University Press.

Toffler, Alvin. 1970. *Future Shock*. New York: Random House.

Turney, Jon. 1998. *Frankenstein's Footsteps: Science, Genetics, and Popular Culture*. New Haven: Yale University Press.

Ulmer, Edgar G., dir. 1934. *The Black Cat*. Hollywood: Universal Studios.

Van Helden, Armand. 1994. "Witch Doktor." SR12295. Strictly Rhythm.

Vlessing, Etan. 2014. "'Maps to the Stars' Director David Cronenberg on Indie Films and Portraying Hollywood." *Hollywood Reporter*, 15 May. http://www.hollywoodreporter.com/news/cannes-maps-stars-director-david-703271.

von Zimmerman, E. A. W. 1787. *A Political Survey of the Present State of Europe*. London: C. Dilly.

Watts, Peter. 1999. *Starfish*. New York: Tor.

———. 2001. *Maelstrom*. New York: Tor. http://www.rifters.com/real/MAELSTROM.htm.

———. 2004. *βehemoth*. New York: Tor.

———. 2006. *Blindsight*. New York: Tor.

———. 2014. *Echopraxia*. New York: Tor.

Weber, Max. [1910] 2005. "Remarks on Technology and Culture." *Theory, Culture, and Society* 22, no. 4: 23–38.

Weber, Samuel. 1989. "Upsetting the Set Up: Remarks on Heidegger's Questing after Technics." *MLN* 104, no. 5: 977–92.

Whale, James, dir. 1931. *Frankenstein*. Hollywood: Universal Studios.

———. 1935. *Bride of Frankenstein*. Hollywood: Universal Studios.

Williams, Raymond. 1983. *Keywords: A Vocabulary of Culture and Society*. New York: Oxford University Press.

Winner, Langdon. 1977. *Autonomous Technology: Technics-out-of-Control as a Theme in Political Thought*. Cambridge, MA: MIT Press.

Wippenberg. 1995. "Neurodancer." From *Neurodancer*. HH 0176. Hyper Hype.

Wolf, Gary. 1996. "The Wisdom of Saint Marshall, the Holy Fool." *Wired,* 1 January. https://www.wired.com/1996/01/saint-marshal/.

Womack, Jack. 2000. "Some Dark Holler." Afterword in William Gibson, *Neuromancer* ([2000] 1984), 265–76. New York: Ace Books.

Wright, Angela. 2005. "Haunted Britain in the 1790s." In *Gothic Technologies: Visuality in the Romantic Era*, edited by Robert Miles. Romantic Circles Praxis series. University of Maryland. http://www.rc.umd.edu/praxis/gothic/wright/wright.html.

Young, Neil. 1974. "Vampire Blues." From *On the Beach*. R 2180. Reprise Records.

Young, Neil and Crazy Horse. 2003. *Greendale*. CDW 48533. Reprise Records.

Young, Nora. 2014a. "Are We Taking A.I. Seriously Enough?" *Spark* 253, 1 June. Toronto: CBC Radio. http://www.cbc.ca/radio/spark/spark-253-1.2848289/are-we-taking-a-i-seriously-enough-1.2848298.

———. 2014b. "Why Your Hands are the Window to Your Mind." *Spark* 266, 23 November. Toronto: CBC Radio. http://www.cbc.ca/radio/spark/spark-266-1.2854081/why-your-hands-are-the-windows-to-your-mind-1.2854088.

———. 2015a. "Surfing, Streams and Clouds: The Dangers of Digital Metaphor." *Spark* 274, 1 February. Toronto: CBC Radio. http://www.cbc.ca/radio/spark/274-twitter-fiction-designing-a-grief-app-the-dangers-of-digital-metaphor-and-more-1.2936726/surfing-streams-and-clouds-the-dangers-of-digital-metaphor-1.2937081.

———. 2015b. "This Is What Happens When Your Boss Is a Piece of Software." *Spark* 279, 15 March. Toronto: CBC Radio. http://www.cbc.ca/radio/spark/279-unlocking-your-creativity-arts-startups-the-future-of-online-commenting-and-more-1.2993979/this-is-what-happens-when-your-boss-is-a-piece-of-software-1.2994175.

———. 2017. "Lessons in Tech Anxiety from Frankenstein's Monster." *Spark* 369, 27 October. Toronto: CBC Radio. http://www.cbc.ca/radio/spark/369-self-teaching-bots-ai-copyright-and-more-1.4373915/lessons-in-tech-anxiety-from-frankenstein-s-monster-1.4373924.

Index

Frye, Northrop, 141
"Funky Drummer" (song), 56
Future Shock (Toffler), 6, 100

Galvani, Luigi, 76, 77
gaming, 41, 43, 44, 123, 126, 163
gangsta rap, 55
García, Pedro Javier Pardo, 37, 41
Gattaca (film), 125
Gehlen, Arnold, 12
"Gettin' Down on the Mountain"
    (song), 180, 182
"Ghosts 'n' Stuff" (song), 168
Gibson, William, 45, 131, 151;
    Idoru, 103, 126–127; McLuhan's
    influence on, 101, 111–12, 122;
    Neuromancer, 9, 103, 104–107,
    110–11, 115–16, 118–20, 125,
    128–30; *Virtual Light*, 126
Gilbert, Jeremy, 16
Gilroy, Paul, 51
globalization, 15, 20, 24–26, 27, 31,
    32–33, 142, 197–99, 204. *See also*
    Canada—globalization
"global village," 98, 110–11, 116–17. *See
    also* McLuhan, Marshall—and
    global village
Godwin, William: *Caleb Williams*, 92
golem (Jewish legend), 55, 152, 196
Good Fences (play), 182
Gordon, Alastair, 97
gospel music, 53, 54
Gotlieb, Phyllis: *Flesh and Gold*, 133;
    "ms and mr frankenstein", 133–34;
    O Master Caliban, 133
Gould, Glenn, 115, 169–70
Grace, Dominick, 126, 153–54
Gramophone, Film, Typewriter
    (Kittler), 136, 195–96
Grant, George, 12, 26
Grant, Peter, 29
Grundrisse (Marx), 63

Guillory, John, 4
Gutenberg Galaxy, The (McLuhan),
    111

Habermas, Jürgen, 66
Handmaid's Tale, The (Atwood), 142
Handsome Boy Modeling School
    (band), 48; "Once Again (Here to
    Kick for You)", 55–56
Haraway, Donna, 13, 63, 139
Hawthorne, Nathaniel, 71
Hazlitt, William, 64, 72
Heidegger, Martin, 12, 63, 194
Her (film), 105
Hideous Progenies (Forry), 37, 48
history, as series of technological
    advances, 23, 95, 152
History of Violence (film), 125
Hitchcock, Susan Tyler, 75;
    Frankenstein: A Cultural History,
    37
Hoeveler, Diane, 76
Hoggart, Richard, 88
Hollywood, 29, 48–49, 118, 124
Holmes, Richard, 79
Holocaust Memorial, Berlin, 196
Hopkinson, Nalo: *Brown Girl in the
    Ring*, 136–37
Hughes, Walter, 158
Hutcheon, Linda, 38, 39, 41–43, 44,
    45, 183; *A Theory of Adaptation*,
    41–44

Ice Cube: "Dr. Frankenstein," 55
"iconflation" (definition), 49
ICTs. *See* information and
    communication technologies
    (ICTs)
iDisorder (Rosen), 19–20
Idoru (Gibson), 103, 126–27
Iggy Pop, 101, 158

Max Headroom (TV series), 115, 136, 173
McKitterick, David, 23–24
McLuhan, Marshall, 42; 1990s revival, 130–31, 156; adaptations, 3–4, 118 (see also *Neuromancer* (Gibson); *Videodrome* (film)); cars, views on, 177; and consumerism, 88; *From Cliché to Archetype*, 95; corporate culture, views on, 197–198; counterculture, influence on (1960s), 8–9, 96–100, 156, 163; discourse of technology, influence on, 8, 9, 14, 26, 85, 90, 95, 100–1, 103, 189–90, 199–200; and global village, 27, 95, 98, 111, 152 (*see also* "global village"); global influence, 8, 10, 96, 189–96, 197–99; *The Gutenberg Galaxy*, 111; and internet, development of, 130–31; *The Mechanical Bride*, 88, 89, 141, 142; media theory, 4, 8, 24, 69, 87, 91, 95, 98, 101, 110–11, 112–13, 115–17, 130, 154, 191, 203–4; *The Medium Is the Massage*, 96, 99; and nuclear weaponry, 87; *Playboy* interview, 94, 95, 99, 100; Poe, Edgar Allan, influence of, 92–93; and popular culture, 3–4, 9–10, 86, 88–90, 96, 103–4, 131–33, 155, 163, 165–66, 197; and the press, 8–9; Romanticism, influence of, 8, 87–89, 91–93; and sound, 44; technological change, hostility to, 87, 91–92, 93–95, 131, 189, 204; technological humanism, 27, 66, 89–91, 112, 116, 123–24, 177, 190, 193; and television, 100, 111, 115; technology, theory of, 12, 33, 63, 70, 89–95, 111–12, 131, 135, 152, 189–90; transferable subjectivity, 115, 117, 136; and underground

press, 98–99; *Understanding Media*, 90–91, 95, 97, 123, 177, 191; *War and Peace in the Global Village*, 94; World War II, influence of, 86–87; writing style, 92–3, 96–97
McNally, David, 18, 51, 176
McQuire, Scott, 60, 63, 65
McRobbie, Angela, 57
Mechanical Bride, The (McLuhan), 88, 89, 141, 142
media, new, 22–24, 86, 96–97, 112, 131, 199–200
Medium Is the Massage, The (McLuhan), 96, 99
Mellor, Anne K., 79
meme (definition), 39. *See also* Internet meme
Merle, Jean-Toussaint: *Le monstre et le magicien*, 80
Messiah (band), 127; "Prince of Darkness," 128; "You're Going Insane," 128
Metropolis (film), 89
Mighton, John: *Possible Worlds*, 136
Milner, Henry: *The Man and the Monster*, 79, 80
"Mind of a Lunatic" (song), 128
Mitcham, Carl, 12, 14
"Moar Ghosts 'n' Stuff" (song), 168
Mohawks, The (band), 55: *The Champ*, 54
Monáe, Janelle, 43; *The ArchAndroid*, 47
Monk, Thelonious, 51–52, 54
"Monster Mash" (song), 50
monstre et le magician, Le (Merle and Béraud), 80
Moody, Jane, 75–76
Moon (film), 125
"Moon-Raker" (song), 165
Moravec, Hans, 135, 136

A book in the Campus Alberta Collection, a collaboration of Athabasca University Press, the University of Alberta Press and the University of Calgary Press.

a PROUD PARTNER in
Campus Alberta  THE UNIVERSITY *of* ALBERTA PRESS  UNIVERSITY OF CALGARY Press

Athabasca University Press
aupress.ca

The Medium Is the Monster:
Canadian Adaptations of Frankenstein *and*
the Discourse of Technology
Mark A. McCutcheon
978-1-77199-236-7 (cl)
978-1-77199-224-4 (pb)

Public Deliberation on Climate Change:
Lessons from Alberta Climate Dialogue
Edited by Lorelei L. Hanson
978-1-77199-215-2 (pb)

Visiting With the Ancestors:
Blackfoot Shirts in Museum Spaces
Laura Peers and Alison K. Brown
978-1-77199-037-0 (pb)

Alberta Oil and the Decline of Democracy
in Canada
Edited by Meenal Shrivastava and Lorna
Stefanick
978-1-77199-029-5 (pb)

University of Alberta Press
uap.ualberta.ca

Keetsahnak / Our Missing and Murdered
Indigenous Sisters
Kim Anderson, Maria Campbell and Christi
Belcourt, Editors
978-1-77212-367-8 (pb)

Trudeau's Tango:
Alberta Meets Pierre Elliott Trudeau,
1968–1972
Darryl Raymaker
978-1-77212-265-7 (pb)

Seeking Order in Anarchy:
Multilateralism as State Strategy
Edited by Robert W. Murray
978-1-77212-139-1 (pbk)

Upgrading Oilsands Bitumen and Heavy Oil
Murray R. Gray
978-1-77212-035-6 (hc)

University of Calgary Press
ucalgary.ca/ucpress

Water Rites:
Reimagining Water in the West
Jim Ellis, Editor
978-1-55238-997-3 (pb)

Writing Alberta:
Building on a Literary Identity
Edited by George Melnyk and Donna
Coates
978-1-55238-890-7 (pb)

The Frontier of Patriotism:
Alberta and the First World War
Edited by Adriana A. Davies and Jeff
Keshen
978-1-55238-834-1 (pb)

So Far and Yet So Close:
Frontier Cattle Ranching in Western Prairie
Canada and the Northern Territory of
Australia
Warren M. Elofson
978-1-55238-794-8 (pb)